Apocalypse Pretty Soon

Travels in End-Time America

Apocalypse
Pretty Soon

Travels in End-Time America

ALEX HEARD

W. W. Norton & Company

New York • London

For information about permission to reproduce selections from this book,
write to Permissions, W. W. Norton & Company, Inc., 500 Fifth Avenue,
New York, NY 10110.

The text of this book is composed in Stempel Schneidler,
with the display set in Universe Ultra Thin
Compostion by A.W. Bennett, Inc.
Manufacturing by Courier Companies, Inc.
Book design by BTD / Ann Obringer

Library of Congress Cataloging-in-Publication Data

Heard, Alex.
    Apocalypse pretty soon : travels in end-time America / Alex Heard.
        p. cm.
    Includes bibliographical references.
    ISBN 0-393-04689-3
    1. Millennialism—United States.   2. United States—
Religion—1960–   3. Two thousand, A.D.   I. Title
BR526.H335 1999
306'.1'0973—dc21
                                                                98-24639
                                                                CIP

W. W. Norton & Company, Inc., 500 Fifth Avenue, New York, N.Y. 10110
http://www.wwnorton.com

W. W. Norton & Company, Ltd., 10 Coptic Street, London WC1A 1PU

1 2 3 4 5 6 7 8 9 0

FOR SUSAN, WHO MAKES
EVERYTHING POSSIBLE

Acknowledgments

Two years before he died, my father decided that I didn't seem to be accomplishing much at the small state college I was then attending in western Kansas. It wasn't the school's fault, but he was right. He declared that I should try my luck at Vanderbilt University in Nashville, Tennessee, I think because, as a native southerner, he associated the place with good writing and English majoring. Whatever inspired him, the idea was a generous gift. I first became interested in journalism at Vanderbilt, and met teachers and friends who changed my life. Foremost among them: James Leeson, James Kilroy, Charles Euchner, Richard Chenoweth, Tom Jurkovich, Eric Etheridge, Scott Story, Jamie Monagan, and Judy McCoy.

In the years since I've been lucky to work with many fine magazine editors, including several who allowed me to write about the subjects in this book. Thanks especially to Michael Kinsley, Jack Shafer, Robert Wright, Mickey Kaus, Jay Lovinger, Leslie Marshall, Alexander Kaplen, Julie Just, Susan Morrison, Kurt Andersen, Andrew Ferguson, Pat Trenner, Charles Freund, Mark Bryant, Laura Hohnhold, Lisa Chase, Dan Ferrara, Greg Cliburne, Brad Wetzler, Hampton Sides, Amy Goldwasser, Hal Espen, Mike Grudowski, Stephen Dubner, Dianne Cardwell, Jack Rosenthal, and Adam Moss.

For this project, I also received invaluable assistance from editors and other staff at W. W. Norton: Gerald Howard, Tabitha Griffin, Hilary Hinzmann, Justine Trubey, and Elizabeth Gretz. Many thanks also to my agent, Mark Kelley.

Equally hearty appreciation must go to my friends in Kansas, Washington, D. C., and New Mexico, whose humor and ideas have kept me going throughout the years. Thanks especially to Jay Benson, Gil Goldsberry, Rex Joyce, Tom Fenton, Tim and Julie Goulding, Scott and Leah Richardson, Scott and "Ernie" Morgan, Lisa Birchard, Nancy Swenton, John and Suzie Gurley, Kent and Debbie Wells, Rick Roth, Dirk Olin, Suzanne Callahan, Gary Grieg, Mike Hiestand, Teresa Kendrick, Teresa Riordan, John Galvin, Chris Czmyrid, Dave Cox, Dave Allen, Mike Bain, Andrew Tilin, and Casey Vandenoever.

Thanks also to both my families, "original" and "extra in-laws." Alan and Marjorie Cheetham welcomed me with open arms soon after I invaded their daughter's life, as did the extended crew of Chris, Pat, Jan, Hilary, and Frank. My brothers Ken and Malcolm, my sister Julia, and my sisters-in-law Cynthia and Diane have always been there for me, even when ritual shunning might have been more appropriate.

Finally, utmost gratitude to my parents, Kenneth and Lois Heard, who gave me everything. I hope at least a little of their defining traits—humor, wisdom, and sympathy—is evident in what follows.

Contents

. . . human beings have always experienced the world as a painful place. We are the victims of natural disasters, of mortality, extinction, and human injustice and cruelty. The religious quest has usually begun with the perception that something has gone wrong, that, as the Buddha put it, "Existence is awry."

—KAREN ARMSTRONG, *JERUSALEM*

. . . the cool world is an iceberg, mostly underwater.

—NED POLSKY, *HUSTLERS, BEATS, AND OTHERS*

Introduction:
An Eerie Tingling

*ANSWER ME THIS: HOW THE HELL DO I WAKE THE NATION AND TELL
THE PEOPLE THAT . . . WE CAN END ALL WARS . . . BRING ABOUT HUMAN
RIGHTS . . . AND ACHIEVE PEACE . . . THROUGH THE USE OF GOD'S
WISDOM OF APOCALYPSE SCIENCE!↙↙↙↙↙*

—CORRESPONDENCE FROM KENNA E. FARRIS, "DIVINE FORERUNNER
PROPHET OF HORSE SENSE ECONOMICS," 1986

One day in the fall of 1985, I was sitting in an office in Washington, D.C., plinking away at a piece of journalism I hated—it concerned public-school reform in Texas, which I hackishly labeled "a process at war with itself"—when I experienced a sensation of hot, head-achy dizziness.

I figured this might be divine retribution for what I'd just typed, but then I realized it was the start of a nasty fever. I left work, staggered to the nearest bus stop, went home, flopped on the floor in front of a TV, and weakly tugged the knob. A rerun of *Gilligan's Island* was on, and I knew I was in trouble when the plot seemed too intricate to follow. As I lay there guppy-mouthed, gasping and half-asleep, for some reason I started recalling themes from Superman comic books, which I'd studied assiduously as a literacy-dodging ten-year-old. Every now and then the Man of Steel accidentally got exposed to Red Kryptonite—a substance that, unlike deadly Green Kryptonite, caused mysterious but nonfatal symptoms, temporarily turning him into Dumb Superman, Fat Superman, or Evil Superman.

When it happened, he knew he was in trouble, too, saying something along the lines of, "Hmmm, an eerie tingling . . ."

Not until weeks later did I find out what my eerie tingling was: viral encephalitis, an inflammation caused by a viral infection that manages to worm into the gray stuff. It's a strange condition, almost always not fatal in someone my age (twenty-six back then), and there isn't much you can do but ride it out until your body's defenses kick in. Symptoms vary, but they can include terrible headaches (your brain swells), disorientation, loss of verbal skills, irritability, and wooziness.

Or so I was told. I didn't quite buy it when I finally got a diagnosis. After the initial bout of fever, I'd ached and brooded and moped for a few days and dropped by an emergency room once (helpful verdict there: it's just fever, stop being a baby and go home) before I finally made an office appointment with a specialist.

I didn't know this doctor and he didn't know me, but he looked reassuringly chubby, pink, and wise. Tapping his fingertips together and squinting, Dr. Healthy listened to my gripes. I could read individual words and sentences but I couldn't make much sense of an entire page. Without warning, even though I wasn't "sad," I would start crying these large, glycerin-consistency tears. And—here was the interesting one—I experienced waking periods of enlightenment during which everything in the universe seemed to come together with the utmost clarity.

"Clarity," he repeated. "How do you mean?"

"I can't explain it," I mumbled.

He nodded and said, "I think you have viral encephalitis."

Great. Could I get a head X-ray or an ectoplasmagram or whatever to verify it? Nope, said the doc. What I had in mind was a CAT scan. But that was very costly, and he didn't think I needed it. "Trust me," he said.

That was tough, since (a) the emergency-room doctor had been fulla crap when he said I "just" had fever; and (b) my other big symptom was a case of hooting paranoia. I squinted and frowned. How did this guy know that my skull didn't contain a pulsing brain tumor the size of a whale's eyeball?

But I shut up and went home, not wanting to whine. A few nights later things came to a bizarre climax. The trouble started when I picked the wrong rental movie to amuse myself with: "Ciao! Manhattan," which stars Edie Sedgwick, the now-deceased Andy Warhol "superstar," who was in the process of killing herself with drugs while the movie was being shot. Sedgwick staggered through her role looking like a flu-stricken zombie, and for some reason, seeing her in that deathly state (and thinking about the cold cruelty of whoever shoved her through her paces) sent me over the edge. Panicking and shouting, I ripped off my shirt and examined my own pitifully skeletal torso. (Already skinny to begin with, I hadn't been eating much during the illness.) Right then I decided I was dying, and I flipped out, seriously and absolutely. I rushed over to the emergency room, where this time they paid attention. They sort of had to, since I was yowling and madly jigging in the reception area. Soon enough they slapped me on a gurney, where I flopped around like an eel on hot asphalt until they tightened the straps.

Ultimately, everything worked out fine. I was admitted and got blood tests, a painful spinal tap, *and* a soothing CAT scan. (A small, foggy patch showed up on my brain. Affirmation!) Still, I was regarded suspiciously. My roommate was a big, crabby jerk who kept complaining into the phone that he'd been paired up with a "nut." At one point a neurologist came by and gave me a narrow-eyed interrogation. He obviously didn't think the physical abnormality he saw warranted the fit I'd pitched.

I didn't say anything, but I thought: Hey, Bud, you don't know.

Something evil had taken my brain, chewed it, swallowed it, shat it, and drop-kicked what was left into a deep, dark hole. Maybe it would happen to him someday. Then he'd see . . .

But, in fact, I didn't care about his opinion. I was released and spent a few days in a state of raptural bliss about my restored sense of well-being. I actually wandered my neighborhood smiling at the sky and saying "hey" to the songbirds and sunshine.

Then something really eerie happened: I started having trouble remembering the precise feeling of any of it, the blissful highs or the hellish lows. A month later, it all seemed dim, gray, and distant.

∞

What does my little Brain Burn have to do with that grandest of themes, the apocalypse?

Just this. The fever amounted to a personal apocalypse—that is, if you stick to the original sense of the word's Greek source, *apoka-lypsis,* which means an "uncovering" or "unveiling."

Among the truths uncovered for me by the illness: the fraudulence of my smug sense that I wasn't especially afraid of death, the fact that I had a pretty weak spiritual life (attempts to comfort myself with the Presbyterian "faith" that I'd lukewarmly explored as a teenager didn't add up to much), and . . . hmmm, what's the best way to put this? Oh yeah, that I hated writing about education, a role I'd sort of drifted into as a means to survive during my post-college career flailings. Thus, my first act after recovery was to sever my remaining ties with that field (ciao, Texas school reform!) and take my chances as a freelancer, concentrating as much as possible on the vast subject area that got me interested in journalism in the first place: weird people. After a couple of years, that focus narrowed into a special interest in millennial and utopian oddballs—that is, people who believe we're heading for a period of dramatic upheaval and change that will lead to a new and improved tomorrow.

I got started in 1987, when I was writing a regular column for the *Washington Post Magazine*. One day an editor received a mailing from an urgent individual named Kenna E. Farris, a self-proclaimed prophet from rural Missouri. Farris had gone to considerable expense to mail news organizations a huge poster that yelped: "'FRIENDLY FEROCIOUS FARRIS.' GOD PLANNED FOR HIM TO SMITE THE EARTH WITH THE ROD OF HIS MOUTH AND TO SLAY THE SKEPTIC WICKED WITH THE BREATH OF HIS LIPS."

I decided to call Farris and yak him up. I did so with two assumptions in mind, both of which turned out to be wrong. One was that Farris would be a raving maniac, a man whose brain was tingling *too* much, whose fever burned him up and left behind a gibbering, smoking husk. Two, that he probably was an off-putting sort, one of those awful, narrow-minded Christians—all that "skeptic wicked" stuff—who would rant that anybody who doubted him would go to Hell.

Not really. Farris was . . . intense . . . but he spoke coherently, and he seemed like a nice person whose real motivation was to help the world. He lived in Savannah, Missouri, where his personal apocalypse had occurred in 1967. Back then Farris owned and ran a restaurant called The Farris Wheel, but one day he heard the call from God, who needed him for an important task: Farris was supposed to alert the planet to momentous changes coming in the years ahead. Without complaint, he liquidated The Wheel and started spreading The Word.

Which was? That Christ would return in the year 3000, not 2000, but that many crucial changes were coming soon. In 1996, for example, a prophet-president would emerge to lead us into a New Age of peace with the Soviets. The man known to the world as Mikhail Gorbachev was really the planet-rescuing "Michael" described in the Old Testament Book of Daniel. Finally, another American leader would pop up who, in a sort of premillennial butt-whup for Christ, would defeat Satan and create a multibillion-dollar, twenty-four-nation trade center that would serve as the world headquarters for a barter-banking system founded on something called "Horse Sense Economics." Farris's role was to be the "divine forerunner prophet" of all these astonishments, a late-twentieth-century John the Baptist.

"Sounds doable," I said. "Where do things stand?"

Not promising. Farris had identified the prophet-president-to-be—he was Edwin H. Smith, a thirty-seven-year-old state circuit court judge in St. Joseph—but Smith was declining to fulfill his predestined role. I called him, figuring he'd holler at me, but he was good-natured about Farris, whom he'd known since childhood. Smith was well aware of the prediction.

"Well, what about it?" I said. "Are you the divinely ordained prophet-president-to-be?"

"I never foreclose any possibility," he replied. "But my wife has said if I get into a major race, she'll kill me."

∞

After meeting Farris, I began a slow process of getting to know an assortment of millennial and utopian strivers—Christians, gloom-and-doomy New Agers, UFO worshippers, new-frontier libertarians, fringe scientists, right-wing radicals, immortality hopefuls—a hobby I pursued off and on from 1987 to 1998. In that period I moved several times, from Washington to Chicago to Santa Fe and then back east to New York City, always keeping an eye out for people whose stories seemed worth telling. In making these choices, I tried to apply what I called the "Farris standard," an ethical commitment that required something of the subjects and of me. I was only interested in people whose beliefs had fundamentally changed their lives—pamphleteers and mere Web-site diatribers need not apply. In exchange for that level of involvement, I set a couple of ground rules for myself.

First, as much possible for an outsider, I would attempt to understand things from the believers' perspective, always based on deep immersion in their canonical texts and first-hand reporting. Second, I would include both millennialists and utopians: anyone who was anticipating or somehow working toward a heroically different world. Third, I would try not to be overly harsh in my judgments, unless harshness seemed warranted.

Meaning what? Meaning this isn't hands-off anthropology. It's journalism, so I've tried to call it like I saw it. Nobody in this book is perfect, including me, and we all come in for criticism, ribbing, and flying elbows. Still, I don't think I've taken any inhumane shots. Some of these people are deluded by astonishing levels of narcissism, and some have done a lot more harm than good.

But I also met a few heroes on this quest, people whose strange commitment to the strangest of beliefs was touching and inspiring in a way that taught me something. Obviously, I wasn't out there shopping for a new off-the-shelf worldview, à la, "Here's the formula: I'll become a fundamentalist Christian *and* believe that UFOs are piloted by angels." I remain skeptical about most of the beliefs millennialists and utopians hold dear, but I think the search that motivates them is still worth contemplating. All of these people are, in various ways, searching for spiritual solace in a world where death is the only available outcome. Who among us isn't doing the same thing?

And what did I learn? That's complicated, but one surprise was this: the millennium isn't all bad. Much of the scholarship and skeptical commentary I've read treats millennialism as, essentially, a form of popular insanity, a disease, one that usually has dire consequences. There's truth to this. I ran into a few dubious, dangerous, and exploitative characters, and I was aware of some scary groups that I decided to steer clear of (mostly on the extreme right). Furthermore, I believe there's a potential for more problems ahead. I'll be surprised if there isn't at least one additional millennial disaster—involving loss of life—before the year 2001.

My main interest, though, was in people who are managing to function peacefully with their ideas, as most millennialists do. Millions of people entertain outlandish prophetic or utopian notions, but only a few have done anybody any harm. Indeed, for the bulk of them, millennialism is a belief system that works, and they don't want to let go of it. Thus the "pretty soon" of my title. It's popularly believed that millennialists tend to set a date, dig in, and wait for the End to come. In fact, most avoid doing that, or they set timetables that can be easily explained away if the prophecy fails. For them, and for the utopian dreamers who pine for a better, brighter future, the key to happiness is for redemption to shine forever on the horizon.

In fact, if I had to identify one unifying theme about what motivates contemporary millennialists, it would be this: they're hopeful. Mainly, they hope for change in a world that annoys them. Everybody I met, whether rich or poor, was in some way an outsider in an end-of-the-millennium American society that they found unacceptable.

To me this was often confusing. Considering all the dangerous, truly apocalyptic upheavals of the twentieth century—especially World War II and the development of the bomb—I think Americans should be grateful for how the millennium is ending. We live in a capitalist, big-government democracy that produces a high standard of living with a modicum of oppression. Science and technology rule, but there's still plenty of room for organized religion and free-lance faiths. Things could be better, but they also could be a lot worse. There might not be anything awaiting us after death, but . . . there might be. Call me Dr. Pangloss, but here's what I think: we're doomed, but it's the best of all possible dooms.

My millennial and utopian friends (and enemies) will look at those words and wince, sneer, laugh, or scream. For them, the future is a battleground. We *may* find Heaven on Earth, but it won't happen without a fight. Otherwise we'll end up with Hell.

Since I first embarked on this project, some of the fighters have fallen. A few have died, others have divorced, lost faith, been pushed into the abyss economically, given up, burned out, or otherwise flailed. Reviewing the toll in my mind, I started wondering about Farris. He was sixty-one when I first talked to him. Would he still be kicking?

Yes indeed. I dialed his number and got his answering machine, which announced that he was now "Prophet King Kenna" and warned the world that the King didn't want to hear from peddlers: "If you are selling insurance, building materials, or siding . . . I am not currently interested."

"Farris?" I said after the beep. "This is Alex Heard. You may not remember me, but—"

He picked up. "Alex? Hey! Heck *yes* I remember you. I've been trying to find you for ten years. I've got important things you need to know about! I've been *trying* to tell Bill Clinton but he won't listen . . ."

Farris opened the floodgates, following up with a thirty-two-page fax, which said, among much else: "IT IS LONG PAST TIME FOR JEWS AND ARABS TO LIGHTEN UP ON THE VIOLENCE AFTER 4,000 YEARS TO PRE-PARE FOR SECURITY IN THE AGE OF AQUARIUS MILLENNIUMS AND THE COUNTDOWN FOR JESUS' SECOND COMING EVENTS!"

Whatever that means, Prophet King Kenna, you're the man to make it happen. Long may you reign.

Apocalypse Pretty Soon

The late Ruth Norman, a.k.a. "the archangel Uriel," Queen Bee of the Unarius Academy of Science.
USED BY PERMISSION OF THE UNARIUS ACADEMY OF SCIENCE.

Welcome, Space Brothers

*What would happen in a world, when upon impacted soil, an angel
touches down to stay a while?*

—FROM *FORTY YEARS OF LOVE AND LIGHT,* A VIDEO EULOGY FOR ERNEST AND
RUTH NORMAN, CO-FOUNDERS OF THE UNARIUS ACADEMY OF SCIENCE

On December 27, 1974, in a moment that must have cheered
somebody up at the Los Angeles offices of the Internal Revenue
Service, a completed IRS form 1023 arrived by mail from a California-based outfit called Unarius–Science of Life. Form 1023 is
mandatory paperwork for groups seeking tax-exempt status, and
one requirement is "a narrative description of the activities presently
carried on by the organization." Most people keep that answer short
and straight. (Why brag when you're asking for a favor?) The
Unarians did too—by their standards—but their unique mission
demanded a splash of Technicolor:

> Planned and masterminded by millions of super-intelligent beings
> from higher worlds, Unariun [*sic*] Mission formally began in 1954.
> . . . [Its teachings] could most accuractly [*sic*] be described as contain-
> ing more information, knowledge, and wisdom than would be con-
> tained in any known pricepts [*sic*] of human knowledge. This Inter-
> dimensional Science exist [*sic*] now in 30 bound volumes and was
> delivered to the earth world by Dr. Ernest L. Norman and his wife,
> Ruth E. Norman. . . . Here . . . can be attained the science of the
> future. . . .

The IRS doesn't require nonprofits to demonstrate that their work will benefit the United States government. Unarius tossed that in anyway, giddily bragging that it could help the country win the cold war.

"The Unariun Science could factually . . . place the United States far ahead of [the] U. S. S. R. in all scientific findings," the application said. Since the previous August, Ruth Norman had received "mental transmissions" from "over 159" departed luminaries, including "Albert Einstein . . . Iwan Petrovich Pawlow [sic] . . . Robert Oppenheimer, President John F. Kennedy, Eisenhower, T. Roosevelt, etc., etc." In the process she had recovered the lost secrets of the Tesla Tower, a 2,000-foot-tall wireless energy-transmission machine—attempted and abandoned on Wardenclyffe, Long Island, in the early 1900s by Nikola Tesla, the late, great engineering genius—that the Normans planned to build using "crystalline substance and gold."

"There are no limitation [sic]," the statement concluded, "to the great aid we can extend to the suffering humanity."

Unarius won its tax exemption, listing both Ernest and Ruth on its initial board of directors. This was rather a stretch in Ernest's case—he had died in 1971—but Ruth definitely made a mark. In 1975 she purchased a building in El Cajon, California, east of San Diego. There she nurtured a remarkably durable utopian group that has worked tirelessly ever since to spread her bizarre but joyous message about mankind's future, which she saw as one of imminent millennial salvation at the hands of "space brothers." Over the years, she attracted dozens of devoted students who helped Unarius find its place in a world that has tended (almost unanimously) to ignore or mock her prophecies, particularly her most famous one. In the mid-seventies she announced that sometime soon, thirty-three spaceships (representing thirty-two other worlds and Earth) would touch down in an interlocking stack near El Cajon. Each would contain infinitely wise extraterrestrials who were coming to launch a

New Age university that would usher in perpetual peace, wisdom, and harmony.

To prepare the way, Ruth bought sixty-seven acres of land outside of town and put up a sign that clearly stated the parcel's function: WELCOME SPACE BROTHERS. At one point, so confident that she placed a substantial bet with a London bookie, she announced that the landing would happen in 1976, but when that prophecy failed she remained unruffled and came up with the year 2001. These pronouncements and flubs made Ruth something of a fringe-world superstar. At various times, print and television reporters from all over the world came to catch her act, which was jazzed up by her speaking style—a cheerful, high-pitched warble—and her wardrobe. As Queen Bee of Unarius, Ruth dressed the part, wearing gaudy gowns and tiaras assembled by loving Unarius students.

Ruth accomplished all this as a very old woman. She was born in 1900, so she was already seventy-four when Unarius began growing in the mid-seventies. At her death in 1993, Unarius's annual filings with the IRS showed a healthy bottom line. The group owns its headquarters, which includes a large meeting space where Unarius students gather for weekly classes, video-production facilities where the students make unintentionally kitsch dramas that bring Ruth's teachings to life (shown on cable-access channels all over the United States), and an endless stream of Unarius publications and books. Unarius's total assets in 1992 bettered $500,000. That's not much by the standards of, say, the Church of Scientology, but it's not bad compared with a more famous outfit whose teachings shared several basic themes with Unarius: Heaven's Gate. During the years that Unarius was attaining Rotarian plumpness, the followers of Marshall Herff Applewhite and Bonnie Lu Nettles were essentially vagabonds living out of cars and in cheap hotels.

As for Ernest Norman, dead or alive he deserved a place of honor on the Unarius roll of honor. Though Ruth's saucer prediction got the media attention, the primary interest of Unarius students, then and now, is a concept Ernest added to the mix in the fifties: "past-life therapy," the study of how your soul's (alleged) past physical incarnations affect you psychologically and spiritually in the present. Unarius students are taught that they've lived many times before in exotic civilizations like Atlantis, ancient Egypt, the planet Vixall, and a distant, long-ago galaxy called Orion. They also believe that by using recovered-memory techniques to examine these lives, they can work toward a more perfect self, a process known as "progressive evolution." In this scheme, the Normans have special distinction. They are both archangels (Ernest's archangel name was Raphiel, Ruth's was Uriel) who came to Earth out of sheer generosity to show debased humans how to advance to a higher level.

But alas, these facts don't fully convey the Unarius style, which was personified by Ruth Norman, a true American original who combined the couture sensibilities of a drag queen with the *joi de vivre* of a Frisbee-chasing Irish Setter. She translates best on film and videotape, but even on the printed page her strange vitality leaps out.

Take, for example, *A Beginner's Guide to Progressive Evolution,* a book-length transcript of a 1978 class in which Uriel guided Unarius students through the wrenching pain of their past-life involvement with drug and snake cults on the lost continent of Atlantis. In it, she assures them that the painful memories are worth the agony: the students are all part of a "nucleus" of Unarian love and light that will eventually brighten up the entire sorry Earth.

"The problems!" she exclaims. "If you stockpile all the problems of the earth world . . . and put them all percentage-wise, and really analyze them, it would make you feel like walking off the end of the pier."

Suicide has never been the Unarian way, so Uriel railed mightily against despair: "[B]ut of course we know that doesn't solve anything and what this world needs now, is Unarius! Well, the majority of the people haven't arrived at the point where they have heard of us just yet but . . . just wait!"

The Unarius students believe it, and they observe the Space Brothers' pending arrival every year with a lavish pageant called Interplanetary Confederation Day. In celebration, they sing a metrically challenged song, "The Vehicles of Light," in which they pledge allegiance to their belief in Ruth's vision:

> *From out of the Spiraling Galaxies,*
> *From the Roaring Seas*
> *Of Connected Energies*
> *Come the Vehicles of Light!*

> *The Prince of the Realm*
> *Ordains Great Gifts*
> *For People of Earth to Change*
> *Our World*
> *And All There-in the Space Ships*
> *Are Lovingly Laden!*

> *The Spacefleet Coordinator,*
> *Uriel Extends the Lighted Hand*
> *Harken to the Welcome Hum*
> *AWAKE! AWAKE!*

∞

I first heard about Unarius in 1987. I was idly flipping through a directory of "experts and spokespersons" and came across the face of Louis Spiegel, an old man whose smiley, droopy features were capped by a badly fitting wig. The ad explained that Spiegel was a Unarius higher-up who had written a spiritual autobiography, a 536-page masterchunk, published in 1985, called *The Confessions of I, Bonaparte.* It appeared to be about his past life as Napoleon. Given

Napoleon's timeless status as a role model for the institutionalized, that sounded like a joke. I phoned Unarius and got Spiegel on the line. It wasn't a joke. In a resonant monotone, he told me all about it, sounding as if we'd been friends for years.

"Greetings, Alex, and may I suggest that your call could not have come at a better time? This is an auspicious moment for our organization, and it may be that you, too, were moved to contact us, for reasons that you do not yet fully comprehend!"

Spiegel explained that Unarius was an acronym for UNiversal ARticulate Interdimensional Understanding of Science. Meaning? He said that it was nothing less than "fourth-dimensional physics" and that I should "come visit immediately to gain a first-hand understanding." That wasn't possible, so to begin my education he generously mailed a copy of *I, Bonaparte*. A baroque, lumbering work, its opening page revealed a Miltonian theme that was heavy on the curative powers of multiple reincarnation.

"I am eternally thankful to my Spiritual Teacher, Ruth Norman," wrote Spiegel, "for the 'immensity' of her accomplishment with the magnitude and significance of my healing! This is clear in my willingness to write and publicize the extensive nature of my previous lifetimes as the negative force, Satan!"

Satan? Yes, and not just him. Spiegel believed he'd been quite a few world-historical figures, his spirit having traveled a long and rocky astral road. It took a while to make sense of it, but with help from him and his book, I finally got the picture.

It all began millions of years ago, at a time when the entire universe was at peace, overseen by goodly beings like Uriel, Raphiel, and their two colleagues Michiel and Muriel. Trouble started on a faraway planet called Tyron, which was experiencing problems with a dawning Ice Age and what Spiegel calls "10-story-high mammals and dinosaurs." An advanced being named Antares observed Tyron's plight and descended to the planet, in physical form, to help out. This was a mistake. According to Spiegel, Antares's decision to "manifest physically" condemned him to an existence away from the realm of light.

Over time, Antares got revenge by incarnating as Tyrantus, a Ming the Merciless–like ruler of the planet Tyron and the larger Orion Empire, an advanced, *Star Wars*-y confederation of planets that existed for eons, starting 800,000 years ago. Through the ages, Antares also existed as, among others, Hannibal, Julius Caesar, Nero, and Cardinal Richelieu—strong men who were all overwhelmed by pride. His last incarnation was less remarkable: in 1921, he was born as Louis Saul Joseph Spiegel, the son of a Jewish family living in Toronto. (Spiegel has used different first names over the years, but most often he calls himself either Charles Spiegel or Antares.)

This all sounds insane to outsiders, but it's important to remember that this prehistory is as real to a Unarius student as Jesus' life and death is to a Christian, and for a select few individuals this belief system is very real—and sacred.

Obviously, it's a rarely acquired taste. Unarius recruits energetically, using magazine advertisements, the World Wide Web, exhibits at New Age expos and on college campuses, television, radio, direct mail, and word of mouth, but most people just laugh and walk away. Or run. Counting "home study" students in the United States and abroad—there has even been a minuscule Unarius mission in Kenya— there are probably only a few hundred believers at any given time. They study a "science" (the Normans rejected labels like religion or faith) that is a lively, eclectic grab-all, drawing on Hindu ideas about karma, the esoteric practice of past-life therapy, and a New Age presumption that higher-level spiritual beings populate the universe. The Normans believed that Earth is a lowly spiritual place—"a kindergarten," Spiegel says—where backward souls are sent to pursue spiritual self-improvement. The hows and whys are complicated, but basically, if a student works at being good in each lifetime, improvements accrue and he or she evolves toward enlightenment. Unarians apply themselves to this task through home study, group discussions, and past-life reenactments called "psychodramas," in which they play-act their actions in earlier civilizations. In the process, they learn that their current behavior and problems are always "relivings" of ancient negative deeds.

Spiegel, of course, piled up more negatives than most people. To cut straight to the worst: he was Pontius Pilate, so he crucified Jesus, who, according to Unarius lore, was a previous incarnation of Ernest Norman. Photographs in *I, Bonaparte* show Spiegel and Unarius students in biblical garb and fake beards, reenacting the fateful trial in Jerusalem. "I had the opportunity at that time," Spiegel laments, "to work with the higher Spiritual Forces and take a stand against . . . the negative forces that lived within the memories of man."

Soul-wrenching though it is, the real message of *I, Bonaparte* is the redemption Spiegel earned through the tender mercies of Uriel and the Brothers, who travel through space and time helping humanity. (Among Uriel's previous identities are Socrates, Peter the Great, Charlemagne, Queen Elizabeth I, Quetzalcoatl, and Mary of Bethany, "the betrothed of Jesus and the 13th disciple.") Sometimes, though not always, Uriel was assassinated and tortured during her intercessions. Unarius belief has it that in various epochs and on various worlds, she was thwarted or murdered, usually at the hands of Antares or other similarly debased Unarius students. For example, in the ancient civilization of Lemuria (the Pacific Ocean counterpart to Atlantis), Spiegel was Ta-Nu, an initially wise and good ruler whose spirit degenerated over time. Uriel appeared on the scene as Ra-Mu, a wise man who established a temple devoted to progressive evolution. One fateful day, Ta-Nu summoned Ra-Mu to his palace, ostensibly to celebrate this new wisdom. After a great feast, Ra-Mu was led into a room "for a private showing of art objects." Instead he was zapped by a "high-energy disintegrator."

Happily, Uriel's spirit prevailed. Uriel declared in the mid-eighties that Spiegel had become "good" Antares again. "Now, as Antares," Spiegel exults in *I, Bonaparte,* "I pledge to assist all persons who formerly suffered at my hands, and help them cross over the 'Rainbow Bridge of Light,' to continue their progressive evolution!"

Uriel's word was law in Unarius, but even for believers, this transition must have been jarring. How could Uriel be sure that after all those millennia of impishness and evil, Antares was truly reformed? Couldn't it be just another trick?

Uriel addressed this in a preface to *I, Bonaparte*: "You may quest or wonder how he can be sure that he has overcome the many horrible . . . tyrannical pasts. Well, the proof of this is in the fact that now he can talk about any or all of the pasts without the usual guilt feeling."

That didn't sound too convincing when I read it, but it certainly increased my desire to visit Unarius. Unfortunately, that had to wait until 1994, when I received an invitation that I couldn't pass up, to the "40th Celebration of Love and Light." Every year, Unarius celebrates the founding of the science, which coincides with the Normans' first meeting around the time of Valentine's Day 1954. The fortieth promised to be especially significant because, after a long and painful decline, Ruth Norman had died in her sleep the previous summer at age ninety-three. This was shattering for two reasons. First, obviously, the Unarians had lost their beloved friend and leader. Second, Uriel had stated repeatedly that she would be on hand to greet the Brothers when they arrived in 2001.

Her death represented what scholars of millennial movements have called "disconfirmation." That is, her prophecy—that she would be around when the New Age dawned—was shown to be false. Disconfirmation is often fatal to millennial movements, but sometimes the loss can actually lead to consolidation and strength. (For example, many non-Christian observers of Christianity think of it as a group that used the myth of resurrection to gain strength after its prophet was killed and failed to rise from the dead.) I wondered: Which would it be with Unarius?

Whatever happened, it would occur under a dramatically different leadership. With Uriel gone, that old devil Antares was now the top entity.

∞

After discussing the mission with my wife, Susan—"Find out if any of her old tiaras are for sale," she demanded—I flew to San Diego, rented a car, and pointed it toward Ruth World. The Unarius headquarters sits in an old, one-story commercial structure on South Magnolia Street in El Cajon, a city of 75,000 people about fifteen miles east of San Diego. El Cajon is a typical semi-arid Southern California sprawlville. The long blocks are crammed with the usual SoCal effluvia that everyone carps about—too many cars, too many shopping centers, too many muffler outlets and burrito stands. But if you come from someplace with gray skies and skinny, bumpy streets—I was living in Chicago at the time—it's a nice change of pace. If nothing else, you can get away with driving 50 in town.

I nosed my rental car into the Unarius parking lot early on Friday afternoon, hoping to poke around before the reunion crush began. The Unarius exterior hints but does not scream that something different is going on inside. A large plastic sign out front reads UNARIUS ACADEMY OF SCIENCE, and one side of the building is slathered with a New Agey mural, "The Eye of the Infinite," which depicts spaceships whizzing about in an other-worldly landscape, all rendered in Easter egg colors. Once you pass through the front doors, though, you've unmistakably crossed a perceptual divide. Walking under a columnar arch hung with fake ivy, a wind chime, and a small disco ball, I saw a bright, airy decorative pastiche that was equal parts outer-space kitsch depot, meditation garden, mad-scientist's lair, branch library, and church meeting hall. The largest room, the meeting space, contained several rows of chairs, a softly burbling fountain, various neoclassical chubbies standing on pedestals, a portable chalkboard, and simple bookshelves groaning with Unarius titles. A narrower room—to the left, on the other side of a row of spaced faux-Corinthian columns—was crowded with strange displays, including a model of a futuristic urban area ("Crystal Mountain City") protected by a plexiglass pyramid. Mounted on the rear wall was a two-dimensional plywood-and-colored-lights representation of the 2001 saucer landing. Up front stood an eight-foot-tall gizmo that resembled a Tesla Power Tower.

And so it was. Tesla is a crucial figure in the fringe world because he combined undeniable genius with equally undeniable crackpotism. Among his achievements, he built the first motor that utilized alternating current and designed the power-generating facilities at Niagara Falls. Among his missteps, he laughed off the research of atomic scientists (calling them "metaphysicians") and claimed to have invented a death ray, a means to split the Earth in half, and (some say) a source of universal free energy that could be transmitted throughout the world without benefit of wires.

Unarians revere him without reservation. They believe, as do many non-Unarian Tesla buffs, that his lost inventions share basic principles with the lost technology of Atlantis, and that Tesla devices will thrum again in the utopian, intergalactic future. "The Tesla Tower," a poem written by a Unarius student, celebrates this dream, saying that the Tower will "Interconnect the vast Inter-Galactic Space Confederation into one united whole."

Hoping that Spiegel would meet me at the center, I'd called him from my room before coming over, but he chucked me a curve. He was at the Light House, a residence leased by Unarius, and he casually mentioned that he wouldn't be coming down "until later." He told me to ask for Carol Robinson, a middle-aged woman who managed the office. After stalling a minute at the bookshelves, I approached an older Unarius student who was reading at a table and asked where to find her. He looked startled and scurried off through a door. He came back with Carol in tow. She looked crabby. No doubt she was busy, and I don't think Spiegel told her I was coming.

"Now, what is it you were wanting?" she said, studying me with the smiley-frowny, quizzical look of Dr. Zaius in *Planet of the Apes.*

"I'm here for the weekend. Mr. Spiegel said I could come down this afternoon and look around."

"What is it you wanted to look *at?*"

Well, in fact, only one thing: the file cabinets full of transcripts. Each Unarius class is taped and typed, and I especially wanted to see how students reacted when Ruth Norman died. Starting with that didn't seem wise ("Fetch me the Uriel death log!"), so I vaguely asked to look at old scrapbooks of press coverage. Carol brought three and whumped them on the table. I started in on a puffy volume that bulged with yellowing clips protected by plastic.

The earliest clips were random science curiosities collected, probably by Ernest, in the early sixties, with headlines like "Scientist's Tests Show Bugs Think" and "Man, Mice Have Much in Common." Before long Ruth takes center stage, and it's easy to see why. In photographs, Ernest wears a charcoal suit and looks kindly, earnest, and dull, like a high-school science teacher circa 1955. Ruth virtually leaps off the page, and it's not just because she's wearing a rainbow mylar empress gown and carrying a scepter. (Though that helps.) There's also an inner glow at work, a star quality, and people noticed. When Ruth became a media darling in the seventies, reporters showed up for a laugh—which they got—but they usually left charmed. She spoke in high-pitched eruptions of dottiness, sounding like a combination of Julia Child, Aunt Clara on *Bewitched,* and a bossy little girl telling other little girls the rules of her playhouse.

Above all there were the Uriel costumes, flabbergasting contraptions that, at their most outlandish, were more stage set than clothing. One of them, "The Cosmic Generator," is a living tableau that illustrates how the planets of the Interplanetary Confederation are linked together. From the waist down, a huge "skirt" of deep blue billows out, studded with bas-relief, brightly colored planets connected by golden star trails. Each planet is labeled with its exotic name: Po, Vulna, Endinite, Severinus, Brundage, El, Deva. From waist level to neck blazes a deep-orange sun "collar," whose far-reaching, glittery flames lick out beyond Uriel's head and shoulders. Her hands are encased by silver mitts twinkling with tiny star lights. On her head sits a tall, swirling peaked cap—also spiraled with lights. The only visible flesh is her pale, contented face, grinning under an ample blonde wig.

It was truly something. My hand cramped just from taking notes about it.

When I looked up, Carol was hovering, clearly annoyed. "Are you finished with those?" she said. Now I was getting annoyed. What was the problem? I decided to counterattack.

"Yes, I am. So I'm ready to look at the files now."

"The files?"

"Yes. The class transcripts. Mr. Spiegel said there was no better way to gain an understanding of the science than to read about the classes in action. He told me to be sure to study them carefully."

Carol didn't like that, but she was temporarily rooked. She escorted me to the office, showed me around, and boiled silently while I pawed. It didn't take long to see that they contained everything I wanted. A class held on July 16, 1993—four days after Ruth's death—was entirely devoted to grief. A summary up top said, "Joseph, Barbara Jarad, David Keymas, Thelma, Lianne, and Neosha give testimonials regarding their experiences with Uriel's ascension." I actually felt overheated.

Unfortunately, trying to take notes on this twenty-nine-page dialogue would be deadly, so I decided to knock off. "Whew!" I sighed, replacing the folders and making a last attempt at good inter-Carol relations. "I am learning *so* much from these classes."

"Yes, well," she said, "good-bye."

∞

That evening the Unarians assembled at the center for "friendship renewal." Spiegel skipped this too, so the master of ceremonies was an affable, nice-looking young man named Joseph Downey, one of several Unarius students who, under Ruth Norman's tutelage, had risen by developing the ability to "subchannel" the Brothers. About a hundred people showed up—adults of all ages, from all over, local students and far-flung home-study types alike—and the evening percolated with the cheerful atmosphere of a successful family reunion. The men wore jackets and ties and were red with happiness. The women wore churchy prints and lots of makeup and solid-colored dresses—light blue, pink, lime-sherbet green—that hinted at somebody's past life as a bridesmaid.

Many of the out-of-towners came from the East. The hub of Unarius influence there is North Carolina, thanks to the tireless efforts of an intense guy named Dan Smith, who often appears on talk-radio shows touting the science. I recognized Smith as the wide-eyed star of *The Arrival,* a Unarius-produced video that uses melodramatic sci-fi to lay out the basic tenets. The main character is Zan, an aboriginal earthling who is hooting around the campfire one night when an immense spaceship drops from the sky. The ship contains eleven bald scientists from outer space who communicate with Zan telepathically. They explain that his apish consciousness traces back to an evil deed he committed 200,000 years earlier: as commander of an Orion battle cruiser, he zapped an entire planet, killing 4 billion people.

I took a long, hard look at Dan, a kindly, fuzzy-haired man who looked about as dangerous as a woodchuck snoozing in clover. Could he really believe he had performed such deeds?

Standing in front of the Power Tower, Joseph brought things to order, asking audience members to introduce themselves before he opened the floor to testimonials. He went first, speaking at length about how the Unarius classes had recently witnessed a procedural revolt that had "brought out some rotting things that have been laying in the psychic anatomy for quite some time."

That sounded juicy, but it wasn't. It was, however, a good example of how Unarius students tend to overanalyze even the tiniest moments. Joseph explained that the instructors had been routinely arriving late. In response, the class members got fed up and complained. Uh huh. He continued: this airing of criticism was very significant, a sign that the students were learning to function without Uriel. Criticism had been one of her main functions, delivered verbally or in detailed letters that Joseph said could be "scathing." They sometimes hurt but they were also "very valuable."

"We are learning to do for ourselves what Uriel helped us do for many years," he said. "It's no accident that Uriel left when she did. I believe that she would have remained if she didn't think we were ready to continue the mission."

Several personal testimonies followed. Brian, a sunny-faced blonde who worked as a gardener at the Light House, generically said Uriel and the house itself gave off an aura that helped heal him. Mark, dark-haired and fidgety, said that when he arrived at Unarius, "I might as well have been wearing a headband that read 'Egomaniac' and a shirt that said 'I am the ultimate materialist.'" Uriel cured that as well.

But there was no mistaking this gathering for just any old New Age revival. A longtime student named David Reynolds stood and described a device that, Tesla-like, he had worked on and abandoned some time back. Called the Bensteveray, it was designed to take musical notes and "convert them to light waves of an appropriate color." This harmless plaything, intended as "a healing object," had aroused guilt feelings in Reynolds. He hadn't known why until one day he experienced a vision. He saw himself as an evil scientist in the Orion Empire, giving a public demonstration of a "tower" very similar to the Bensteveray. Among those in the audience was . . . Uriel.

"Suddenly," said Reynolds, eyes widening in his friendly, waxy face, "I saw her to say, 'He's gonna kill us all! He's gonna murder us!' And so she made a mad dash to get out of the room. But it was too late. All the doors were sealed shut and she was doomed at that time to a horrible murder." Pause. "*I was the one who pulled the trigger!*"

Topping this for sheer gruesomeness was Lianne, Joseph's wife and another Unarius student leader. A dark-haired and stern-looking young woman, Lianne said she had recently suffered a bad flu, so she asked the Brothers for a "reading" about it. They complied and she learned of a past life in which she was a "mean, big, fat king." Tired of her guff, a mob dragged her into the streets and chopped off her head.

"And that's where I got the coughing," she said sweetly. "From my severed head."

Such anecdotes are typical of Unarius therapy in action. Students tend to identify dramatic, often violent past events as sources for ordinary faults or problems like drug use, unemployment, envy, sloth, weight gain, moody pets, general unhappiness, and (an oft-mentioned theme) masturbation. The old anti-Freudian cliché that sometimes a cigar is just a cigar doesn't apply to Unarians. With them, it's more accurate to say that a cigar is never *merely* a penis. It's more likely to be a 20,000-volt torture probe that was jammed up Uriel's rectum in Lemuria. Examples of how the mundane becomes the macabre are found all through *A Beginner's Guide to Progressive Evolution,* the book about the Atlantis drug and snake cults. A student named Roberto Gaetan describes a terrible revelatory memory in a restaurant. A person he was with served himself some "red and yellow" Jell-O. Gaetan started to feel sick. He flashed back to an image of himself as a priest at an ancient "sexual orgy," and realized he had ripped a breast off a human torso and "squeezed it like a lemon over my head."

After the evening broke up, I tried to socialize with the Unarians, to gingerly begin the long process of getting to know them, but I got nowhere. I spoke to Dan and Lianne, among others, but beneath surface friendliness they seemed guarded. Dan gave me tense, short-sentence answers until he managed to get away. Lianne was friendly but evasive. She asked what I was writing about. I told her I was interested in people who were interested in the millennium.

"Millennium," she said, tasting the word. "I don't know what that means."

Eventually I gave up and trudged a few blocks to a bar, where I sat drinking and brooding while drunks from a wedding party sang karaoke. I was confused. Usually I had to *earn* people's dislike. Why had it come so automatically here?

∞

Saturday at the Unarius headquarters turned out to be a long, grueling experience that ended with me whipped and whimpering in the progressive-evolution doghouse. As I realized later, it had been wrong to think the Unarians took a personal dislike to me. They just didn't like journalists in general, and for good reason. But in a few hours on Saturday I made a breakthrough: they definitely disliked me for me.

I didn't mean to be naughty. But I had to see those files without Carol bugging me, so I was on the premises and hard at work, beavering through the cabinets and melting down the photocopier before she showed up. By the time she came, I'd compiled a cubic foot of goods, but I kept chugging anyway, slapping down page after page as her temperature rose. The boil-over happened quickly. Carol made a call (to Spiegel, probably), yanked the copier's plug, and angrily told me to vacate the file room. I skulked out—*with* the nefarious load, which went straight into the rental car's trunk. After that I went back inside and crept around silently, looking at the exhibits, trying to go unnoticed until the day's big event started, a complete tour of the Unarius facility.

The fun began at the 2-D model of the thirty-three flying saucers, where Lianne told about two dozen listeners—most of whom were Unarians and knew this already, including Dan Smith—that the bigger landing will be prefaced by the arrival of a giant starship from the planet Myton, which will land on an "island mass" rising from the Caribbean. (Later, after people have had a chance to "adjust" to the new reality, the thirty-three confederation ships will land outside El Cajon.) The thirty-three themselves varied in size, but were designed to fit together in a stack. "The way the ships have been constructed," she explained, "the bottom ship will be 3,000 feet in diameter. Can you picture how big that's gonna be? Huuuuuge. And then they reduce in size on the way up, to 300 feet for the top ship."

She rattled off more stats. Exactly 33,000 higher spiritual beings will inhabit the ships' various levels, with the "earth people" granted a place of honor on top. "Surrounding this starship configuration," she added, "will be an entire city that will be built, and you will see a replica of this in the next room."

We shuffled over to the burg-under-glass, Crystal Mountain City. Arthur, an older-gent Unarian, took over and described it as a sort of progressive-evolution enterprise zone, "a halfway house between this world and the higher spiritual world." He gestured sweepingly at the surrounding space, a lavish, mural-lined room that was chock full of Unarian artistic statements. This, we learned later, was the Star Center Room, which had been refurbished ten years before by a former Unarian named Stephan Yancoskie, a talented artist who conceived of the mural. Strangely, despite this obviously large contribution, mention of Yancoskie's name made a couple of people cringe. I later found out why: he was a rising Unarius star who had left the group under a dark cloud years before.

"Is there any reason the Crystal Mountain City is encased in a pyramid?" a woman asked.

"No," Arthur sniffed congenially. "There wasn't any grand metaphysical idea behind it. It was more practical than anything else. The plexiglass is to keep the dust out, and it's easier to make a pyramid than a sphere."

There was no shortage of metaphysical significance at our next stop: Uriel's jewelry case, which contained baubles and costume-jewelry crowns. A Unarian named Crystal, a blonde with thin hair and a trembly bearing, explained that each of these "personal treasures" are "polarized to Uriel's higher consciousness." She showed us a red glass rose. "This was one of many gifts the Unarius students gave Uriel in appreciation. The red rose represents the red rose that Ernest Norman gave her—"

At this she started sobbing—hard. Dan Smith stepped up to offer comfort. Giving her a cozy sideways hug, he said, "Crystal's overcome with the love that she's feeling for Uriel and the Brothers right now."

The tour continued, to a second building that contained the pressroom, costume shop, and Unarius's video and sound studios. A Unarian named Dave explained that the studio space was once a trashed-up attic, and that many, many hours of manual labor were required to convert it to its current spiffy splendor. And yes, as usual this tied in with a "reliving." Dave said the demolition crew realized "we were living through negative lives of having destroyed a temple."

But at the moment I didn't feel like snickering about that. I kept thinking about Crystal, and the awful reality of her grief.

∞

"Nooooo, Alex! Don't you see? You're reliving! I suspect that in a past life, you were an evil scribe."

But first, the awful reality of my grief. It was later that afternoon. I was sitting alone in my hotel room, steeped in the lonely odors of boiled sheets and mildewed carpet, taking high, hard ones over the phone from Spiegel, who was madder than a wet Tyrantus. The more I whined defensively, the madder he got.

"But you *said* I could look at the files. What's the difference between making copies and taking notes? It's just a more efficient way to do the same thing."

"No! You're masking the truth as part of your reliving."

"I'm not reliving anything."

"Yes, you are!" Pause. "Your denial is *part* of the reliving!"

It went on like that, with specific punishments meted out among the circular chastisement. Spiegel had promised to let me interview him at the Light House and see the fabulous "Space Cad," a customized Cadillac with a flying saucer mounted on the roof, used to transport Unarius dignitaries on important occasions like Interplanetary Confederation Day. That was out. Obviously, I was banished from the file room. I offered to hand the files over as a gesture of reconciliation, but Spiegel said that wouldn't be necessary.

"The photocopies aren't the point"—good, I was bluffing—"I just want you to take some time and examine your motives." Click.

Fair enough. As Spiegel commanded, I did think about it seriously, then and over the next few hours, as I pawed through some unread press clips about Unarius and absorbed the full horror of who Stephan Yancoskie was. In the process I realized why the Unarians might be tense. To them, I was just another in a long line of outsiders come to plunder their sanctuary.

To understand what I mean it's necessary to put Unarius in historical context. The group is certainly distinctive, but it's not unique. It's one of many similar outfits that sprouted on the American scene after the first major reported sightings of flying saucers occurred in 1947. As Jerome Clark explains in *The UFO Encyclopedia,* Unarius is a "contactee" group, one whose members are less concerned with the hard metal edges of UFOs than the gauzy spiritual significance of their pilots, whom they assume to be not amphibian-fingered ETs but tall, wise, and kindly Space Brothers—essentially, as Clark puts it, "angels in space suits." The details vary, but the Brothers' message (usually delivered telepathically) is that Earth is in trouble and they can help. Anyone who listens is promised enlightenment, salvation, and elevation to a higher level, and as is true with most millennial believers, this deliverance is almost always coming "soon."

That was the basic theme of Heaven's Gate, of course, but that group, founded under a different label in 1972, was a relatively recent arrival. One of the first significant contactee players was the late George Adamski, a California occultist who in 1952 claimed that he had experienced physical and mental contact with an extraterrestrial from Venus. It all started when Adamski and six like-minded friends were driving around in the desert near the California-Arizona border. They saw a "huge, silvery cigar-shaped object" pass overhead. Adamski wandered away from the group and returned later with a spectacular tale. According to the *Encyclopedia,* he claimed he'd met a "beautiful-looking being of human appearance, with long blond hair and an 'extremely high forehead.'" The being said it and other entities were "coming here in peace, out of a deep concern about humanity's atomic weapons and warlike ways." Adamski used this alleged encounter to launch a long and controversial career as a flying saucer prophet.

Plenty of similar tales and movements followed. The Aetherius Society, founded in 1956 in London and in existence today in Los Angeles, dispenses wisdom channeled from a Venusian, Aetherius, who is part of a larger cosmological brotherhood. On the contemporary New Age scene, the contactee message is so common that it's become almost a bore. Heaven's Gate was a typical contactee group with one very novel element in its theological mishmash: the dark suicidal note. Usually contactees are sunny and harmless, for obvious reasons. They're awaiting a happy fate—angelic blessing.

In terms of understanding Unarius, the most significant contactee outfit was a short-lived but famous group that coalesced in 1954 around Dorothy Martin, a suburban Chicago housewife who believed she received messages from Sananda, an ascended being who, apparently, was the same spirit that inhabited the historical Jesus. Sananda was part of a larger corps of "Guardians" who, Martin was told, were watching the Earth from a higher spiritual plane. They were especially alarmed by the development of nuclear bombs. Eons before, mad scientists on the planet "Car" had blown it up using similar weapons, and this time the Guardians were determined to stop the insanity.

This aid would come with a price, however. Martin was told that on December 21, 1954, terrible floods and earthquakes would disrupt the entire planet, killing billions of people and reshaping the Earth. Anyone wise enough to heed the warning would stand a chance of being beamed into flying saucers and saved at the last moment.

Contactees are usually well-meaning people, and Martin decided it was her responsibility to warn the world, so she sent out a press release. Martin and her tiny band thus came to the attention of reporters and townspeople who, as the months rolled by, subjected them to ceaseless ridicule as they monitored the crashing failure of her prophecy. (The same thing happened in March 1998 to members of the Chen Tao group, a Taiwanese saucer cult that moved to Garland, Texas, in anticipation of the arrival of God that month.) She also came under the gaze of three academics, Leon Festinger, Henry W. Riecken, and Stanley Schachter. In short order, using graduate students and department staff posing as believers, they infiltrated Martin's group and documented its rise and fall.

The result was *When Prophecy Fails,* a classic 1956 sociological study of the dynamics of millenarian belief. The authors were careful and fair—they changed the names of everyone involved—but from the believers' perspective the book must have seemed cruel and inhuman, especially since they had been spied on. Even in the antiseptic language of social science, they came off as buffoons.

Consider, for example, this description of the night before the predicted catastrophe, when a dozen or so believers gathered in the home of "Mrs. Keech" (Martin's pseudonym). Sananda had said that all those planning to board the saucer should remove any traces of metal from their persons, so they got to it: "All the believers complied painstakingly with this order. Arthur Bergen . . . carefully unwrapped the tinfoil from each stick of chewing gum in his pocket. Coins and keys were removed from pockets and watches from wrists. . . . At about 11:15, Mrs. Keech received a message ordering the group to get their overcoats and stand by."

By 4:00 A.M., with no saucer in sight, despair crashed down. "Mrs. Keech broke down and cried bitterly. She knew, she sobbed, there were some who were beginning to doubt but we must beam light on those who needed it most and we must hold the group together. The rest of the group lost their composure, too. They were all, now, visibly shaken and many were close to tears. It was a bad quarter of an hour."

Mrs. Keech tried to keep up her spirits. At 4:45 she called everyone into her living room and announced that she had received a good-news message: the cataclysm had been called off. Why? Because God had spared the world, moved by the faith of the believers. "Not since the beginning of time upon this Earth has there been such a force of Good and light as now floods this room," the message said, "and that . . . now floods the entire Earth."

The authors of *When Prophecy Fails* called this "an adequate, even an elegant, explanation of this disconfirmation." That it was, but it didn't keep the group from disintegrating. As disappointed believers drifted away, Mrs. Keech started taking heat from local authorities. Her neighbors complained about the ongoing mob of curious spectators, schoolboys, and hecklers who assembled at her house. Threatened with forced deposit in a mental hospital, she moved away.

Thinking about Dorothy Martin made me realize two things. One, it's amazing that Unarius even exists. Founded in the same year that Martin's saucer group rose and fell, it ran on vapor for twenty years before it finally amounted to something. Two, for Unarius believers, the publicity that Ruth generated probably has been a mixed blessing. At best it has brought attention, new members, and the sort of way-out stardom that she seemed to thrive on.

At worst . . . well, there were two varieties of that: cold-blooded academic scrutiny and what might be called journalism-with-intent-to-kill. By the eighties, academic study of contactee groups was commonplace, and Unarius was discovered by two southern California academics, R. George Kirkpatrick and Diana Tumminia, who as usual worked hard to be fair and objective. But the Unarians hated what they published, which they found wrong, stupid, and offensive. One typical paper is called "Space Magic, Techno-animism, and the Cult of the Goddess in a Southern California UFO Contactee Group: A Case Study of Millenarianism." Among other things, it concludes that Unarians are low-watt losers, usually holding "working-class jobs" and often in recovery from drugs and alcohol: "From all indications, the majority . . . have a troubled background which may have lead [*sic*] to their susceptibility to the collective fantasy of flying saucer contact."

But that indignity was nothing compared with "The Gods Must Be Crazy: The Latter Days of Unarius," a 1991 article published in the *San Diego Reader,* an alternative newspaper. The piece was written by Adam Parfrey, a prolific and funny chronicler of fringe groups who visited during a dramatic period. Parfrey dropped in on Uriel at the Light House and described her as an incontinent and ridiculous old bat with a "broken leg elevated, [and] a bladder bag hidden discreetly behind the Barcalounger." Worse, he elicited a scandalous tell-all from Stephan Yancoskie.

As Parfrey explained, Yancoskie was a favorite of Uriel's and had risen high in the group. By the time Parfrey found him, he had departed after a feud and was ready to debunk every aspect of Unarius's holy image and dump on his former pals. He said he'd accelerated through the ranks easily because "the other members were weak . . . washouts." He also said Unarius was teeming with dysfunctional homosexuals and that he had served as Uriel's boy toy and wardrobe designer. The article never made it clear whether handsome young Yancoskie and old, bewigged Uriel were lovers—I doubt it, but mainly I try not to think about it—but he spoke in a leering sneer that left an impression of her as a vain and grotesque hag.

"I did her from top to bottom," Yancoskie sniped. "When I first came, she looked something like a country singer down on her luck. Then I designed her dresses, her wigs, the whole thing. She loved what I could do for her."

∞

If Yancoskie's catty talk makes you feel sorry for Uriel, that's fine. But save a few tears for the students, because old Ruth didn't always behave like an angel. Whatever her private life was like (and in the end, who wants to know?) she was, like almost any effective religious leader, a disciplinarian, capable of being harsh and exacting, and she had a knack for making the Unarius students feel Uriel's pain.

This isn't to say that Unarius is a dark cult in the style of Heaven's Gate. It's basically harmless, and the adoration of Ruth was not necessarily a bad thing. She and Ernest created something tangible—a brand-new faith—and the students got (and get) something in return. Unarius has been a second home and sanctuary for people who might otherwise be spiritually disenfranchised. Unfortunately, that comes with a price. In Unarius's case it isn't one of the usual cultic entry fees (your life savings, your slave labor) but one that is often used by mainstream religious groups: guilt.

Guilt certainly pervades *Effort to Destroy the Unarius Mission Thwarted,* a 1984 book that documents how Uriel cracked down on the Yancoskie heresy, which began when he trashed her in an impromptu speech at an evening class. It begins with a reprint of Yancoskie's forty-minute diatribe. It's not very shocking stuff, and I suspect it was edited for publication. Basically, he apologizes for doubting Uriel's divinity, for wondering if she was just a "glitter girl" who "wears purple hair and . . . doesn't really do much more than try and make everybody think that she is a great person." At the end of his milky criticism he chides himself for doubting her and vows to toe the line—a promise that doesn't last.

In response, Uriel fought back hard, making several descents from the Light House to condemn Yancoskie and terrorize the students for listening to him. "I am wondering why all of you students sat here and let this constant defamation and hate oscillation go on for forty minutes last Sunday?" she said. "Dear students, aren't you aware of what is said against me is to the entire Infinite? I am not a separate entity from the Infinite."

And yet, she understood. He was merely acting as the mouthpiece of "countless thousands of . . . lower astral forces" who wanted to destroy the Unarius mission. The students had failed to react properly because they were—yes—reliving an episode on the planet

Tyron, where Stephan had been a female leader named Shimlus who "robotized" her followers.

The rest of the book consists of the students "working out" this realization, trashing themselves relentlessly to earn forgiveness. One woman blamed herself for an old problem that had dogged her in the "Elizabeth I cycle," the "Hsuan cycle," and the "Ra-Mu cycle": she too wanted to "be" Uriel.

But David Reynolds topped that, in a testament that suggested that Unarius doesn't do quite enough to help its students emotionally. He said the Shimlus cycle made him understand his own serious problems with women and sex: "under [Shimlus's] regime . . . I got involved in these horrible sex experiments. . . . I've had a very difficult time in this life relating to the opposite sex, coming into this world very shy and timid with respect to women, which indicated a great imbalance in my psychic." In 1984, trying to conquer the problem, David met a girl and they started going out. But, regrettably, the relationship hit a snag when he realized that he had sexually tortured her on Tyron.

Amid all the moans and gnashings, one person extracted some joy from the situation: Spiegel. By the end of *Thwarted* Yancoskie hit the road permanently (I've been told he's dead now, but I couldn't confirm it), giving Spiegel a chance to hollowly eulogize his departure.

"We all know that about ten days ago," he said, "Stephen [*sic*] suddenly left town and did not show any courtesy to those to whom he owes his very livelihood, you might say, his ability to stay 'on his own two feet'! Stephen is an extremely unbalanced person, not only a nymphomaniac but also a schizophrenic. . . . A homosexual person is one torn between himself and his identity. It is an unfortunate and miserable kind of life to live! On top of that, he has the problem of alcoholism!"

Sniff.

∞

Traditionally held at the Unarius center, the 1994 Celebration of Love and Light took place at the fancy-pants Westgate Hotel in downtown San Diego, an expensive upgrade of venue. Unarians with cars volunteered to act as chauffeurs for their wheelless friends, so at dusk drivers and passengers gathered in the Center's parking lot to form carpools. As engines ticked and the late afternoon sun glanced gold off fenders, people socialized and chuckled. The men were dressed the same as the night before. The women had ratcheted things up a notch: from thrift-store bridesmaid to thrift-store prom date.

For my part, I caught a few frosty glances (word had spread!) and was assigned to drive three middle-aged women whose names I didn't catch. Two of them were very unfriendly—they may have heard I was evil—so I talked to the other one, a tiny sparrowlike creature who perched on the front seat and strapped in nervously. With nothing to lose, I tried a blunt opening.

"I had an interesting afternoon. Antares gave me a barbed-wire enema because I used the copying machine without asking." That amused her. A tiny crinkle of a smile formed. "Antares seems like he can be a pretty scary guy. What's the deal?"

Quietly: "Antares has changed a lot in this lifetime." Pause. "But because of who he had been and his position with Uriel and who he was in his past lives, he can be . . . domineering."

"Who was this Stephan Yancoskie?"

"Stephan . . . left Unarius." She winced. I knocked it off.

"It's a nice evening, isn't it?" I said.

"Yes, it is." Then she relaxed and proceeded to tell me all about how her marriage had collapsed because her husband didn't accept "the Science."

After a half-hour drive into San Diego, we parked in an underground tomb and shuffled to the hotel, the women advancing very slowly thanks to the hobble of their finery and footwear. Inside the Westgate, the Unarians were gathered in a large meeting room that was festively filled with white-clothed tables, flowers, candle glow, and gabbling comrades. I took a seat next to a hyper-friendly man named Alonso, who regaled me with Unarius lore. I'd heard it all before, but I was grateful anyone was even speaking to me.

"Unarius essentially began forty years ago because Ernest and Ruth Norman met on Valentine's Day 1954," he said, pointing at an old painting of the couple reprinted in the program.

"One thing I always wondered," I said. "Unarius started in 1954, but as far as I can tell nobody much heard of it until the seventies. What took so long?"

His instant reply: "For the first several years, the Normans spent a lot of time by themselves because they had so many past lifetimes where they were killed."

At a dais up front sat the Unarius brass: Spiegel, Joseph, Lianne, David Reynolds, and Dan Smith. I walked up to take my medicine.

"Charles Spiegel, I presume?" I said, extending a hand.

Instead of shrieking he took it and smiled, addressing me in the same weirdo-profundo monotone that he used when I phoned in 1987. "Greetings, Alex! Are you enjoying the evening?"

"Very much."

"Wonderful! I do hope to speak with you more later!"

And that was that. Let no man say Spiegel is entirely without mercy.

In addition, let no man say Spiegel is entirely without leadership qualities. In the early nineties, as Ruth Norman passed away, he faced the tricky task of maintaining order while Unarius struggled toward its uncertain future. Many religious movements have died at this moment—when the disconfirmation of the dead prophet cannot be explained away—but Spiegel kept this group together. As the transcripts show, he did it by displaying a combination of grace, discipline, and genuine love for a decrepit archangel whose demands must have been trying. In one transcript, there's mention of such depressing realities as Ruth's impacted colon and her "little electronic signaler," which she pushed "almost constantly" to summon her various Unarian caregivers at the Light House.

For a long time Spiegel was reluctant to tell me anything about his biography in this life, but when he finally did it was obvious he felt deep, sincere love for Ruth. Like many Unarians, Spiegel was predisposed toward the occult. As a student at the University of Southern California in the late forties, he had a vision that foreshadowed his eventual involvement with the Normans. He was working the night shift at the main post office in Los Angeles, walking in a dimly lighted hallway, when "all of a sudden a picture emerged out of the air. Full sized. Six feet tall. And there was a picture of a woman. It was a beautiful woman smiling at me. That was my first definite psychic experience."

What it all meant didn't become clear for years. Spiegel took a degree in psychology, moved east, got established as an insurance broker in Boston, got married, and worked while he continued to dabble in metaphysics. He sampled various beliefs but found a home in 1960 when he came across *The Voice of Venus* by Ernest Norman. Its wisdom rang true for him: "At first I said, 'This is just fiction, it talked about people who lived on Venus and they didn't have physical bodies,' but then one day I said, 'This is real, this is *real!*'"

He wrote the Normans and eventually visited in 1965. Result: instant, life-changing epiphany. "When Ruth Norman came to the door, she was wearing a tiara and she was beautifully dressed. I said, 'My God! That's the vision I had back in 1949.' That's when I decided this was where I was supposed to be." He visited a few more times in the sixties and moved out in 1972. His marriage didn't move with him.

Maintaining a personal devotion to Ruth was not as demanding as maintaining Uriel's immortal gloss in the face of obvious physical decay. Spiegel's method was to play the role of loving hardass. For example, in February 1992, when Ruth was still more than a year away from death, he came down to the Center to update the students on her health, which wasn't good.

"I'm not telling you that Uriel's dying," he said. "I'm just saying the physical body has a limit. It has a life cycle. Eventually, we will experience that transformation ourselves."

Spiegel opened the floor for questions. Unexpectedly, a student named Ken Bond came on strong, implying the worst: that Uriel's pending death cast doubt on her divinity. "Antares, maybe I'm confused a little bit on this," he said, "but I remember very clearly in 1986 IPC Day . . . that the mission is for her to be [here] until the year 2001."

Spiegel didn't like that. He shouted Ken down, thundering, "So what?!" and "Can you heal Uriel's body, her physical body?"

Ken babbled haplessly that he was only asking about a promise, but Spiegel shut him up with a radical restatement of what Uriel had, in fact, pledged. She would be here, *but in spirit*. "She wanted to greet the Brothers, but Kenneth, that physical body is not the real Uriel," Spiegel said. "She will be here, but in a way that will be much greater than it could be with a body that is not functioning. Don't you see, a higher being."

Ken evidently couldn't "see." He later left Unarius. But those who bought the new line faced a difficult test when Ruth finally died on July 12. On the sixteenth, Joseph and Lianne led the students in their grief discussion at the Center. Lianne's reverie was typical. She said she was at home when Uriel died, and there was a sign from above. She was writing in her journal when, near her, a flower in a vase fell off its stem. She later realized that this was a wink from Uriel's spirit, an indication that "Uriel is working with me just as closely" as before.

Dorothy Mandragos—a physical therapist who helped take care of Ruth—was present at the post-death scene with Spiegel and Dorothy Ellerman, Ruth's personal secretary. She described exactly what happened at the end.

> Antares and I sat there in the room and just talked. . . .
>
> I said, "Will you help me turn her?" We washed and put every-thing clean. Then I said, "Gee, you know, she was such a lady. Her hands are so beautiful, and her nails are all chipped." So, I redid her nails. . . .
>
> . . . We sat in there, just quietly with the music until [the under-taker] came. Then we left. Of course, they covered everything up, and when she went out the door, the body went out the door, Antares said to the man, "You're not covering up that beautiful face?"
>
> He said, "Body fluids, body fluids," and had everything covered and went out. But we sat down after she was gone. Dotty, Antares, and I, and we just talked and the Power in the room! I had no skull. There was nothing in the top of my head, and all I felt was the ener-gies pouring into my head, and oh, so sleepy! . . .
>
> The next morning . . . I went to work and I . . . wrote this:
>
> "You are free. Oh, beloved one, you are free! Free from all the bondage, the pain and misery of being imprisoned within a third dimensional body living on an earthean plane. . . ."

Very eloquent. In fact, Spiegel might be well advised to hire Dorothy as a speech writer. As he demonstrated Saturday night—and again on Sunday night, when lower-key festivities continued back at the Center—he's no toastmaster.

At the banquet he talked about the meaning of Unarius in a cou-ple of long, foggy harangues and emceed the presentation of awards. (Carol Robinson got one for running a tight ship back at the office. I applauded that with a deep sense of "inner knowing.") On Sunday he "channeled" the Space Brothers for a half hour of somnambulistic droning. Finally, the contrast of his style with Ruth's was dramatically illustrated by the world premiere of *Forty Years of Love and Light,* a video hagiography of Ruth and Ernest that showed precisely how much loopy pizzazz was lost when Ruth died. You see her in dozens of fabulous dresses, blinking under enough wigs to supply an entire college theater department. You see her charming David Susskind on his show ("My staff said you were *completely* sincere about all this, and I think they were right") and not quite charming a grumpy David Letterman, who cuts her off when she starts talking about the Power Tower. You see her laying healing hands on sobbing Unarius students. You see her at the 1989 Interplanetary Confederation Day, where students sob at her touch and celebrate the Space Brothers with the release of white birds from inside a hollow model of a flying saucer.

"We send *alllll* of our love to *alllll* of the people of *allllllll* of the worlds," she shrieks. "So fly away, dove, fly skyward!"

And at the end, in a moment that illustrates the powerful emotional hold she had on the students, you see a suitably togged Uriel—gold dress, glittery crown and scepter, gargantuan wig—marching through a double line of Unarians who are singing "You Light Up My Life."

Could she ever be replaced? At the banquet Saturday night, as Spiegel talked, I studied the dais and wondered if he might be on his way out. Would the aching contrast between him and Ruth prompt the followers to ditch him in favor of a new, livelier leader? I sat there handicapping which one of the four might fill the role.

David Reynolds? Nope. Too loopy.

Dan Smith? No, he still seemed too sobby from his past-life failings to take command. "There have been times," he confessed that night, "that I thought I'd never crack the shell of this monster ego I live inside of."

That left Lianne and Joseph, who definitely did possess what a sportswriter would call "superstar-type tools." They were young and good-looking, both were accomplished leaders, and Lianne obviously had drive and determination. That night she spoke in lilting boilerplate—"Something has been reignited within us and that's what's so exciting"—but my mind drifted back to a comment she'd made during the Uriel post-mortem meeting in 1993. It read like a prophecy of turbulent times to come: "In case it's not clear . . . obsessional forces are going to attempt [to] . . . divide us, divide from each other, and divide us in opposition to Antares or fear or memory of him."

Yeah, I thought: you. I made a mental prediction. In two years, if Spiegel hadn't already died, he would go down in a palace coup.

∞

I was half right. Lianne and Joseph did make a move, but it was more in the nature of self-imposed exile. As of mid-1998, Spiegel remained in charge, while Lianne and Joseph were living in purged removal from Unarius, making a living as freelance editors. The Center and its resources remained under Spiegel's control, and plenty of students (including David Reynolds and Dan Smith) decided to stick with him. Whether the loyalists acted out of love or fear I can't say, but I suspect that for many of them the determinative factor was that Spiegel had the keys to the castle. The idea of losing touch with the Center—the hallowed ground—was probably just too much.

I found out about the feud the same way I first learned about Unarius. Out of the blue one day I called Spiegel just to check in. After a few pleasantries I asked about Lianne and Joseph.

"Oh," he said blithely, "they're not with Unarius anymore."

What? What went wrong?

Ego crimes. "If you're interested in growing, mentally speaking, you have to accept the negative side of yourself. Everybody has a dark side. Lianne thought she was an advanced being. Her ego was her block. She really couldn't put down this attitude that she was right." That was about as specific as Spiegel got. He claimed to have no idea where they were living.

I eventually turned them up in Dulzura, California. Notably, unlike Stephan Yancoskie, they weren't eager to trash their former leader and only agreed to talk after I agreed that some topics would stay off limits. Basically, the dispute came down to theological minutiae, clashes about business decisions, and a whopping disagreement—as significant in its way as the split between Constantinople and Rome—about what the Brothers intended for the future direction of Unarius.

The fracas started, Joseph said, soon after the fortieth anniversary celebration. He was helping proofread a reprint of *Voice of Venus,* one of the early foundation texts of Unarius, written in 1954 by Ernest Norman. He noticed that the text had been altered to make Ernest's style more contemporary. Sacred words were being altered.

"I freaked out when I saw he was changing the books," Joseph said. "I confronted Antares and yelled at him and he denied it. I tried to confront all the rest of the students and nobody cared but me!"

How did they rationalize it?

"They said: You're emotional and he's the leader. See, by this time they had decided that Antares had taken on the 'psychic anatomy' of Uriel. People were heard saying this. They were already beginning to equate him with Uriel, like he had ascended to her role in some kind of weird religious situation.

"I had a couple of conversations with him about this. You know what he said? He said, 'Joseph, if you disagree with me, you're disagreeing with Unarius.'"

The final break came in 1996, during preparations for Interplanetary Confederation Day. Lianne and Joseph decided Spiegel planned to spend too much on frippery—including a $98,000 direct-mail campaign, professional grading of the landing sight, and rental of a big party tent—so they resigned their positions on the Unarius board and walked out.

According to Lianne, Spiegel phoned her on August 18, 1996—Uriel's birthday—poised for a weepy reconciliation. "He said he'd been in great physical pain and he called up and said, 'I really love you.' He asked me to come and serve as a channel so he could talk to the Unarius Brothers. I was more than willing to do that. I went to the Light House and he asked me to ask them about his upcoming plans for IPC day. The response from the Brothers was: no. They spelled it out in a really beautiful way. They said everybody was reliving following his orders."

Indeed they did: "You have attempted to strike out far into the future with your massive mailing pieces and your grand schemes in the desert," they scolded, "but you have, by doing so, struck deeply into the negative and have become entrapped there."

The upshot was twofold. First, Lianne says, Spiegel spoke to the Unarius students, admitting that the Brothers had rapped his knuckles. Then a few days later he reversed field, telling the students that the Brothers had been mischanneled by Lianne, obviously for her own devious ends of rewriting the "truth."

What it came down to was a simple but fundamental struggle over who would inherit the spiritual legacy. Lianne and Joseph lost, but as far as they're concerned the battle isn't over. "Unarius isn't about the Center," she told me. "It's about the teachings of Ernest and Ruth Norman. We'll keep that alive and thriving wherever we are."

You could think of this split as Unarius's version of the Great Schism, the period between 1378 and 1417 when there were two, and later three, rival popes in Catholicism, each with a dedicated following. Whether the anti-Unarians will prevail or vanish into excommunicated obscurity remains to be seen, but one equally likely outcome is that both factions of Unarius will wither and die, especially after 2001 arrives and the spaceships don't.

In fact, it's almost as if the whole thing were a cosmic plot to "thwart" the Unarius mission. Does Lianne ever wonder about this? Or about what it says of Ruth Norman's infinite wisdom? After all, why would she let Spiegel take over and mess things up? Did he trick her yet again?

They don't see it that way. First off, Uriel can't be thwarted—she *is* the infinite. Second, in spite of everything, they don't see Spiegel as evil, and in this they're remaining faithful to the teachings. "I don't think he's trying to create an empire for himself," Joseph said. "Any mistakes he's making are part of a battle that goes on within everyone. It's the duality of human nature."

"The Center was a great gathering place when Uriel was there," said Lianne. "Maybe it will go that way, maybe it won't. Maybe it's not needed anymore. Maybe it's like a baby that's outgrown its bassinet."

What about the spaceships—are they still coming?

"Oh, yeah, I think they are," said Joseph.

When they don't come, will you still believe in Uriel?

"Sure," said Lianne. "If it doesn't happen in my lifetime, it's gonna happen eventually. It wouldn't faze me all because I'm still growing spiritually."

You'll have to decide what that means on your own. For my part, I'm filing it under the unfathomable wonders of belief.

The Reverend Clyde Lott (left), Rabbi Chaim Richman, and a very special apocalypse cow.

2
The Sunny Side of the End

Whenever the sun shines brightly
  I rise and say,
Surely it is the shining of His face,
And look unto the gate of His high place
  Beyond the sea,
For I know He is coming shortly,
  To summon me;
And when a shadow falls across the window
  Of my room . . .
I lift my head to watch the door . . .
  And the Spirit answers softly
  In my home,
"Only a few more shadows,
  And He will come."

—FROM THE HYMN "HE SHALL COME," REPRINTED IN *THE SECOND COMING OF CHRIST,* BY THE REVEREND CLARENCE LARKIN (1918)

"They like to have their bellies scratched," said Clyde Lott, a softspoken Pentecostal minister and cattle breeder. It was May 1997, on a bright, warm, breezy Saturday morning, and Lott was showing off a few head of prize livestock inside an enclosed pen on his farm, a tidy layout just east of Canton, Mississippi, the town where John Grisham set *A Time To Kill.* Using a "show stick," a modified golf club with a dull point on the tip, he tickled the belly of a Red Angus cow named Harvey, who moved slowly around the pen with three other happy beasts. Harvey paused to blink and enjoy the scratching, and one of her colleagues seized the moment to liberate a prodigious green pie, which hit the dirt with a wet *plap-plap*.

"Now, see here?" Lott continued. "Her length and her structural correctness are two of the things we're trying to produce." He used the tool as a pointer, tapping flanks and legs and rump.

I leaned over for a squint. Harvey was a heifer, which means a young, virginal cow, and she was a nice-looking animal. She had a wide, muscular back that looked solid enough to dribble a basketball on, sturdy legs, and an all-body, velvety redness, down to the tiniest detailing—hoofs, whiskers, eyelashes. Even her skin was red, the color of blush wine. Earlier, Lott had shown me a picture of Harvey taken a few months before at the Dixie National Junior Livestock Show in Jackson, the nearby state capital (and, as it happens, the city where I was "calved" and lived until junior high). Harvey whipped all comers that day—she was named Grand Champion in her class, English Cross—and you could see why. She looked glowing, inspired, beatific even, like she'd been dipped in buttermilk and fluffed by a team of yackety, gum-popping hairdressers flown in from Oz.

Granted, in the glaring sunlight, Harvey looked more ordinary, what with all the flies buzzing around her. Still, the big gal had a quality.

"She's something, all right," I said, a comment that drew affirmative grunts from three other men who, just now, stood behind us: the Reverends Alfred Bishop and Guy Garner, Jr., red-faced and gray-haired Pentecostal ministers both, from Waverly, Tennessee, and Porterdale, Georgia, and Rabbi Chaim Richman, a pale, middle-aged, American-born Israeli who had traveled all the way from Jerusalem to be here. Why? Partly to check out Harvey, who in his mind was, as E. B. White might have put it, "some cow."

Lott, a husky forty-one-year-old with a neat cap of tightly curled gray hair, went on with the lecture. "And then there's the thickness of the animal, the width. Here again"—he tapped a shoulder—"is your muscle. In that particular pitcher you showed me earlier, I would say that muscle is one of the things you'd fall short on."

Lott was politely trashing a picture of a skinnier red calf named Melody, whose image had been published in *Newsweek* just a few days before my visit, under the headline, "The Strange Case of Israel's Red Heifer." The strange case involved Melody's supposedly miraculous birth (it was said she was the first all-red calf born in Israel since biblical times) and her possible role as a sacrificial animal in a restored Jewish Temple in Jerusalem. These offbeat matters tied into something that was flat-out bizarre: the potential fulfillment of apocalyptic and messianic prophecies that captivate millions of Christians and a much smaller (but significant) number of Jews. When I visited Lott, many messianic Israelis were in a tizzy about Melody's all-over redness—was she a sign that it was time to rebuild the Temple?—but he wasn't much impressed.

"She's a little swaybacked," he diagnosed when I pulled out the Melody pic. "I don't imagine she would be a very . . . sturdy animal."

Then *I* noticed a flaw.

"Are those white spots on her face?"

"Yessir," Lott said.

"Wouldn't that disqualify her from being 'perfectly' red?"

"Yessir," he said. "Those spots there would probably be from worms."

∞

It's strange but true: these four men are convinced that an animal like Melody or Harvey will play a crucial role in the End of the World as we know it. Stranger still, they're looking forward to this event with great joy. That part sounds confusing to untrained ears, but it points up a fundamental paradox of millennial beliefs: the way they can be terrible and wonderful at the same time.

Obviously, the rabbi and the preachers put different spins on
What Will Be. When Richman thinks end-of-this-world, he's hoping
the Messiah will show up—for the first and only time, making Himself known as an infinitely wise and righteous man who will banish
evil from the planet. The Christians think the Messiah, Jesus Christ,
has already come once and will soon come again, also to banish evil
and to usher in a kingdom of peace. Big, big differences. But for now
the men have decided to overlook them on behalf of a shared belief.
For all of them the major focus of longing, and the stage for a dramatic star turn by a heifer like Harvey, is the Temple Mount in
Jerusalem.

You've probably heard of the Temple Mount. A vast, raised trape-
zoidal wall, enclosing ruins and standing structures, it is perched on
a plateau alongside Mount Moriah in the Old City of Jerusalem, and
it is arguably the world's most famous religious site. Its underlying
millennial significance is not so widely known, but it has everything
to do with the unique confluence of sacredness on this holiest of
spots.

The Mount was home to two great Jewish temples that existed
in the ancient world before they were destroyed, in turn, by the Baby-
lonians (who tore down King Solomon's Temple in 586 B.C.) and the
Romans (who razed Herod's Temple in 70 A.D.). There's no Jewish
temple up there now, of course. Since the seventh century A.D., the
Mount has been under Moslem control. Muslims call the site the
Haram esh-Sharif, and it contains two important Islamic holy places,
the Dome of the Rock (also known as the Mosque of Omar) and the
el-Aqsa mosque. Because of these, Jerusalem is referred to as the
"third holiest city in Islam," after Mecca and Medina.

The various faiths find the Mount holy (or at least quite interesting) for conflicting reasons. The Dome is built over a rock that the
Muslims believe was the site from which Mohammed ascended on
a flying horse to visit Heaven, after his famous Night Journey from

Mecca to Jerusalem. To many Jews, the plateau is where Abraham, patriarch of the Hebrew people, prepared to sacrifice Isaac. Or they revere it because it was the site of the Holy of Holies in the Temple. For their part, Christians have a deep, Old Testament respect for the Mount, but it mainly symbolizes the spiritual revolution brought by Christ. They believe that by atoning for the sins of man with his blood, Jesus forever did away with the need for the priestly sacrifices practiced in the Temple.

The rabbi and the revs get moony-eyed about the Mount's Judeo-Christian heritage, but they're downright cranky about those mosques, which in a way are slaps in the face to both faiths. (The irritation factor for Jews is obvious; the Dome also contains a Christian-insulting inscription denying God could have a Son.) To them they're glorified eyesores, and they'd love to see them swept away, leaving the Mount miraculously rezoned for construction of what they optimistically call the "Third Temple." Richman's study of Judaism's writings and oral traditions tells him that it must be so. When the Messiah comes, He will reign inside a fully functioning Temple, a grandiose structure kept humming by a latter-day Temple priesthood and filled with long-lost treasures like the Ark of the Covenant, the box in which the ancient Israelites carried the Ten Commandments. (Opinions vary about whether the Messiah will come before or after the Temple is rebuilt, but Richman says, "To me it's like *Field of Dreams*: 'If you build it, he will come.'")

The reverends also want a Third Temple, but for a Christian cause: they believe it's a crucial "trigger" setting for the events preceding the Second Coming. Their prophecies indicate that a worldly, evil being known as the "Antichrist" will one day inhabit and desecrate the rebuilt Temple, an episode called the "abomination of desolation," and that it will be destroyed during the violent End-Time happenings described in the New Testament's Book of Revelation. But this calamity, awful as it will be (the bulk of humanity is doomed to die during a "great tribulation"), is supposed to be followed by something wonderful for all righteous people: a millennium of peace, with Christ returning to reign over a planet reborn into perfection.

Whichever version comes to pass, it's a drag for a cow like Harvey. Call it *A Time to Be Killed.* As explained in the Old Testament's Book of Numbers, which contains descriptions of ritual practices adopted by the ancient Israelites, the ashes of a sacrificed red heifer were needed in rites to purify priests who had been made "unclean" by contact with a dead body. In Numbers 19, God tells Moses and Aaron to order a priest to kill and burn "a red heifer without spot, wherein there is no blemish, and upon which never came a yoke." Much later, the ashes of the heifer became an integral part of Temple rituals in Jerusalem.

Richman, who moved to Israel in 1982, devotes much of his time to studying the ritual requirements of the Temple, with a special focus on the red heifer. He believes nine red heifers were sacrificed to produce ashes for the first two Temples, and that no appropriate animal has been born in the Holy Land since the Second Temple was destroyed. Before forming his own messianic group, Light to the Nations, he was a longtime affiliate of the Temple Institute, a Jerusalem-based outfit that has produced replicas of the implements and robes used by the ancient priests. Richman insists that the location of the all-important lost Ark is known—he won't say where it is, but many messianic Jews believe it's hidden under the Mount—so all that's missing to make the Temple viable is the red heifer.

"[I]n truth," Richman wrote in a 1997 book on the subject, "the fate of the entire world depends on the red heifer."

A surprising number of people in the United States and in Israel monitor these red heifer doings, which is why Melody caused a commotion. But alas, she was a dud: as Melody grew, she sprouted white hairs on her tail. Harvey didn't stay perfectly red either—she nicked herself on barbed wire, and white hairs sprouted where the wound had been. But that was all right, because there's no need for a heifer until the Temple is built. For Lott, Harvey was really just a test run of his ability to breed a suitable "Numbers 19" heifer on demand, when the time is right. Lott had also cooked up an ambitious plan to ship Red Angus to Israel, as the nucleus of a starter herd that, as a bonus, would improve the overall quality of Israel's second-rate livestock.

Interesting visions. Unfortunately, there's a problem that robs the scene of any Pooh Corner coziness. As Richman knows, his dream of rebuilding the Temple is, by definition, extraordinarily combustible. Islam never intends to abandon the Temple Mount, and any attempt to remove the Dome or build a Temple would probably touch off a major war in the Middle East. (Along these lines, one Israeli newspaper melodramatically referred to Melody as a four-legged time bomb.) Israel captured the Mount during the Six-Day War in 1967 but relinquished control in the interest of keeping future peace. The vast majority of Jews in the world want nothing to do with Temple visions, either. For them the idea isn't just dangerous, it's silly and backward. The temples are a fascinating part of Judaism's past, but not part of its future.

Nonetheless, unchecked "take back the Mount" enthusiasms have generated a considerable amount of violence over the years. In 1969, Michael Dennis Rohan, a fundamentalist Christian from Australia, set fire to the el-Aqsa mosque, citing a religious conviction that Jesus would return to Earth only when Jerusalem became completely Jewish and a Third Temple was built. In 1982, Alan Harry Goodman, a U.S.-born Israeli soldier, went on a deadly shooting spree inside the Dome of the Rock, claiming that he was on a holy mission. In 1984, members of a small messianic group called the Lifta Band sneaked onto the Temple Mount to blow up the Dome of the Rock, but the plan was aborted when they were detected by a Moslem guard. That same year, members of a much larger messianic cell called the Jewish Underground—made up of twenty-seven men, many of them from the Israeli army—were arrested before they could carry out a plot to blow up the mosques. In 1990 the Temple Mount Faithful, a messianic group, marched on the Mount, unfurling a banner that denounced the Moslem presence. During the riots that ensued, seventy-two Palestinians were killed.

Thinking about the potential for mayhem, I looked at Lott and Richman and contemplated the weird mix of harmless longing and dark peripheral possibility that, in my experience, often gets stirred together in the escapades of millennial believers. Could *these* guys be terrorists?

I doubted it very much. Many people who pine for a Third Temple are essentially religious hobbyists who spend their time getting the props ready. When you ask them how the mosques will be razed, they say loud and clear that setting the stage is God's prerogative, not theirs.

Still, any Temple buff is playing a dangerous game. To preach the need for a Third Temple is, by nature, to run the risk of "exciting" the wrong kinds of people.

Richman and Lott don't see it that way: they're just doing what their faith compels. At one point I asked Lott how he figured the "problem" of the mosques would be solved. He said, predictably, that God would take care of it. No telling when, but Lott hoped to live to see the day.

How would God do it? By precision-hurling an asteroid?

"Wellsir," Lott said, polite as always, "that's something I'd have to leave up to Him."

∞

The inspiration for Lott's beliefs is scriptural prophecy, a timelessly popular literary form that in our day involves a complicated mix of Bible thumping, crackpot theology, contemporary paranoia, and a wide-ranging sense of shuddering delight about the violent changes that will occur when mankind is finally delivered from evil. Prophecy belief is an institutionalized part of many branches of Christianity, but it's also a folk practice, believed in and acted upon all over the United States by quiet players like Clyde Lott.

To understand what motivates him, a good place to start is with a handout that the Reverend Guy Garner, Jr., gave me during my visit to Lott's farm. It was a slender, floppy collection of materials called *The Key to Understanding Endtime Prophecy,* which he had assembled himself by photocopying pages from the Bible and various other texts and pamphlets, forming a personalized handbook on the Last Days.

"Understanding" seems impossible at first. The *Key* is an inscrutable jumble of Bible quotations, mysterious charts, drawings, labels, and confusing diatribes. The cover shows a statue of a Babylonian man, with a head of gold, a chest of silver, thighs of brass, legs of iron, and feet of iron and clay. Near the statue there's a timeline showing something called "The 70 Weeks of Daniel," which features carefully marked-off points in history with labels like "69 WEEKS," "MESSIAH CUT OFF," and "1000 YEAR MILLENNIUM." Inside are more charts, crude drawings of loathsome beasts, and feverish quotation of biblical texts and conspiracy tracts:

> The vials Rev. 16:1-21 . . . Boils Blood Blood Heat Darkness
> Euphrates Hail . . . JUDGMENT NO. 3 OF THE "JEWS" (UNDER ANTICHRIST)
> Ez. 20:34–36, 22:19–22, Jer. 30:4–7, Dan. 12:1
>
> A VERY, VERY URGENT MESSAGE! YOU MAY NOT HAVE A COUNTRY AFTER
> 1995! . . .
> 1 Did You Know . . . There are four massive crematoriums in the
> United States of America NOW complete with gas chambers and guillotines?

Garner didn't make up the *Key*'s mode of analysis himself. Except for the conspiracy stuff, most of it comes from an inherited tradition of scriptural interpretation that attempts to tie together the enigmatic prophecies scattered throughout the Old and New Testaments. Books like Daniel and Revelation are known as "apocalypses," and as the scholar Paul Boyer explains in *When Time Shall Be No More,* a history of Christian prophecy belief in the United States, this genre has ancient roots. The word "apocalypse" comes from a Greek word meaning "to uncover" or "unveil," as in unveiling the future plans of God for ever-curious, ever-trembling men. (Since these plans tend to involve destruction, it also means cataclysmic mayhem.) The origins of apocalyptic writing go way back, predating the Bible. For example, Hesiod, a Greek poet from the eighth century B.C., wrote of history playing out in a series of devolving stages, with mankind becoming more and more debased until Zeus stepped in to destroy it for its wickedness.

But it was the Jews and Christians who showed the greatest aptitude for the form, which has it that the bumps and grinds of existence are signs that evil is running amok in the world, and that good will eventually win out. Boyer points out that the Jews produced at least sixteen apocalypses, perhaps as many as seventy, most of which are lost. Christian writers drafted several more that didn't make the cut during the slow process of canonizing the New Testament—for instance, the Apocalypse of Paul, which featured a horrific vision of Hell.

Despite these losses, the Bible is still bulging with doom. The apocalyptic bumper crop includes parts of the Old Testament books of Daniel and Ezekiel, portions of the New Testament's books of Mark (specifically chapter 13, known as the "Little Apocalypse"), Luke, and Matthew (notably Matthew 24–25, where Jesus warns his disciples that "famines, and pestilences, and earthquakes, in diverse places" will precede "the end"), and of course, the Big Unit, the most famous apocalyptic work of them all, the Book of Revelation.

Revelation is a spooky and difficult piece of writing, and the source for almost all the apocalyptic imagery that has entered the popular imagination through books, art, and film. The Beast whose number is 666. The Whore of Babylon. The Seven Seals. The Four Horsemen. The Battle of Armageddon. The Second Coming. The very idea of a millennium—which refers not to the year 1000 or 2000, but to the thousand-year period of peace that will follow the final conflict between the dueling powers of God and Satan—comes from Revelation 20, where "thousand years" is referred to six times. In Revelation 20:1–2, after the triumph of good, an angel descends from Heaven holding a chain and the "key of the bottomless pit."

"And he laid hold on the dragon," the passage says, "that old serpent, which is the Devil, and Satan, and bound him a thousand years." According to the revelation, after this period of calm Satan will escape for a "brief season" to fight again, but he's doomed to be defeated and cast into a lake of fire. Later, all of mankind, both the living and the resurrected dead, will be lined up for the Last Judgment, with dire consequences for the unworthy—eternal damnation—and eternal life for the blessed. Finally, the old world will be swept away, replaced by a New Heaven and a New Earth.

Revelation is usually attributed to St. John, author of the fourth Gospel, or (by most secular scholars) to a first-century Christian named John who was exiled to the Isle of Patmos, a Greek island, as punishment for performing Christian missionary work. Its composition is usually dated during the Christian-hostile reign of Domitian (81–96 A.D.) or Nero (54–68 A.D.).

Either way, it's been confusing people ever since. The problem is that once you get past the relatively simple plotline, Revelation is as baffling line by line as "The Wasteland." The action starts in chapter 4, where John announces that angels have shown him blinding visions of "things which must be hereafter." The visions describe the triumph of Christian martyrs over evil; soaked with symbolism, they play out with a heavy emphasis on sevens, apparently a numerical symbol of perfection to ancient writers. There are greetings and warnings to seven Christian churches in Asia Minor, seven seals, seven trumpets, seven bowls, seven plagues, a seven-headed whore of Babylon, and a seven-headed dragon. But there's much more going on in Revelation than number games.

Among the highlights: John sees a vision of a heavenly throne surrounded by twenty-four white-robed elders. The throned figure, God, holds a book with seven seals that are successively broken by Christ, who is represented as a slain lamb.

Each broken seal, blown trumpet, and spilled bowl brings forth visions of terrors to come. These include the Four Horsemen, a glimpse of martyrs murdered for their beliefs, earthquakes, a "black" sun, and falling stars. When the seventh seal is broken, John learns that 144,000 faithful Jews, 12,000 from each of Israel's twelve tribes, together with great multitudes who "came out of the great tribulation," will ultimately appear before God, who promises them salvation.

Throughout the action, a chilling array of prophetic detail is chucked out. It's said, for example, that two "witnesses" will appear during the Tribulation, who will be killed by a beast and, after lying unburied on the streets of Jerusalem for three and a half days, ascend to Heaven. Later, the Whore of Babylon shows up, drunk from the blood of martyred saints, and two beasts arise from the sea. One of them, presumed to be the Antichrist (contrary to popular belief, Revelation doesn't use this word; it's found in the First and Second Epistles of John), is the beast whose "number is 666." This evil being requires everyone who wishes to buy and sell goods to "receive a mark in their right hand, or in their foreheads."

On and on it goes. There are dozens of other details like this, some of them utterly indecipherable. The climax begins in chapter 19, with Christ finally charging down from above to knock heads together, bearing little resemblance to the kindly-if-opinionated hippie presented in the Gospels. He's riding a white horse at the head of a heavenly host. His eyes are flaming, he's wearing blood-stained clothes, and, creepily, he has a sword coming out of his mouth, which is usually taken to symbolize the power of the Word.

∞

What does it all mean? Religious thinkers have puzzled over that one for centuries. St. Augustine, the great theologian, basically elected to grab the apocalyptic pigskin, drop back deep, and punt. He believed in a Second Coming, but not in a literal millennial kingdom on Earth, and he said Revelation should be read allegorically, as a symbol for the ongoing spiritual war in the hearts of men. This take, called "amillennialism," dominates Catholicism and mainline Protestant sects.

Other choices that avoid making the tough call include "preterism" (the Gospels and Revelation were real prophecy, but they pointed to events that have already happened, especially the destruction of the Second Temple in 70 A.D.) and "idealism." Popular among academics and other weak sisters, the latter says that Revelation was a vivid pep talk from John to fellow Christians, allegorizing the ongoing battle between good and evil, which will culminate in the return of Christ.

In response to these rather bloodless interpretations, many faithful Christians, including millions and millions of fundamentalists, Pentecostals, and evangelicals, have essentially said: Uh, thanks, but we'll stick with the truth. *It's all going to happen.* These are the rockribbed "premillennialists," who are sure that we live in an age prior to the literal establishment of Christ's millennial kingdom.

For premills the big question is when. The Bible doesn't say, and Jesus gives hints but never clearly spells it out. In the Olivet Discourse, after a stretch of moody talk about the coming tribulation, he says that "this generation shall not pass, till all these things be fulfilled," words that have caused plenty of head-scratching. Did Jesus mean the generation of people he was talking to? That seemed to be the case (and the early Christians sure expected Him to come back soon), but when it didn't happen, other explanations arose. One was that Jesus spoke in veiled language about things that would happen in the distant future. Though He warned against predicting exact dates or obsessing on the fulfillment of prophecy—"of that day and that hour knoweth no man"—predicting and obsessing have been impossible for men to resist.

In fact, the prophecy-decoding game has entranced some of the finest minds in history. Luther was an ardent millennialist, as was Isaac Newton, who spent the better part of his golden years analyzing Daniel and Revelation to figure out the date. At one point he leaned toward 1948.

In our day, many people have claimed to "know" when Christ will return—David Koresh thought he *was* another Christ, and Marshall Herff Applewhite believed that he and his sidekick Bonnie Lu Nettles were the enigmatic "two" of Revelation—but this is nothing new. It's been going on almost continuously since the crucifixion. In the second century A.D., for example, Montanus, a self-proclaimed prophet from what is now Turkey, founded a heretical sect based on his belief that the thousand-year reign of Christ was soon approaching. In preparation, the "Montanists" emphasized a starkly ascetic religious existence, "much given to visionary experiences" as well as "fasting and prayer and bitter repentance."

The amount of millennial hubbub surrounding the year 1000 has long been debated—some scholars say not much happened, others insist Europe suffered widespread panic—but it's widely agreed that the post-1000 world periodically saw outbursts of millennial theory, hoodoo, and disruption. One of the most influential promulgators of the genre appeared in the twelfth century: Joachim of Fiore, a prolific Italian abbot who expected a literal Second Coming, and who divided human history into three ages, the Age of Law, the Age of

Grace, and a future, millennial Age of Spirit. Other manifestations were less bookish. In *The Pursuit of the Millennium,* a 1957 study of millennialism in the Middle Ages, Norman Cohn catalogued a procession of hysterias and murderous popular rampages, often directed against Jews, who were deemed by some Christians to be in league with the Antichrist.

One of Cohn's larger points, though, was that the deadly variety of millennial delusion did not completely disappear with the Middle Ages or the Reformation. In a controversial thesis, he argued that it infected the twentieth century in a defining way, mutating into the killer utopian bacillus that poisoned Hitler and Stalin, who believed they were cleansing the world of evil. "For Cohn," writes Michael Barkun, a contemporary millennial scholar, in his book *Disaster and the Millennium,* "[millennialism's] reappearance in secularized form has been its most sinister incarnation."

"Here is the final transmutation of millenarian scholarship," Barkun concludes, "from exotic sects on the margins of society (in that pregnant phrase, 'the lunatic fringe') to forces at the very center of great events."

∞

My own small contribution to millenarian theory doesn't have that much clang and bang, because I was interested not in big-time bad guys but in the little fellers, the grunt millennialists who, more often than not, are harmless. People like Guy Garner, Jr., with his homely doombook, or Clyde Lott with his beloved apocalypse cows.

Throughout the nineties, many scholars and (especially) journalists seemed to assume that millennialism automatically means darkness and destruction. Obviously, it *has* meant that at times (Jim Jones and David Koresh are good examples), and it may mean that again. To name just a couple of quite scary millennialists whom I think we'll hear from before 2001: Yisrayl Hawkins and Charles Meade.

Hawkins, who runs a Christian cult in Abilene, Texas, called the House of Yahweh, teaches that most of the world will perish on October 13, 2000, flaming out in a nuclear holocaust. Meade is the leader of a church in Lake City, Florida, called End Time Ministries, which teaches that the world is headed for an apocalyptic drought that only church members will survive. Unfortunately one of Meade's "truths" appears to be a rejection of modern medicine. Lapsed End-Timers claim that several people in the group, including children, have died because they didn't receive proper care, a charge that is often leveled against another millennial sect, the Jehovah's Witnesses.

But to me, the real surprise of the nineties was the fact that millions of "millennialists" managed to do their thing without hurting themselves or anybody else. In my opinion, they were usually engaging in something more corrective than deadly: elaborate self-therapy. Self-therapy about what? In part about their fear of death in a modern world that, by and large, says death has no meaning. Above all, they were expressing a need to believe that the awful things that happen here on Earth are being watched by a higher power that has a redeeming purpose in mind.

This is an important point, because it helps explain why people preoccupied with doom so often seem sunny. Reverend Garner's booklet talks of genocide, of innocent children going under the Antichrist's guillotine. But in person he's as happy as a chubby uncle on his way to a family reunion. Along the same lines, the *Key* contains reprints from old premillennial works by the Reverend Clarence Larkin, a Pennsylvania minister who in 1918, amid the horror of World War I, wrote an odd little book called *The Second Coming of Christ*. Like Garner, Larkin—who lived in a house he called "Sunnyside"—assumed everything was getting worse and that the End would arrive at any time. True to form, this made him glad. "In short," he exulted, "'The Blessed Hope' helps us to cling lightly to this world.

It will not make us idle and negligent, but will fill us with zeal to be found a faithful servant at His return . . . [it] fills the heart of those who believe it with Joy."

It took me a while to understand how this works, and that this joy didn't necessarily involve a selfish attitude of "I'm saved, you're not." I got the drift at a church in Harlem called the Bethel Gospel Assembly, where I attended Thursday night Bible-study classes and the occasional Sunday service for a couple of months in early 1997. Bethel is a black Pentecostal church housed in a defunct school near 125th Street. I'd read about it in a book called *Apocalypse: On the Psychology of Fundamentalism in America,* by a New York–based psychoanalyst and history professor named Charles B. Strozier. I picked it because, to be honest, I expected it to be a pyrotechnic funhouse, full of bulge-eyed End-Times nuts rolling in the aisles. The church's pastor, Bishop Ezra N. Williams (called "Reverend Charles" by Strozier), certainly promised to be colorful. Among other things, he seemed convinced that white people had conspired to destroy Harlem by flooding it with drugs.

"There's been times," he told Strozier, when "I've felt in my heart that this drug thing is a planned genocide by the white man to just wipe us out."

In fact, Bethel was a fascinating place but it was no freak show. I jumped in by cold-calling the church office to request an appointment with Bishop Williams. This was flatly rejected—nothing personal, he just didn't have time—so I asked if it would be all right to show up at Bethel's Thursday night classes for "New Believers."

"Oh, sure," said a sweet, old, distracted-sounding church lady.

It wasn't all right, but the Bethelites were extraordinarily hospitable given that I was a stranger who just dropped into their laps like some gawky, sticky spider. The classes were run round-robin style by a trio of hard-charging sub-pastors—one man, two women—whose job was to lay out what the church believed and what was required of members. The doctrine was clear, tough, with no room for compromise: Jesus is Lord, love it, live it, believe it. Joiners had to make a solid commitment to worshiping Him *and* to steering clear of the problems (booze, drugs, marital infidelity, crime) that deviled some of my classmates, twenty or thirty low-income people who basically were there looking for strength and love. My favorite was a large, loud, and ecstatic man named Dwight, who, in classic fashion, had found Jesus in prison and was now trying to redirect his life.

At first the teachers paid me no particular mind—Bethel has a few white members—but after a couple of classes, one of them, the Reverend Walter Wilson, firmly told me to see him after class. When everybody cleared out (Dwight giving me a "humorous" look that said, "Uh oh"), I approached Wilson sheepishly and said, "Am I in trouble?"

"No, no! But Sister Viola indicates that you are planning to *write* about the church?"

Sister Viola was the woman I'd talked to on the phone. "Right, yes. I told her that up front."

"She didn't completely convey that part of the *message*," he said, smiling aggressively.

I groaned, figuring I was in for another Unarius-style tussle, perhaps an ejection. But it wasn't as bad as all that. Wilson was simply being careful. As he explained (then and later, as I got to know him better), Bethel had been burned in the past by journalists who played up the church's more caterwauling aspects—the swaying in the aisles, shouting, and speaking in tongues that often occur during Pentecostal services.

"These things are not what is important," he said. "The message of Jesus Christ is what's important."

Boilerplate language, I suppose, but he meant it very seriously, and I didn't want to cross him. Wilson vibrated with sincere moral purpose that actually jolted me. He was an ex-con himself, a former drug dealer, and he ran Bethel's outreach program for men in trouble. He wasn't getting rich doing it, and he *was* doing more to help his fellow man than I ever had.

Taking the hint, I holstered the toxic pencil and spent my time at Bethel just watching and listening—taking the classes and attending a couple of Sunday services, as well as a nighttime "salute to school graduates" and a full-dunk baptism ceremony for new members, including some of my orientation classmates.

The biggest surprise to me was that, for an "End-Times" church, Bethel's preachers didn't talk about the End very often, mainly because there was so much else going on. Bethel was a seven-days-a-week place—anytime I went there, something was afoot, whether it was a class, a service, a rehearsal, or a special event—and the church's focus was your basic "street-level" saving of souls. For the most part, that involved preaching the positive aspects of Christ's message rather than the doom that must inevitably overtake this world.

In fact, during my time at Bethel I heard the End mentioned only twice. Once in a sermon by Bishop Williams, who pointed to the year 2000 date crisis—the built-in glitch that could shut down computers all over the world when the millennium clock rolls over—as a troublesome sign of looming catastrophe. And once during class, when Wilson interrupted his lecture on man's "two natures" to share a little sunny gloom.

"The Bible tells us that things are going to get worse and worse," he said. "There will be no peace in the world. Just as there is always warfare in the world, there is always warfare within you—your life is a battle ground for the two natures."

A student asked the obvious: since destruction is inevitable, why not just say to Hell with it and party all the time?

Wilson said that's what "they" (the agents of evil) want you to think, but God wants you to fight them off. "Let's say you were a dope fiend up on 129th Street," he declaimed, "and they were going to *throw* you away. But God said, 'I'm gonna *raaaaaise* you up to show you that they were *wrong* to throw you away!'"

This heady talk got people worked up. They wanted to hear more about the End-Times stuff.

"No, no," Wilson said. "Prophecy is *meat*. This class is only ready for the *milk*."

∞

At Clyde Lott's farm, after viewing the cattle, we trooped inside. Lott and I sat down in his living room, a cozy Mayberry space filled with puffy furniture, family pictures, and an upright piano. Everybody else peeled off to read or rest for the big event that night: Rabbi Richman was scheduled to lecture on the Third Temple to a Pentecostal congregation in Thomastown, a tiny crossroads community a half hour north of Canton.

As we settled in, Lott shared his biography and conversion story. His dad was a veterinarian and cattle expert who worked with farmers in the area. (Indeed, he was the vet for my late Uncle Vernon, who had a farm a half hour from Canton.) Lott the Younger studied animal science at Mississippi State and came back to the family spread to make a living breeding calves, steers, and heifers for sale to 4-H kids who showed them in competitions.

Religiously, he was raised Southern Baptist, but converted to Pentecostalism after college. That may not sound like much difference— both faiths are strict, emphasizing the inerrant truth of the Bible— but it's fair to say that Pentecostals bring a good deal more wiggle to the dance floor. One distinguishing factor is that Pentecostals believe in what Lott called "the infilling of the Holy Spirit."

"We believe that once you repent and turn yourself over to God he will literally put his spirit in you," he said. "According to Acts, this is evidenced by the speaking in . . . You're familiar with the term 'speaking in tongues'?"

Pentecostals are famous for their belief that the gift of tongues—literally, speaking spontaneously in an unknown "language"—is called for in the New Testament's Book of Acts, Luke's account of the doings of various disciples in the period after Jesus' death. Pentecost was an important Jewish feast day in the spring. According to Acts 2, on the first Pentecost after the resurrection, followers of Christ gathered in Jerusalem, in an "upper room," for what amounted to the first Christian prayer meeting. On hand, among others, were Peter, James, Andrew, and Jesus' mother, Mary. The big event happened on the day of Pentecost:

> And suddenly there came a sound from heaven as of a rushing mighty wind, and it filled all the house where they were sitting. . . . And there appeared unto them cloven tongues like as of fire, and it sat upon each of them. And they were all filled with the Holy Ghost, and began to speak with other tongues, as the Spirit gave them utterance.

The majority of modern Protestants, especially in middle-of-the-road denominations like the one I grew up in, Presbyterianism, teach that this and other gifts were reserved for the apostles, not for us. Pentecostals believe that "signs" are still the proper manifestation of the power of faith.

The sect, which today is one of the fastest-growing Christian denominations in the world, emerged from the enthusiasms of a former Methodist Episcopal minister named Charles Parham. In 1900, in Topeka, Kansas, he founded an institution called Bethel Bible College, whose students were urged to investigate the "baptism of the spirit," an activity that led to an outbreak of speaking in tongues. The modern Pentecostal movement was formally born on January 1, 1901, when a woman named Agnes Ozman became the first person since biblical times to publicly seek and receive the miracle of tongues.

Pentecostalism's association with End-Times belief also has old roots. In 1906, an African American minister named William J. Seymour, who had studied under Parham, began preaching at a long-running revival held in a rented church on Asuza Street in Los Angeles. Speaking in tongues broke out at the revival on April 9, just nine days before the San Francisco earthquake—a coincidence that did not go unnoticed. "More than 125,000 tracts relating the earthquake to the Asuza Street happenings and the 'endtime' were promptly distributed," says the *Encyclopedia of American Religions*. Appropriately enough, given that dramatic gestation, a sense of doomsday urgency has permeated the faith ever since.

∞

The premillennial Christian materials that support such conclusions are staggeringly complicated; it's easy to get lost in the terminology alone. "Premillennialists" break down into various camps whose members quibble, among many other things, about the sequence of events during the End Times. The most popular school goes by the unwieldy name "pretribulational dispensationalism," which refers to two separate but intertwined beliefs that were popularized in the early 1800s by John Nelson Darby, an English minister affiliated with the Plymouth Brethren movement, an important source for modern-day fundamentalism. Darby believed that history had played out, and the future would play out, in a series of "dispensations," divinely ordained historical epochs in which man is tested by God and fails, leading to the next dispensation.

Darby thought in terms of numerous "ages and dispensations," among them: the Paradisaical State, Conscience, Noah, Abraham, Israel under the Law, Priesthood, Kings, Gentiles, the Church Age, Millennium, and the Eternal State. We're living in the Church Age.

Next up, leading to the Millennium, is the Tribulation, when the Antichrist will bring wrack and ruin to this world. Pre-Tribbers believe that the starting gun for the Tribulation will be an event called the Rapture, when Christ will rescue the souls of righteous individuals by descending from Heaven "with a shout." When the Rapture happens, the chosen will physically disappear, with their souls ascending to Heaven. "[T]he dead in Christ shall rise first," says a passage in First Thessalonians. "Then we which are alive and remain shall be caught up together with them in the clouds to meet the Lord in the air."

Historically, much of the argument in the rarefied world of pre-millennialism has been about whether the dominant "pre-Tribbers" are correct in their timing of the Rapture. Some people who also fit under the broad heading "premillennialist" think it will happen afterward ("post-Trib"). A camp called "mid-Trib" or "pre-Wrath" claims that the Rapture will occur *after* the Tribulation but *before* an event called the Wrath of God. These thin-slice distinctions sound silly, but they're achingly serious to believers. In *The Pre-Wrath Rapture of the Church,* Marvin Rosenthal, a converted Jew-turned-premillennial-evangelist, writes that his decision to abandon pre-Trib in favor of pre-Wrath essentially meant walking away from beliefs—and friends—that he'd cherished for a large part of his career.

"[N]ow I had a problem. Word would spread quickly that I was rethinking my view of the Rapture," he wrote. "One Bible teacher, on hearsay alone, suggested to a friend that I had come up with a new doctrine that was 'off the wall.'"

This malleability exists because the basic framework established by Darby and the chief American popularizers of his ideas—especially Cyrus Scofield, whose hugely popular *Scofield Reference Bible* (1909) featured marginalia that explained how it all fit together—lends itself to innumerable permutations and personalized style statements. There's no uniformly agreed-upon "formula" for how or when the End will happen, but crucial sources for the most popular sequence of events include the Old Testament books of Ezekiel, Zechariah, and Daniel, and the New Testament books of Matthew, Mark, Luke, I and II Thessalonians, II Peter, and Revelation.

Of these, Daniel is crucial for establishing the timing of events. In *The End: Why Jesus Could Return by A.D. 2000,* premillennialist writer Ed Dobson calls its prophecies "the most important in the entire Old Testament that deal with the end times." The logic of why Daniel applies to the End is hard to fathom, since its action is set during the Babylonian Captivity (sixth century B.C.) and mainly refers to future glories for the people of Israel. In one famous episode, Daniel, a captive Jew, is called in by King Nebuchadnezzar to interpret a vexing dream. The king saw a great statue of a man, with a head of gold, chest and arms of silver, abdomen and thighs of brass, legs of iron, and feet of iron and clay—the same statue that the Reverend Guy Garner used on the cover of the *Key.* The statue's feet shatter when a huge stone lands on them. Daniel tells the king that its various elements represent four kingdoms, including his, that will fall as history unfolds.

What does this have to do with the Christian End? Just this: premills believe that prophecies like Daniel have "near" and "far" implications, so they can be applied both to biblical events and future events. "[O]n a second level," writes Robert Van Kampen, a pre-Wrath premillennialist, in his book *The Sign,* "there is a corresponding 'far' prediction that will be fulfilled at a later time, or in the events of the end times."

Obviously, this near/far principle complicates things. With it, almost any prophecy in the Bible can be applied to any future event, and Daniel thus becomes the source of several crucial concepts that make their way into contemporary premill timetables. Among them is the explanation for the strange statue (to some, its elements represent four ancient empires, Babylon, Medo-Persia, Greece, and Rome, whose power was smashed by the "rock" that is Christ), the almost ubiquitous notion that the Tribulation will last seven years (based on Daniel 9, which speaks of the Messiah taking seven weeks—"week" taken to mean a year—to restore Jerusalem), and the very murky concept of "the 70 Weeks." This also comes from Daniel 9, in which Daniel prays for the forgiveness of his people and the restoration of Jerusalem. The angel Gabriel descends and tells him how much time will pass before Israel is restored.

The answer: "Seventy weeks are determined upon thy people and upon thy holy city, to finish the transgression, and to make an end of sins." Gabriel also says that sixty-nine weeks will pass before "Messiah the Prince" returns and "the street shall be built again, and the wall, even in troublous times."

Many prophecy writers of the past took "seventy weeks" to mean seventy weeks of years or some other flatly numerical figure. Premills declare that the church represents a "time gap" or "parenthesis" between the end of the sixty-ninth week and the beginning of the seventieth, or Tribulation week. Forget about why—it's too complicated, like quantum scripture—just focus on the conclusion: the Church Age is basically a pause between the Age of Mosaic Law and the Tribulation, when God will accomplish the final dispensation of His chosen people, the Jews.

The Jews? Yes, they're crucial. Following Darby's lead, modern premills believe that the Jews are God's most important chess pieces. There are sunny and dark shadings to this. On the one hand, premills believe there was no chance of the final dispensations happening until the Jews were restored to Palestine—because the Jews are supremely important to God, they *are* his Chosen People, and history cannot end until their story has run its course. On the other hand, the Jews rejected their Messiah, so they're in trouble during the Tribulation. They won't be Raptured, of course, but as you'll recall, Revelation does speak of 144,000 sanctified Jews who will gather around the throne.

And the rest? Opinions on that vary. Some premills say that salvation is open to all Jews, not just the 144,000. Others say that the majority of Jews will perish in a super-Holocaust. Some premills gloss over that idea, but as Boyer makes clear, the genre's history is rife with this icky theme. "During the Tribulation, John Darby taught, Antichrist will slaughter two-thirds of the Jews regathered in Palestine. . . . Six million Jews died at Hitler's hands, observed a prophecy-conference speaker in 1963, but their 'greatest sorrow is yet to come.'" More recently, John F. Walvoord, one of the grand old men of premillennialism, wrote that "two out of three Israelites will perish" during the Tribulation.

As for the starting time, most premills avoid date setting, but inherent in their work, almost always, is a sense that the End is "imminent," and that the signs of the times are auspicious. The creation of Israel in 1948 was a watershed, but premills also point to a general sense that things are getting worse, which would be typical of the Last Days.

Of course, if you look at the world hard enough, things are *always* getting worse, and every generation can find evidence to support this claim. The early Americans were famously millennial. Boyer writes that Cotton Mather, the Puritan theologian, preached a sermon called "Things To Be Look'd For" that "found portents of the Second Coming in local and world events" and "tentatively predicted the end in 1697." The most famous outburst of American millennialism was the Millerite movement, named for William Miller, a self-taught New York State farmer whose reading of scripture convinced him that Christ would return to set things right sometime between March 21, 1843, and March 21, 1844. Starting in the 1830s, Miller traveled all around the Northeast and Midwest, attracting followers and eventually settling on the updated date of October 22,

1844. That date came and went, an event known as the Great Disappointment.

These days, almost any unsettling thing can qualify as a sign—including the existence of the Soviet Union, the collapse of the Soviet Union, the Gulf War, the use of microchips for pet identification tags, the "globalization" of the economy, emerging viruses, and even environmental problems.

"The Secretary General of the UN recently told us that man has perhaps ten years to solve the problem of survival," wrote Hal Lindsey in *The Late Great Planet Earth,* a famous mass-audience pre-Trib book that intertwines biblical prophecies with world events. "He pointed out three great crises which are unique to this generation—the problem of nuclear weapons, the problem of over-population . . . the problem of pollution of our air and water."

Silly stuff, but *Late Great* has sold millions of copies since it appeared in 1970, and its success has inspired a horde of imitators. I have two dozen titles in my relatively modest collection of premill lit, which includes nonfiction, novels, and even some movies. Start reading and studying, and you quickly realize that anything can be a sign of the End. And almost everything is, according to current pop-apocalypticists like Lindsey, Pat Robertson, Jack Van Impe, Timothy LaHaye, and Peter and Paul Lalonde, who produce a news program, "This Week in Bible Prophecy," that tirelessly correlates current events with End-Time events.

Most of us never see any of it, but the amount of "product" out there is amazing. Typically, books of recent vintage avoid dates, but some don't. The book *88 Reasons Why the Rapture Is in 1988* added 40 (a "generation") to 1948 (Israel restored) to conclude that 1988 was, no doubt about it, the year of the Rapture. And *1994¿,* by Harold Camping, applied the same wrong certainty to that year.

The Temple business is a subcategory of the genre, and not all premills buy into it—mainly because the scriptural "evidence" is so murky. The books *Ready to Rebuild,* by Thomas Ice and Randall Price, and *The Coming Temple: Center Stage for the Final Countdown,* by Don Stewart and Chuck Missler, both cite Old and New Testament verses in support of the idea that a Third Temple is necessary. Ice and Price acknowledge the unavoidable truth that "there is no Bible verse that says, 'there is going to be a third Temple.'" The ones that seem to suggest it indicate that the Antichrist will desecrate "the holy place" during his Tribulational reign. (One typical passage is Matthew 24:15–16.) Another important citation is Revelation 11, which says, "And there was given me a reed like unto a rod: and the angle stood, saying, Rise, and measure the temple of God, and the altar, and them that worship therein."

Meaning? "This is an important reference," Stewart and Missler write. "John wrote . . . Revelation approximately A.D. 90, *after* the Second Temple had been destroyed. He envisions the Third Temple existing during the time immediately *before* Christ comes back to earth."

That's it? Basically. Not to be churlish, but as prophecy, I'd have to call that something other than meat or milk. How about: thin gruel.

∞

For his part, Clyde Lott fully believes that the End is near, but he doesn't seem particularly riled up about it. "I can't say that such and such a date's going to be when they build the Third Temple," he told me as we kept chattering in his living room, "but I can say I feel the pressure of time to begin our project, and I look forward to that goal every day." I asked Lott if the "pressure of time" meant the year 2000. No. Lott is not a date setter. He believes the Second Coming could happen 339 years from now or $333\frac{1}{3}$ seconds from now. But he is certain of two things: the world will continue to devolve, and there is an urgent need to accomplish his work.

"You really think things are always getting worse?" I asked, citing both world wars and, for good measure, the disco era.

"Sure I do. Very strongly."

I posed a couple of specific questions, starting with the idea that the Jews would be singled out for a special thumping during the Last Days, which seemed inconsistent with his buddying up to Richman. "Singled out is not the right way to put it," he said, very concerned. "The land of Israel is going to suffer because of the battles. But everybody will suffer during that time."

How about the criticism that this belief breeds a selfish, defeatist attitude?

He shook his head. "The Bible says we must occupy until He comes. That means living a relationship with God, leading a holier, purer life that would be an influence to your neighbor or a stranger or a friend."

In his case it also meant self-sacrifice. Before I came down, I assumed Lott was still a prosperous cattleman raising red heifers as a hobby. Not so. Red heifers were his full-time ministry; he and his wife and daughter were basically living off gifts from benevolent fellow believers. The Angus I'd seen were actually raised by breeders in Nebraska; Lott was paying for them himself, not raising them for profit, and he estimated that the heifer operation cost between $40,000 and $50,000 a year.

That caught me flat-footed. "So to do this you gave up—?"

"Everything. Everything. It's been a miracle. God has always provided for us financially when we needed something. It's been a real faith walk for us."

"But you do run a church?"

"No. I would be considered an evangelist in the field, with a ministry toward the restoration of Israel."

Lott said his life-changing ministry began in earnest in 1989, when his study of passages in Genesis convinced him that the Israelites, before their exile to Egypt, owned "ringstraked, speckled, and spotted cattle" whose traits "would not, on a consistent basis, yield red calves."

"So the question was," Lott continued, "where did their Numbers 19 red heifer come from? I just began to wonder. Where did that red cow come from, and did Israel have it?"

Having heard the godly cattle call, Lott realized he didn't know whom to get in touch with in Israel. So he contacted a state agricultural official in Jackson, Roy D. Manning, who offered to type up Lott's goal under an official letterhead and zip it off to the American Embassy agricultural attaché in Athens, Greece.

"Dear Sir," it began. "We have been approached by a producer and seller of cattle from the State of Mississippi and I am quoting him in the following: 'Red Angus cattle suitable for Old Testament Biblical sacrifices, will have no blemish or off color hair, genetically red will reproduce red, eye, nose pigmentation will be dark. . . . also excellent beef quality.'"

The letter bounced around a while before finally landing on the desk of Chaim Richman at the Temple Institute, who was instantly intrigued. Letters flew back and forth, travel plans were made. Lott and some Christian colleagues flew to Israel in 1990. Richman pilgrimaged to Canton for the first time in 1994. A friendship formed and an unlikely ecumenical plan was hatched. After getting up-close looks at the reality of Israel's modern cattle stock, Lott conceived of "gifting" Israel with his superior breeds, consistent with his belief that in the Last Days the Holy Land will be as healthy and teeming as the Garden of Eden.

"We're talking about a very large number of cattle," he told me, his eyes widening. "In fact, I'd say our single most important goal right now is us raising our finances."

How much financing would be required?

"If our vision is correct, it could easily come close to $100 million."

∞

Reverend Lott might never pull off this grandiose dream, but the intent itself is interesting, because it illustrates what I call the "potential energy" problem of premillennialism. The prophecies point to the most staggering events imaginable. The prophecies also say that your role is to be good, love your fellow man, and otherwise wait. But as you might imagine, the act of anticipating the Second Coming produces considerable amounts of nervous energy. What do you do to work it out?

Clyde Lott raises heifers. Other people throw themselves into church work, some read teeth-chattering thrillers like *The Late Great Planet Earth*. But the most kinetic peaceful expression of millennial fever I've run across, by far, is the work of a globe-trotting evangelist who calls himself Arthur Blessitt.

I first became aware of Blessitt in 1995, when his press kit landed on my desk, announcing the imminent completion of his mission to carry the cross of Jesus to every nation in the world before the year 2000. The kit was stuffed with pictures of Blessitt—a tall, thick-limbed, smiling man with long gray hair—doing just that, in some of the strangest places. The first picture showed a much younger Blessitt on the day he started: December 25, 1969, preparing to drag his cross from coast to coast across America.

Then there was page after page of countries Blessitt had knocked off, often rubbing shoulders with the famous. I saw Blessitt with Billy Graham in Northern Ireland in 1972, with Yasir Arafat in Lebanon in 1982, with Muammar Qadaffi in Libya in 1988, with President Mobutu in Zaire, no date given. I started counting off countries and locales: Spain, Poland, Israel, Colombia, Brazil, Egypt, the Great Wall of China . . . ah, there was no use counting. According to the kit, he'd taken his cross—eighty pounds of wood with an inflatable tire attached to the base, to reduce the drag—through 223 countries, on seven continents, covering 30,942 miles. Anticipating everything a reporter might want, he included a sheet of fun facts.

"'Who is Arthur Blessitt?' He's a 55-year-old resident of North Fort Myers, Florida, who accepted Jesus Christ at age 7. In 1969, the Lord told him: 'Carry the cross on foot—identify My message in the highways, road-sides where the people are.'

"'Average shoe life.' 500 miles.

"'Average tire life.' 2,000 miles.

"'Biggest animal scares.' Green Mamba snake in Ghana; baboon attack in Kenya; elephant chase in Tanzania; crocodile attack in Zimbabwe.

On a mission from God: Arthur Blessitt (with his wife, Denise) is determined to carry the cross to every nation before the year 2000.
USED BY PERMISSION OF ARTHUR BLESSITT.

"A few memorable scenes: Firing squad in Nicaragua; stoning and beating in Morocco; Civil Guardia attack in Spain; LAPD choking . . ." A firing squad? I wanted to hear more about that, but it had to wait. I called Blessitt's office, but his assistant said he was "out."

In his case "out" meant for several months: Blessitt was humping the timber somewhere in South America.

Eventually I found him and got to know him fairly well. Blessitt had burned with religious intensity since age seven, when he accepted Jesus at an old-fashioned tent revival in Louisiana. As a kid, he helped pray his dad off the bottle and then accompanied him, now reformed, on forays into bars to rescue sodden souls. After college Blessitt moved to California, where he evangelized North Beach beatniks and, in the late sixties, Los Angeles hippies in a Sunset Strip coffeehouse called His Place. He received the call to walk the United States from coast to coast in 1969, though he wasn't exactly in peak condition for the journey.

"I had been very ill with a brain aneurysm, a small seepage of blood in my brain," Blessitt told me, in a voice that was oddly high-pitched for a man his size. Despite experiencing "numbnesses," he flushed his medicine down the toilet and took off on Christmas morning, dragging a 12-by-6-foot, 105-pound cross made of creosote-soaked wood.

Blessitt went international in 1971, with a trip to Northern Ireland. The mission expanded after that, but not until 1988, in Germany, did he formally hear the voice of the Lord tell him to take the cross to *every* nation. These days, as the final triumph or failure looms, Blessitt is well funded by a solid core of private religious donors who underwrite an operation that costs about $150,000 a year. Along the way he has experienced many, many things that, if true, could only be called miracles.

For example, in Nicaragua in 1978, Blessitt says he was almost shot. "I was walking the Pan American highway," he told me, "and it was the day that my parrot died."

"Your parrot?"

"Yes, I had gotten him in El Salvador, and I was trying to teach the parrot how to preach. My plan was to release him and he would preach to the other parrots. El Salvador del Mundo was his name."

Unfortunately, del Mundo, who sat on Blessitt's shoulder as he trudged, succumbed when a mosquito-spray truck rolled by and fogged them both.

Darker events followed. Blessitt was accompanied and supplied by a couple of colleagues driving a truck and trailer. One night as they slept, armed gunmen rousted them out of bed, yelling, *"Narcotica policia,* open up!"

"I got up and opened the door, and saw that these were just guys in regular blue jeans. They had guns. They lined us up and said, 'We're going to kill you,' and I realized these guys were really serious." Anticipating death at any moment, Blessitt scrambled to get inside his truck, which contained a box of Bibles, because he wanted to die clutching the Word. During the confusion and shouting that ensued, Blessitt konked out . . . or something.

"When I looked up nobody was standing there," he said. "All I saw was six guys laying on the ground about fifteen feet away. And then they jumped onto a truck and took off."

"So who knocked them out?"

"People from a little village started coming up," he said. "They said, 'We saw a bright light.' And they said, 'God was here.'"

Little village? What little village? I didn't bother asking. Blessitt's stories tended to go like that—the narrative was a bit choppy—but I liked them anyway.

The stories sound insane, but I don't think Blessitt was crazy at all. I think he was . . . burning brightly from within. I finally got a chance to meet him in late 1997, when he and his wife, Denise, passed through New York on their way back from a major lugging: into Afghanistan. With that one in the bag, he had six left, all of them tough-to-crack places like North Korea, the Sudan, Iraq—all very difficult, all very risky. The grim reality was that Blessitt really could get killed doing this.

As Denise drooped from jet lag, Blessitt described his latest adventure. He'd been unable to get permission to enter Afghanistan, so he hired a guide to take him in by way of a mountain pass.

"What kind of distance and altitude are we talking?" I said, buttering a piece of bread.

"We walked about 23 miles up and 23 miles back. Up to 18,200 feet." Whoa. To put that in relative terms: Mount McKinley, the highest point in North America and a world-class climbing challenge, is 20,320 feet up. I had trouble believing this, but I decided, based on his calm sincerity, that I did believe it.

"It was cold and I had to wear layers," Blessitt said blithely. "We crossed a glacier to get to the pass. It could have collapsed. It was verrry dangerous, but there was no other way."

But why do all this? Jesus spelled that out clearly to Blessitt, but this is his Big Secret: he won't reveal the stakes. Every indication and hint, though, is that Jesus told Blessitt that He will return if Blessitt gets the job done. So according to his beliefs, he's hiking for the salvation of everybody in the world.

"Jesus said the gospel of the kingdom must be preached in all the world to every nation, then the End will come," Blessitt said. "Now, I'm not saying that this means my walk necessarily, because the gospel's been to every place I've been. But for the first time in human history, one person, with an open symbol of the message of Christ, will have gone through every nation with that gospel."

That settled, I pestered Blessitt with questions about the tinytype details of his final challenges. If he was absolutely barred from a place like North Korea, would it be fair to, say, sneak in at night as a frogman, carrying only a cross made of matchsticks?

He thought about it, then nodded. Sure, that would qualify, but he preferred to roll in the big guy, the forty-pounder.

How determined was he to finish? Completely. He said would do whatever it took, even if it meant running into a hail of bullets.

"If I'm alive and physically able to complete this journey before the year 2000," he said, "I *will* give my life rather than not attempt it."

∞

"You need to go see Dr. John Fischer of the Union of Messianic Jews in Miami," a man was shouting into my right ear. "In *Florida*. You need to know something, you can just call him up on the phone!"

The speaker was a big, booming Christian evangelist named Ballard who introduced himself as we sat waiting for Rabbi Richman. I was sitting next to him on the back pew of the Wake Forest Pentecostal Church in Thomastown. It was Saturday night, around 8:00, and the place was jammed with Pentecostals who had come to hear the rabbi. The music was starting, the fever was building, people were swaying, and suddenly . . . an announcement. We'd have to wait a while longer. Unbeknownst to the event's schedulers, the rabbi's Sabbath restrictions prevented him from riding in a car until after sundown. It would be at least another hour.

At a rock concert, this news would prompt boos and a storm of pennies. Crowd reaction here? "Whooo!" "Amen!"

I turned back to Ballard, who introduced me to his wife and shouted out the nature of his ministry, which involved carrying the Word to hairy parts of "Old Mexico." I mentioned the Third Temple, and he started roaring out helpful imperatives about all the things I had to purchase or do immediately to further my studies.

"There's a book about prophecy that's already been written. His name is *Smith*. It's about Jesus. That is a very good book.

"The Temple will cost trillions. Yes, trillions. You been to Jerusalem? No? The awesomeness and the breadth and height of the Temple Mount is unbelievable. There's one group that has rebuilt a model of the structure like it was in 66 A.D. You need to see that."

I asked him if he'd heard of the red heifer. His face turned stony. "I cannot talk about this."

"Wait, I should mention: I already know about it. I was over at Clyde Lott's farm today and he showed me the heifer."

"I'm not supposed to talk about that. I don't know where they are at and do not want to know where they're at. The reason for it is we've got too many Palestinians who want to get rid of this heifer." Pause. "OK, did you *see* the heifer?"

"Yeah."

"Where are you from?"

"New York."

"Oh, really?" He squinted, amazed. "You come all the way down to Mississippi for this?"

"Yup."

Pause. "Are you Jewish?"

Before I could answer, the tambourines kicked in, and the Reverend Bob Ellis took over up front. The chapel was a shoebox-shaped enclosure with tiny windows, paneling on the walls, and two wide rows of pews leading up to the preacher zone, which looked like the set-up for a wedding band. There was a simple pulpit, microphones scattered around, and a variety of instruments, all manned: a piano, an organ, a guitar, a bass, drums, and a tambourine. Combos like this are common at many Pentecostal services, which tend to flow along on a tide of peppy music that rarely stops. Even when the preacher is really going at it, yelling and screeching, the organist or tambourine player will accent his words with a riff or a jangle. In Thomastown, between stretches of preaching, there were long singing intervals—joint shouting of hymns whose words lent themselves to wave after wave of repetition.

Reverend Ellis was a handsome, robust man who filled out his clothes nice and fatly, like Jerry Falwell. His style alternated between hushed insights and howling, growling climaxes. The effect on the crowd was electric; from start to finish the worshipers were a writhing part of the action.

Ellis juiced them up right away by hollering, "Praise the Lord, hallelujah, HALLELUJAH! Ohhh, let's praise the name of the Lord, hallelujah!" Just like that, everybody in the place went wild for twenty minutes, singing simple hymns with a total-being elation that, multiplied times a crowd of two hundred, struck my lapsed-Presbyterian eyeballs as a genuine religious orgy. Most of the congregation stood and swayed, arms waving loose in the air, but there were dozens of individual styles on display. Ballard jiggled, smiled, and clapped. Reverend Garner was up front with Ellis, clapping and bouncing. A baldheaded man playing the bass performed a sort of stiff, lock-kneed hop. In the back, near me, a woman dressed all in red whirled and screamed ecstatically. Various people worked the aisle, including a teenage girl in pink who funked out with a hypnotized chicken dance. At some point during the general bedlam, a boy, a blond-haired, sunburned kid in wire-rimmed glasses, took over the mike up front for a screeching vocal solo—"Why don't you LOOK what the Lord has DONE"—that extended the singing for another fifteen minutes.

Things eventually quieted down and Ellis got going. "Ayyyyy-men," he said, mopping forehead sweat. "*My.* Well, the Bible did say make a joyful noise and we are quite noisy, but that's all right. It don't get on God's nerves a bit. Amen! If a celebrity can traipse across the stage hearing the words of 'encore, encore,' people stomping their feet, clapping their hands, screaming at the top of their lungs, whistling as loud as they can, lightin' lighters to show their stamp of approval—"

Organ squiffle.

"Then why in *Heaven's* name can we not *wur-*ship God with *evvurthing* we have?" Riffs, applause, cheers. Ellis started yelling. "Amen! Amen! Hallelujah! Praise the name of the Lord! Hallelujah!"

Then he hushed up, tamping it down, slowly working back up into a sustained bellow about how Rabbi Richman was a beloved brother, despite his obviously different "tradition." This was a significant ecumenical statement, and nobody seemed to have any problem with it. The crowd cheered, and when Richman finally showed up—during the preaching he, Lott, and others filed quickly to a place up front—the audience strained to glimpse him, their faces aglow. Some people I spoke to before the service had read about Jews all their lives, but they had never actually seen one.

The Reverend Alfred Bishop, who spoke after Ellis, built on this theme, with a preaching style marked by big, toothy grins and heavy use of "amen" interjections and the syllable *hah*, which he throatily (and unconsciously) added to create an urgent, syncopated rhythm. ("One God Pentecostals is doing something that no other denomination has done-*hah!* Amen! Amen-*hah!* It has opened up, hah, a door, hah, and we're beginning to *talk* to people, hah.") During his inspiring harangue, I heard the first faint, ecstatic stirring of "tongues"—a woman started keening like a tormented cat—which broke out in earnest soon enough. The first to deliver was a heavyset, red-faced man in a plaid shirt who, eyes closed, stood in the aisle near me and produced roughly a minute of guttural gibberish.

"Yellabootsia yellabootsy-iiiiii," he said, drawing a deep, anguished moan from down around his ankles. "Yellayalbootsia yellabotesiuh!"

Richman stepped up to the mike soon after the tongues orgy. Wisely, he didn't try to reach the same emotional pitch as the preachers but stuck to his own style. Wearing a dark suit and a yarmulke, he took the podium and spoke quietly and seriously, stressing the shared strengths of Judaism and Christianity, the prophetic urgency felt by messianic Jews like himself, the details of the red heifer. Mainly, though, he trashed Islam. Which got me worrying again. Was this guy a dangerous crank?

I decided he probably wasn't. His Muslim-bashing was generic. He said it was a "myth" that Jerusalem is especially holy to Muslims. Then he ripped into Yasir Arafat.

"You know, I don't really understand Americans allowing Arafat into their country," he said. "Aside from being the ugliest man in the world . . . I mean, I don't understand why he can't take a shave . . . the man is essentially one of the most terrible war criminals in this century." Later he said, "There is *no* redemptive Messiah in Islam—there is only a destroyer" and "I don't have any confrontational aspirations toward Islam, but I think that God might."

Judging by Richman's theatrical pause, I think that was supposed to be an applause line, but the Mississippians didn't get it. Either that, or they were so good-natured, so sunny, that they weren't in a mood to boo Arabs. Richman's line drew a sickly "amen" from one of the tongue-speakers, who sounded like he was drifting off to sleep.

∞

As the months passed after my Mississippi trip, Richman's "confrontational aspirations" line gnawed at me. I kept wondering if he was potentially dangerous after all.

I can't be certain, but I still doubt it very much. In 1998 I had a chance to talk to a famous Israeli named Carmi Gillon, who directed Israel's General Security Services from 1994 to 1996. Gillon was an instrumental figure in the bust-up of the Jewish Underground, which had plotted to start a war by blowing up the Dome of the Rock, so he certainly knew the territory. Sitting across from him in a cafeteria in New York, I asked him if he'd ever heard of Rabbi Richman.

No, he said, waving the name off, but the Temple Institute shouldn't be lumped in with messianic terrorists, or with more insistent Temple groups like one called the Temple Faithful. "To the Temple Institute it's God's decision to make," he shrugged. "They focus on the particulars of what will go in the Temple when the time comes."

So did he mean that Richman was completely harmless?

Gillon frowned thoughtfully. No, no, he couldn't quiiite say that either. "I don't know Richman," he said. "But the problem comes when people listen to him and think, 'Well, there's a short way to do that.' He doesn't intend someone to do a radical act, but someone else may reach the wrong conclusion."

I leaned in and put it to him straight: How dangerous is this stuff?

"This is the most dangerous thing to the future of Israel, it's really explosive," he said without qualification. He leaned in, locking eyes with me. "It's *nitro-glycerin.*"

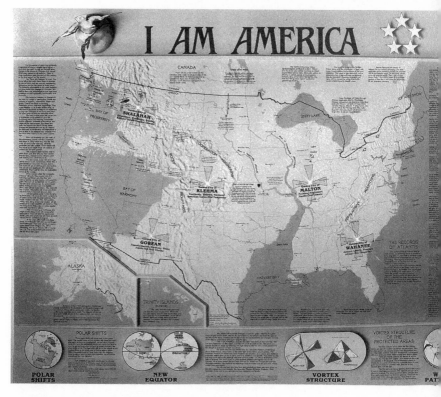

Lori Adaile Toye's "I AM America" map—one of several
that envision bad times for this old planet.
USED BY PERMISSION OF LORI ADAILE TOYE.

3

Earth Is a Mother

(and She's Sending You to Your Room)

The Earth felt glutted, abused.

The units of the scurrying life form on her crust had doubled by the decade over the past six thousand years until they had become swarms.

. . . Now the swarms nested everywhere. Now they had harnessed the lightning and shot electronic arrows through her bowels . . . changing the stately manner of her seasons. . . . They sprinkled obscene matter across her skin, buried arsenals of hate, fouled her waters. . . .

They were in their billions . . . and reproducing on an exponential scale. . . . Man, the only animal that dirties his own nest.

—FROM *BLINDSIDED,* A 1993 NOVEL ABOUT THE COMING "EARTH CHANGES,"
BY DICK AND LEIGH RICHMOND-DONAHUE

"This conference is like a Lamaze class," Annie Kirkwood said as she peered over a raised podium, her face a serene oval, her round head topped by a nimbus of graying perm. A short, plump woman in her fifties, Annie sighed and squinted like a tough-love bombardier eyeing newcomers at an A.A. meeting. Then she dropped a payload. "You can't just sit there with your legs crossed," she said. "Sometimes you have to get into the blood and guts of it. And that's what we're going to do now. After that we'll get to the *joy* of Earth Changes."

A spooked murmur rose from her audience, some five hundred people assembled on a sunny Saturday morning in the dim ballroom of a hotel north of Dallas. The people in the crowd, mostly middle class and Caucasian, had traveled from thirty-six states and as far away as Australia to be at this event, a March 1995 conference innocuously labeled "Earth Festival: A Celebration of Earth's Future." Don't be fooled by the perky title, though. The agenda was a strange stew of beliefs, collectively labeled "Earth Changes," whose message is simple but starkly apocalyptic: Mother Nature is tired of mankind's blighting presence, so she's planning to kill most of us off in the next few years by "willing" a rise in natural disasters, strife, and disease.

It's a frightening idea—*My planet wants me dead*—so you can see why the crowd whimpered a little. Annie, who had organized the conference with her husband, Byron, was warning people bright and early that rough talk was about to commence, and the words put her listeners in a metaphysical pinch. Conscientious students that they were, they wanted to hear it. Being only human, they also sort of didn't.

That's because, in its uniquely weird way, Earth Changes packs scarier oomph than Christian premillennialism, predicting equally horrible upheavals in the near future, but for paganish reasons that play on people's deepest fears about the future of the environment. The driving force is the planet itself, an avenging goddess who, according to Earth Changes theology, is possessed of an actual "consciousness" and an ability to crank up the severity of earthquakes, storms, and microbes in her own best interest. Various prophecies— the Book of Revelation, the quatrains of Nostradamus, ancient Hopi Indian predictions—seem to confirm this, indicating to believers that the Earth Changes have already started and will only get worse as the millennium turns. Before long, the foreboding burps and rumbles of the eighties and nineties (global warming, for instance, and all that weird weather in recent years) will escalate into a level of physical destruction that will alter the face of our world. Lately, some Earth Changers have hopped on the "Y2K" bandwagon—the increasingly popular notion that the millennium computer date crisis will cause so much trouble that survivalism will be necessary.

This is most often meant literally, not allegorically. One leading Earth Changes writer, a now-deceased New Age shaman who called himself Sun Bear, described the process as a "great big shaggy dog" shaking off fleas. He predicted an unimaginable period of hurricanes and tornadoes, continent-cracking earthquakes, melting ice caps, floods, barfing volcanoes, famines, plagues, even a possible "pole shift," a flipping of the planet on its axis. Earth Changes believers produce terrifying maps that show what the continents will look like after the dust settles. One of these, Gordon-Michael Scallion's "Future Map of the United States: 1998–2001," depicts a much-widened Mississippi River, a flooded East Coast, and an ocean-covered West and Southwest. New York City is completely underwater. A lot of Florida is gone. California has sunk, and only hangs on in scattered land chunks with telling names like the "Island of Mount Shasta." The "new" West Coast cuts a gruesome arc through Arizona, Colorado, Nebraska, Wyoming, Utah, and Idaho.

So where's the joy? Like Christianity, Earth Changes offers believers hope. Christians talk about the Rapture, a moment sometime before the Tribulation when the righteous will be whooshed safely into Heaven. Earth Changes holds out two possibilities. One is that the changes don't necessarily have to happen. As Annie Kirkwood explained in her 1991 book, *Mary's Message to the World,* a compendium of channeled communications about Earth Changes from the Virgin Mary, the Big Bop could be significantly reduced, perhaps delayed indefinitely, if people would start living in peace and harmony.

If we don't, Earth Changers will be better off anyway, because they'll have made sufficient physical and spiritual preparations. That's where Byron Kirkwood comes in: he specializes in readiness. His 1993 book, *Survival Guide for the New Millennium,* is all about using classic fallout-shelter techniques to make it through the hard times. Annie's main focus is the blissful "aftertime" that comes after the Changes.

"All will live in harmony," Mary told her. "All will be cared for intelligently. . . . Future generations will have no conceptions of hatred, anger, and war."

Still, Mary made it clear that we're probably in for it, that the Earth will be "moved by violent forces which will cause many to lose their physical lives."

How many? Annie didn't offer a figure at the festival, but plenty of others have been willing to chuck a dart at the number board. Within the movement, many believers have decided that we've already crossed the line of doom, so they've taken refuge on safe ground away from obvious no-no spots like coastlines, big cities, or anywhere near a nuclear power plant. One typical evacuee I spoke with was Leigh Richmond-Donahue, an elderly metaphysical thinker and writer based in Maggie Valley, North Carolina, a small town in the southern Appalachians that became an Earth Changes hotspot during the eighties. With her husband, Dick, Leigh wrote a 1993 novel, *Blindsided,* which dramatized a couple's survival saga after the Earth Changes whomped New York City. Soon after the festival I called her and asked: How much trouble are we in?

"Well, the Earth is a living entity," she explained, sounding as brisk and no-nonsense as a veterinarian probing a cat's behind, "and when you pass the 3 percent mark in terms of ecological change there's a reaction—a violent reaction. As they say, Earth Changes is a birthing process, but it's going to be a bloody birthing."

How bloody?

"I think billions will be killed."

∞

I first heard about Earth Changes at a 1989 New Age expo in New York, where I sat in on a lecture by a man named Matthew John Stenger, a thirtysomething guy from Baltimore who seemed to be offering something different from the standard menu of dolphin telepathy, wheat grass–juice diets, and chakra healing. The brochure said Stenger had studied "Native American Shamanism with Navajo, Cherokee, and Aztec Medicine Men" and would discuss how various prophecies pointed to planetary "changes" that would soon reshape civilization.

The expo was held in a regal-but-rundown old hotel near Penn Station. Stenger, a nice-looking, physically fit type with blonde hair and a sun-crinkled face, did his thing inside a small, stuffy meeting room, where he used a slide show to cover all the basic horrors. In a routine drone, he talked about earthquakes, storms, disease, scary prophecies, unbalanced planetary ecosystems, and how his own spiritual quest had convinced him he had a responsibility to warn the world.

"I was a former life-in-the-fast-lane businessman and I realized my acquisitive, yuppie ways were killing me," he told a small, somewhat puzzled crowd of New Age fans. "My major organs were dysfunctioning and it looked like I might, ah, start developing signs of cancer." Searching for a new path, he embarked on Native American–style "vision quests" in Arizona that clarified his life's purpose. Subsequent searches led him to the Northwest, where he studied under Sun Bear in Washington State. Henceforth he was committed to spreading the word about Earth Changes, particularly as expressed in the prophecies of the Hopi Indians, who apparently saw all this coming 10,000 years ago. He was also committed to making a living at it, a goal that would prove elusive in the years ahead. To that end he was marketing himself as a spiritual half-breed—the vision quests, he said, directed him to adopt a new "spirit name," Matthew Mooncloud.

Sun Bear, who died in 1993, led a "Bear Tribe" of New Age followers who tried to live according to the tread-lightly style he advocated in books like *Black Dawn, Bright Day: Indian Prophecies for the Millennium That Reveal the Fate of the Earth* (with Wabun Wind). Sun

Bear was a controversial figure; he claimed to be a Chippewa Indian, but some Indians doubted his bloodline and dismissed him as a white "wannabe" who ripped off their traditions. Still, many New Agers put great stock in the harrowing forecasts he received from an entity called Spirit.

"Spirit is telling me, a Native person, to stand in front of [the mainstream culture] and say, 'Hey, this isn't working, kids,'" he wrote in *Black Dawn, Bright Day*. Spirit told him that volcanic activity, desertification, insect invasions, flooding, hurricanes, tornadoes, famine, animal deaths, chemical and nuclear accidents, epidemics, drought, and tidal waves were all going to increase soon, and there was no turning back. "Then Spirit went further and . . . said, 'You speak of 7.0 and 8.0 on your Richter scale for earthquakes. We speak of 10.0 and 12.0.'"

The Hopi prophecies warned that the Great Spirit would come down hard if the planet moved "too far out of balance," as it has obviously done in the twentieth century. The Hopi foresaw "two shakings" (World Wars I and II), precursors to a "third shaking" whose severity would dwarf those conflicts. The "third shaking of the Earth" could be staved off, Stenger said, but only if the people of all nations came together immediately in a spirit of harmony and peace.

Chillingly, there was no sign this would happen. Hopi representatives had traveled to the United Nations in the past to warn humanity to unite, only to be turned away at the door. Frowning, Stenger said that if they were ignored by the world, the shaking would begin.

And if that happened, he said with a tense laugh, New York wouldn't be a choice locale: "Once the super-earthquakes start, glass box skyscrapers will *not* be very safe. You might want to think about that."

∞

The authors of *Blindsided* obviously thought about it. A prophetic yelp written in an insistent, often-italicized style, the novel isn't much as literature, but it's very valuable as a record of how Earth Changers see the future playing out, and how they rationalize a relatively selfish attitude toward the apocalypse.

It opens in Manhattan, where a fiftysomething couple named Craig and Lex Gallagher notice the first sign of trouble while relaxing in their swank apartment overlooking Central Park. Craig is a prosperous engineer. Lex is his equally accomplished wife, a snazzy intellectual whose latest book of cutting-edge social theory, *Electronic Anthropology*, is on the best-seller list.

As I've learned over time, this steely duo represents an idealized version of how Earth Changers like to see themselves. They're intelligent, professional, financially self-sufficient, hard-headed, loving, and tough when they have to be. Craig is also quite icy about the worth of other people. Lex is more the gooshy "liberal" type, but she eventually comes around to his way of thinking, and the novel unintentionally dramatizes an attribute that Earth Changers probably wouldn't claim: they don't much care for their fellow man.

As the action begins, Craig is sprawled out watching a football game; Lex is preparing to deliver a lecture that night at Lincoln Center. Wrapped in a nubby towel and looking crabby, she tells him the water pressure is down. Craig laughs. Women, even this brilliant woman, just don't understand infrastructures. He patiently explains that it's half-time of a big game, so millions of toilets are probably glugging in unison. But he checks the faucet anyway, realizing as he does that, dammit, both of them are pretty darn special. Even if something terrible happens, they'll probably survive it.

"Lex would take it in stride. She always did. She'd given herself almost as rough a life as he had had—learning welding at ten in his uncle's welding shop. Climbing the high steel by the time he was sixteen. Earning his way through Stanford . . ."

A virtual coiled spring of can-do, Craig is forced into action the next night, when a total blackout creates citywide panic. As the jabbering herd fills the streets, Craig and Lex pile into their car and prepare to scoot to their son's rural home in the mountains. Getting out of town is a nightmare. Everyone seems to sense, as does Craig, that something vast and grotesque is taking shape. "This was not to be compared with the 1964 blackout," Craig broods. "This was the time of gang rapes and senseless murders. . . . When frustration was the daily gridlock; with helplessness of every kind. . . ."

They eventually make it, but not without a scare or two. At one point, as their car creeps through the howling night, a beast-man with a crowbar tries to pry open Lex's door. "These are human beings!" she cries. "Normally sane people!"

Craig isn't so sure about that one. For him, individuals are little more than a mob waiting to happen. He mulls their awful power.

"Mindless. Primitive. Huge dinosaurs made up of individual bodies, wasting, destroying, without purpose except a lust for revenge. Against what? Against 'them.' . . . Yes, unless this was brought under control, quickly, the mobs would form."

Aiming the car west, Craig shudders at a world gone mad.

∞

I thought a lot about what Matt Stenger said, and soon came to an important, life-altering realization: Hey, if people take this stuff seriously, doesn't that mean they have to dig in and prepare for the worst? To actually build Earth Changes survival shelters? About a week after Stenger's presentation I called him and asked.

"For some it definitely means that," he said. "I tend to believe that you should trust in your spirit and be prepared to live lightly off the land." To that end he said he and his "soul mate, Veronica," were planning a move to Maggie Valley, the Earth Changes nexus in western North Carolina where Leigh Richmond-Donohue lived.

Great. Back to the point. "Do you know anybody who's going the shelter route?"

He didn't want to discuss that, but over time I pestered him until he yielded the names and number of Leon and Lois Blackwell, a pair of wealthy retirees he'd met on the New Age circuit. (I've changed their names to preserve their desire for anonymity.) He said they were preparing to flee suburban Maryland and move to a full-blown Earth Changes redoubt in the mountains of West Virginia. I phoned, introduced myself to Leon, and slowly tacked the conversation toward the pod or bunker or pillbox or whatever it was. Had they really built one?

"Yep, yep," he said amiably. Sounding like Water Rat bragging about his riverside digs in *The Wind in the Willows,* he described an earth-toned dome built on a geophysically stable rock ridge in the Appalachians. "We're comfortably equipped for everything," he sniffed. "Two-hundred-and-fifty-mile-an-hour winds, and earthquakes, and fallout, and even energy saving."

The Blackwells hadn't moved yet, and they invited me to visit them at their Maryland home, a huge converted dairy barn that housed a New Age foundation they owned and operated. I was then living in Washington, D.C., so I drove out the next morning.

As my car crunched to a stop on their gravel driveway, Leon and Lois bounded out, waving hello. Neither fit my mental stereotype of what pod-bound doomsayers might look or act like. Leon resembled the late novelist Walker Percy—sturdy and hale, with gray, close-cropped hair and clear eyes. Lois was a jowly woman with blue-gray hair; she wore a wide-eyed, fish-mouthed expression that made her look alarmed, but not out of it. Overall, they looked like what they were, happy retirees who wanted to enjoy their golden years in comfort and security. Only difference: in their case, comfort and security required the ability to survive everything from nuclear meltdown to an attack by mutant whitetails.

The Blackwells had done well financially—Leon was a Craig-like person, a retired engineer—and they were smug about their place in life, not worried in the least that the majority of mankind couldn't afford to prepare for Earth Changes. Both reacted testily to my questions about Earth Changes details; they were impatient with my relative ignorance of the teachings.

"Do you expect the Earth Changes to happen soon?" I asked as we sat down in a sunroom.

"*Soon?*" Leon gasped. "We wouldn't prepare if we didn't think it was soon." He squinted. "Look, I don't know where you are with this material. I have no idea where you are so I have no idea what to tell you or what you would understand."

"I'd like to educate myself. Where do I start?"

"Have you read George Green? *No?* He's head of a California group that has chapter and verse on why this is going to happen sooner instead of later. Get their newsletter, the *Phoenix Liberator*. But there's no point just calling them up—all you'll do is waste their time. They've put out about thirty or forty books on this, plus weekly updates. We have this material and you can look at it here. You can call them up once you understand the gist, the magnitude of it. But right now, you're so near the beginning that you're only going to waste people's time."

I took these shots with a passive grin. I wanted to avoid any mouthing off that would jeopardize my chances of seeing pod. "Thanks for the advice. I'll do it."

Next, an interrogation about motives. "What are you trying to do here?" Lois said. "What are you after?"

"I'm interested in sociological responses to the year 2000," I said, a response that was carefully calibrated to be meaningless. It made them frown. "What kind of thing do you mean?" Leon pressed.

"Well, for example, last year in Russell, Kansas, a couple of women decided the world was about to end in a nuclear holocaust. They heard this from archangels who fly around in UFOs. The angels told them to go to Israel immediately, because Israel alone would survive the destruction." (A true story.)

Leon stared at me and then erupted, but not because I had compared him with blatant kooks. "Good grief, Israel is the *last* place you'd want to be! That's where the Mossad is headquartered!"

That sounded strange. People drag all sorts of stray themes into Earth Changes, but I hadn't heard any Israel-bashing before. Perhaps the Blackwells were borrowing the fundamentalist Christian belief that the Antichrist will attack Israel first during the Tribulation?

Perhaps, but they were also reading materials that struck me as anti-Semitic. After some additional chat, the Blackwells took me up to a second-floor office, where they laid out back issues of the *Phoenix Liberator.* They talked about the paper and its editor, George Green, with utmost reverence.

"It's all in here," Lois said, gently fingering open an issue.

Yes, it sure was. Green received his copy for the *Liberator* from "pulsed short-wave transmissions" dispatched by entities in the Pleiades who, for some reason, hated Jews. The top banana was "Phoenix Commander" Gyeorgos Ceres Hatonn-Aton, whose stated mission is to pave the way for the return of a being—"the messenger, God, Christos"—who will usher in a New Age of peace. The outer-space teachings are designed to protect us from "alleged" Jews who will help the Antichrist bring wrack and ruin, and the paper brimmed with David Duke endorsements, Holocaust revisionism, and "the truth about" *The Protocols of the Elders of Zion,* the long-debunked document that was alleged to be a transcript of a secret nineteenth-century meeting of Jews plotting to rule the world. (Green's "truth" is that the debunkers were liars.) As near as I could make out from my brief glimpse, the Earth Changes would be part of a worldwide cleansing of these dark forces.

"Interesting," I said, willing my eyes back into their sockets.

Suddenly pleased, the Blackwells hauled out pictures of their pod, displayed in a grandmotherly photo album. Painted adobe brown, it looked like a simple Bucky Fuller dome with windows. They gave me directions and we set a date for my visit.

Alas, they broke the date. The Phoenix Commander must have heard me snickering when I drove off—and tattled—because the Blackwells yanked the invitation the morning I was scheduled to come out.

"Indefinitely," Lois chirped on my answering machine. "But God bless, and best of luck with what you're trying to do!"

I drove out anyway, rationalizing that they were backing out on a "deal." The trip took five hours and ended with my creeping up winding, wooded West Virginia backroads. Finding the town was easy enough, but finding the pod was tricky. My directions seemed garbled, and I got lost, hopelessly confronted with a choice of long, posted roads that seemed to match the description of the Blackwells' road . . . or maybe not. This was an area of hillbillyesque right-next-to-the-road home zoning, and people were noticing me as I tooled back and forth, stopping frequently to check my map and curse.

I gave up and headed for a general store I'd passed. Inside, a helpful old lady named Nellie said yes, she knew the Blackwells. They were nice people who were putting up a real-estate development on 250 acres next door to her son's 400. They hadn't found many buyers, though, owing to the low demand for domed houses made of concrete.

"Now me," she said, "I'd rather have a nice A-frame."

Her directions took me down a road that again led to a confusing array of options. As I executed yet another clumsy K-turn, a huge middle-aged man in overalls wobbled in my direction from the front yard of a roadside house. I rolled down my window, grinning feebly.

"Hi, I'm looking for the Blackwells place."

"The Blackwells expecting you?"

"Uh, yeah," I lied. "In fact, I'm late for my appointment."

"They're good people," he said, nodding. "My son's up there now, working for them." He pointed at the correct lane, which ran right by his house. "It's about a quarter mile to their place." Pulling away, I watched him staring at my back bumper.

With visions of a phone alert, alarm bells, barking dogs, and this guy's truck blocking me when I came back out, I floored it up the lane, verified that the Hunkerdome did exist—it was squat, brown, and round, like a dirt dauber's nest—floored it back, and beat it out of town.

∞

Chastened by their stiff dose of reality, Craig and Lex, the *Blindsided* duo, pick their way to a mountain community where they hole up with their son, Jeff, and his wife and kids. But simple escape is not enough. A central theme of *Blindsided* is that hard-core protective measures will be necessary as human vermin scatter from their disrupted urban nests. Away from the women, Craig gruffly tells Jeff about New York, and in short order they drive to town and buy a few guns. "I keep hoping that Lex is right," he sighs, handicapping the looming collapse, "that these are the birth pangs of a new and better civilization. That what we see is the fetus separating itself from the structures that have supported it . . . the afterbirth . . ."

For all her comforting visions about the "aftertime," Annie Kirkwood also understood that we won't get to Heaven without hitting a few gaping potholes. After her opening spiel on Saturday morning at the Earth Festival in Dallas, she yielded to her husband, Byron, a portly, friendly fellow whose job was to verbalize Earth Changes' hunker-down aspects. Taking the podium to light applause—Byron is a nice guy, but his words are not easy to hear—his first chore was to yield the floor to a more famous prophet of the hardball message: Gordon-Michael Scallion, the "future map" psychic who is one of the best-known Earth Changes visionaries. Scallion was patched in live via satellite from the Matrix Institute, his Earth Changes think tank and hideaway in the solid granite hills of Chesterfield, New Hampshire.

As an image of Scallion flickered onto a large screen, Byron mumbled his introduction. Scallion wore a tie and a navy blazer and looked dapper and corporate. Mounted on a wall behind him, his "Future Map of the United States, 1998–2001" showed a cracked and woeful fruited plain.

"Gordon-Michael is considered one of the most accurate futurists of our time," Byron said in a soft Texas accent. "He's been featured on the NBC show *Ancient Prophecies* as well as *Sightings* and *Encounters.* He predicted the June 1992 California earthquake. He also predicted Hurricane Andrew, many floods, and more. Live from his studios in New Hampshire, please welcome futurist Gordon-Michael Scallion!"

Vigorous applause. Scallion nodded and smiled.

"Gordon-Michael, welcome to the great state of Texas!"

"Thank you, Byron."

"For those that are not familiar with the work, would you tell us how you came to be a futurist?"

Cued, Scallion told his revelation story, an important aspect of the Earth Changes style. Almost without exception, Earth Changers claim that their knowledge of the doctrine came to them through an intense personal spiritual experience as opposed to, say, picking up one of the numerous books on the subject. Why that's so is hard to say. It may be an impossible question, because the answer would require a believer to step out of his skin and examine his faith as if it were a mental condition. ("You believe X. *Why* do you believe X?")

My own guess is this: Earth Changers tend to have very healthy egos and a large measure of narcissistic delusion; for several reasons, Earth Changes and its "revelatory moment" resonate with both traits. First, Earth Changes is esoteric. Only a few people know about it, so knowing about it delivers an insider's thrill. Second, it allows you to attend to your own needs—through spiritual self-healing, pleasurably cathartic states of terror, or, if you have the resources, the soothing construction of survival pods—while telling yourself that what you're really doing is working to save mankind.

Third . . . it's just nice to receive secret spiritual commands. In our essentially godless world, most people don't, and when it happens it must be genuinely riveting. Annie Kirkwood says Mother Mary picked her as a messenger in 1987, despite her protest that "I'm not Catholic!" ("Nor I," Mary responded.) Matt Stenger got the news during a vision quest. Claire Applegate, a young Earth Changer I met during a break at the Earth Festival, told me that Earth Changes awareness simply "happened" to her one day in the late eighties when she was sitting on her couch in Houston despairing about the environment.

"A voice came to me and said, 'Claire, something really, really bad is going to happen to the Earth.' I had never heard of Earth Changes, but I felt the truth of it all at once, and I knew that I would help in some way." (So she wrote and recorded a song about the peaceful aftermath of the Earth Changes, "Mary's Lullaby.")

For Scallion, predictably, the conversion experience was more intense—as a top visionary, he would naturally have a top vision. It started in Florida in 1979. Back then, Scallion said, he was a successful professional involved in electronics, moving through life in a nonspiritual schlep. Then one day he lost his voice "abruptly" and checked into a hospital for tests. His great epiphany happened that night, when he saw dream visions of "disasters occurring on planet Earth. I remember seeing Dan Rather reading a news bulletin that said Mexico City had just been hit by a major earthquake."

Later, a luminous, floating woman appeared over his bed, instructing him to write down visions that he would receive on behalf of all mankind. By 1982 he'd seen thousands, "most dealing with great changes in the Earth that would occur in the nineties." At first he resisted his prophet's calling, but eventually made a career of it, releasing maps, tapes, and a regular newsletter, *Earth Changes Report,* which provides specific dates about earthquakes, floods, and other disasters. Scallion explained that his revelations came in handy color-coding: "Deep colors if the thing will probably occur, gray if not."

Lately, he said, more and more visions had been in "bright, colorful images." The crowd murmured again; one man actually said "Whoa."

"What is the cause of all this?" Scallion asked rhetorically. "We've all heard about the millennium of peace that's coming, a thousand years of peace that's been prophesied by every major religion and culture. The Hopi Indians, the prophecies of Nostradamus and Edgar Cayce, all are talking about the same kind of changes at this time.

"Sometime between 1998 and 2001 we'll see the emergence of a new kind of man," he said in his conclusion. "All the value systems that are established in the next three years will literally set the framework for the next thousand years."

At that, the floor was opened for questions. The highlights: two that drew specific predictions from Scallion about the remainder of 1995, both of which didn't happen. (One was that "in 1995 there won't be *any* question that there is life on other planets. We're gonna know, proof positive.") The lowlights: everything else. Annie had specifically admonished, "Please, no personal questions," but people flouted that rule—"Will Hot Springs, Arkansas, be destroyed?" "Would you comment on the area between Buffalo, Niagara Falls, and Syracuse?"—so I took a break and checked out the exhibits area, where various purveyors of Earth Changes literature and survival equipment were showing their stuff.

First I scanned the bookshelves for treasures (this is where I found *Blindsided*) and bought a few titles by or about two old-timers who helped start it all. One of them being, of course, Nostradamus, the sixteenth-century French prophet who crystal-balled the future in hundreds of mysterious four-line poems called quatrains, and who predicted Earth Change-y turbulence at the end of this millennium. The other was Edgar Cayce, the famous "sleeping prophet" and the man who appears to have first conceived of Earth Changes. Born in 1877 on a farm near Hopkinsville, Kentucky, Cayce was a true American original, an alleged clairvoyant and healer whose method was to lapse into a trance state and start talking. These "readings" were written up and typed, and today some 14,000 of them are stored at the Association for Research and Enlightenment, Inc., in Virginia Beach, Virginia, the throbbing center for the world's continuing fascination with Cayce.

Edgar Cayce on Prophecy, a 1968 book published by the ARE, describes one of his more astonishing visions. In 1936, Cayce dreamed he was alive as a young boy in Nebraska in the year 2100. He told his elders that he had existed as Edgar Cayce in the twentieth century. Their interest piqued by this, a group of bald, bearded, chin-scratching scientists loaded him into a "long, cigar-shaped metal ship" and took him on a high-speed tour of the United States.

"On this venture he saw that New York had been destroyed and was being rebuilt," *Prophecy* says. "Alabama was partly underwater. . . . The group returned to Nebraska, now America's west coast!"

Later, Cayce interpreted this dream with a reading that told him the sights were real and that, despite the coming cataclysm, everything would work out for the best: "Though the very heavens fall, though the earth shall be changed . . . the premises in Him are sure and will stand."

That's a nice outcome. Whether it's true is open to serious debate, since Cayce made several predictions that have already konked. For example, he once said that the Lost Continent of Atlantis would rise again in "'68 and '69. Not so far away." The expo shelves were full of similar boo-boos, including a few vintage offerings. In *Secret of the Andes,* written in 1961, a UFO-obsessed mystic named George Hunt Williamson (writing under the name Brother Philip) was told by channeled entities that the elements would soon rebel against man and that the "entire face of the Earth will change," with the loss of millions of lives. According to *We Are the Earthquake Generation,* a metaphysics masterpiece written in 1978, almost all of the West should be underwater by now. If you save back issues of Gordon-Michael Scallion's *Earth Changes Report* for a few months, you'll see that he constantly misses. Howlingly, he predicted "volcanic activity" for Mount Rainier in 1994 or 1995.

How do Earth Changers respond to these mistakes? With a shrug, basically. Prophecy is a tricky business, they'll tell you. Certain dates may be off because the fallible human messengers were mistaken, or because the good will of many people helped forestall disaster. The latter tactic is significant. With it, Earth Changers have removed all the risk from the prophecy game. If a prophecy comes true they claim credit. If it doesn't, they say it might still come true, or claim credit for its not coming true.

What do they get from this? I can only theorize about that, but my sense is that there's something deeply satisfying about the Earth Changes mindset, and that believers don't want to let it go. In the past, failed millennial prophecy has often meant the end of the prophetic movement. With its built-in fail-safe clause, Earth Changes can continually reinvent itself for an audience that seems to respond positively to the idea that naughty mankind is on the brink. It's a way of living on the edge of apocalypse forever, and never losing the twin thrills—the pang of impending disaster, the anticipatory joy of ultimate redemption—that can make millennialism terrible and enjoyable at the same time.

Little wonder, then, that the audience was primed and alert when

Byron stepped back up to the mike to do his bit. I took my seat as he got going with his version of an ice-breaking anecdote.

"When you first learn about Earth Changes it brings up fear, and that's OK, that's quite natural. The two greatest fears are the fear of death and the fear of change, and Earth Changes has both of these associated with them."

He ticked off the major prophets who have seen the changes coming and asked, "How many of *you* have had a dream or some sort of premonition about the changes?" Many hands went up. "Ohhhhh. Cold chill time."

Byron got serious soon enough, with his spiel about the need for hard hats, dust masks, respirators, goggles, walkie-talkies, Red Cross first-aid training, food caches, and long-term shelters. About the threat of rising oceans, high winds, and mass death.

But before that, he indulged in one final riff of introspection. Byron said his role wasn't to bum people out, but to protect them from the natural tendency to avoid thinking about the hard reality of Earth Changes. He acknowledged that many people hope the "physicals" of Earth Changes won't take place, that the planetary transformation will occur symbolically in the hearts of men.

Byron respected that viewpoint, but other people, he said, had even suggested that merely *talking* about destruction is bad karma that will somehow "help make it happen."

"To those people I'd only say this," Byron parried. "Does a squirrel cause winter by gathering nuts?"

∞

Byron could have a point. In the nineties, it *has* often seemed like the planet is punishing us, regardless of whether Mother Earth "thinks" we deserve a spanking. I know I've worried about it, and to keep a check on my tendency toward knee-jerk anti–Earth Changes mockery, I keep a file labeled "Hmmm," which bulges with newspaper clippings and magazine articles about real-world events that happen to dovetail with Earth Changes prophecy. Stuffed in there, along with reminders that the oceans *are* rising, that an asteroid *could* hit us, and that one out of every three plant species *is* considered "threatened," is a 1998 beauty from the *New York Times* called "Climatology Guru is Part Curmudgeon, Part Imp." Its focus is Wallace Broecker, a widely respected geochemist at Columbia University's Lamont-Doherty Earth Observatory, who believes that if mankind warms the planet as much as computer models predict—just a few degrees—this could set off a chain of events with "disruptive results for much of the world," including temperature changes that "could mean disaster for world agriculture."

"The climate system is an angry beast," Broecker has warned, sounding a lot like Sun Bear with his image of a flea-maddened dog, "and we are poking it with sticks."

During an interlude in my longer-term "quest for pod," nudged by such statements, I decided to try a front-line experiment in feeling the apocalyptic burn. The vehicle: a weekend workshop called the Council of All Beings, a relatively milder form of ritualized enviro-guilt-expiation that is popular among environmentalists, modern pagans, and various Native American wannabes.

Earth Changes and the Council of All Beings are inspired by the same planetary angst, but the similarities end there. Earth Changes is about digging in and hunkering down. The Council's rituals teach you that man is harming the planet, yes, but there's still hope—that is, if we grovel, mope, say we're sorry, and start behaving properly.

The message at the heart of the Council goes by the label "deep ecology," a term coined in 1973 by a Norwegian philosophy professor named Arne Naess, who believes that the first step toward redemption is for humans to roll over, expose their bellies to the godhead, and admit they aren't so special. "Within the framework of deep ecology, and contrary to key assumptions of Judaeo-Christian/Marxist/humanist tradition," says *Thinking Like a Mountain,* a Council of All Beings manifesto and how-to manual written in 1988 by Naess and others, "humans are not to be viewed as the ultimate measure of value or as the crown of creation. We are but 'a plain member' of the biotic community."

My Council was held in a private home in Malibu, California, on a chilly weekend in 1992. The kickoff event was an introductory Friday night lecture held at a church in Santa Monica. There, I sat in the pews and listened to a service that was part rain forest–preservation lecture, part enviro-spirit hootenanny, and part guilt trip. Our leader was John Seed, a pudgy, balding forty-seven-year-old Australian with elfin features and twinkling eyes, who had helped co-write *Thinking Like a Mountain.* Using the same tools that Matt Stenger did (a slide show, a somber voice, and enough terrifying information to make Chicken Little hurl himself off a cliff), Seed laid out the grim eco-realities about the ozone layer, the greenhouse effect, rain forest depletion, species extinction.

As I listened, I felt a twinge of apocalyptic déjà vu, but it wasn't a flashback to anything I'd heard in a church. I was recalling a class I took in college, called "Can Man Survive?" The course featured a couple of with-it professors who delivered a message of undiluted environmental alarmism, circa 1976. Their aim was to drive home the didactic scold that we students were overprivileged brats whose wasteful habits threatened the world, and it worked. For months afterward I felt guilty every time I went near a McDonald's.

Obviously, these profs weren't millennialists, but they sounded an apocalyptic note that the world heard loud and clear starting with the first Earth Day in 1970. The year 1972 saw publication of *The Limits to Growth,* a best-selling book by a team from the Massachusetts Institute of Technology—sponsored by the Club of Rome, a priestly sounding collection of industrialists and scientists—who used computer models to plot out the likely fate of the planet by the turn of the millennium. Their conclusion: unless the exponential growth of population and consumption stopped, mankind was fated to suffer an "uncontrollable decline" in population and production—a mass die-off, like the crash of a deer herd that lacks sufficient browse. Paul and Anne Ehrlich echoed this secular doomsaying in 1981 with *Extinction*, where they warned: "By the end of the century the extinction of perhaps a million species in the Amazon basin could have entrained famines in which a billion human beings perished. And if our species is very unlucky, the famines could lead to a thermonuclear war, which could extinguish civilization."

In the eighties, one by-product of such rhetoric was the formation of distinctly spiritual political movements—some tiny, some large—centered specifically on environmental concerns. For example, Earth First!, the now-mostly-irrelevant radical-environmental group, was created in 1980, driven partly by the belief that humans amount to a planetary cancer that warrants a "cure." Earth First! pushed a heretical reading of the Gaia Hypothesis—the well-shy-of-Earth-Changes notion, popularized in 1979 by British scientist James Lovelock, that the Earth is a unified system that tends to regulate itself when planetary changes throw things out of balance. In Earth First!'s view, Gaia was an angry lady with a vengeful side, and it was possible that global calamities like starvation, AIDS, and thinning ozone were, as Earth First! co-founder Dave Foreman once put partly tongue-in-cheek—like antibodies against "the human pox."

John Seed was a gentler sort, but only slightly. He got his start in 1979, when he took up with protesters who were attempting to stop a government-sale logging operation at Terania Creek, a virgin stand of tropical timber in New South Wales, Australia. That protest featured pioneering use of direct-action tactics that later became commonplace among environmental radicals—lying in the path of bulldozers, chaining protesters to trees—and for Seed, who was living nearby in a Buddhist meditation community, it was the end of what he called his "Buddhist detachment" from the real world. He got involved with other, similar protests and in 1981 founded the Rain Forest Information Center, an international rain forest–preservation group.

For his Santa Monica audience, he laid the guilt on thick, extrapolating current trends to a distant point of nullity. "The real destruction of the rain forest began in our lifetimes and will end in our lifetime," he said. "*One million* species are going to go extinct before the year 2000.

"We can, we *must* regain our sense of deep ecology, or discover it anew. Without it, we have already died a death more horrible than any we can imagine."

The preaching was undeniably scary, but the Council itself didn't really work for me. It consisted of play-pretend ritual exercises that were supposed to make us "see" reality from the perspective of animals and plants, but in fact it generated more cringing than tremors. We got going early on Saturday morning, with a loosening-up exercise called "Eco-Milling," which involved wandering around in circles and stopping occasionally to hug a stranger, staring into his or her eyes and saying, "I love this person! This person is a valued member of the biotic community!" In the afternoon we nestled in for part one of our "despair work," in which each of us, speaking "as humans," talked about our planetary grief in long, foamy-lipped confessionals. That night we were supposed to meditate and establish a spiritual link with whatever entity wanted us to speak for it. On Sunday morning we would make masks—using a table full of kindergartners' art supplies—in preparation for the high mass: the Council of All Beings itself, which unfolded in two parts. First, we would bitch at mankind. Then we'd empower ourselves by discussing things the Demon Species could do to set things right.

As we sat down for the initial talk, I checked out my fellow critters. Most of them struck me as well-meaning people who were involved in some tangible realm of do-good, like environmentalism, and needed a morale boost. There were, of course, a few overly emotive workshop saps on hand—like the woman who became Elephant, and who tried to upstage everybody with her grieving—but there was also that rarest of birds, an oddball character who didn't seem to belong here at all.

This was Caged Dove, a tubby, goateed hipster who was never quite able to let go of his original self, which he described to me as "bohemian." During the Eco-Milling, when he had to lock eyes with and declare his love for my biotic-ness, he couldn't quite handle it, so he refused to remove his blackberry-dark sunglasses.

Seed kicked off the Saturday morning session with a recollection of his own Saul-on-the-road-to-Damascus experience at Terania Creek, with emphasis on the epiphany. "Somehow," he recalled, "I found myself in the rain forest, and I could hear the trees screaming." Inspired by this, everybody pitched some woe.

"I'm tempted to let my rage make me say, 'Fuck you—let the people of the Earth die,'" said one woman, who was "deeply into Native American spirituality."

"Sometimes," said a burly guy wearing a windbreaker from the Sea Shepherds, a radical sea-going outfit that tries to sabotage whalers and seal hunters, "I just get overcome with the guilt and the sorrow."

Before we "got primal," Seed warned again that we would soon grapple with grief like we'd never grappled before. "To some," he said, "what's about to happen here will sound like Gestalt therapy, but it's actually more like standing in a front of a tree with someone waving a chainsaw at you."

That was a bit much, but I'll admit to feeling "threatened" when I woke up Sunday, Council of All Beings Day. For no particular reason, I decided to represent a California Quail. Using stuff from the supply table, I made my mask, cutting holes in a paper sack, gluing on a beak, and using crayons to draw "angry eyebrows."

The Council officially opened with everyone's statement of creature identity. Caged Dove, the hipster gent, skittered down his own unique and eloquent path: "I cost $19.95 at the pet store. I cringe. I poop. I realize this is my life. I'm a bird in a cage. I'm the dove." Elephant, predictably, had spent a long time fashioning her mask: a mammoth construction project featuring a long trunk made of tightly twisted newspapers. But on this day she was upstaged by the quiet dignity of Pond, who, after listening to Elephant's long, tearful bugling of despair, turned up her tiny cardboard Pond face and whispered, "Lick *me-e-e,* Elephant."

The rhetoric boiled over soon enough, with entities like Baboon, Lizard, and Road Kill giving it everything they had. (Especially Road Kill, who wailed: "Three hundred fucking million of us a year! Deer, moose, birds, countless insects who are killed every day by the two-leggeds who have no fur, feathers, or wings and who drive their cars over us!") Then, after a half-hour of shtick, fury, and keening, Seed gave us the cue for final healing to begin.

"I wonder about the two-leggeds," he said. "Have they fallen asleep? What are we going to do?"

The brood's members were supposed to heal at this point, but in the end they couldn't get a grip on the demons they had hauled, like lunker bass, to the surface. The general mood drifted toward a dour apocalypticism that infected even that perky guy, Caged Dove.

"I wonder if the two-leggeds are trainable?" Worm asked.

"They can change," said Lizard, a man who in real life liked lizards. "My human friend learned to love me."

"No! Look at the Dove."

"They're going to die. A lot of them are going to die."

"I'm a Caged Dove," Caged Dove added inexplicably. "But I'm sure as heck glad I'm not a chicken."

"The disease they call AIDS came from the rain forest. We must destroy them in a way that reflects their despoliation."

"I've almost given up on them. A lot of them take those white sticks and blow smoke in their own bodies. So how are we going to get them to stop creating the machines that poison the air?"

"Those two-leggeds are going to start killing themselves! Civilizations have come and gone, and this one will, too."

"Yeah," sighed Caged Dove. "It's the day before the Sacrifice."

∞

The *Blindsided* crew has no intention of being sacrificed. Making like the Swiss Family Robinson with a Rambo complex, they call a family meeting to discuss practical questions (how large a freezer will they need? should they store propane or gasoline?) and the essential philosophical dilemma of whether survival entails a willingness to kill. Lex gropes for a stance of peaceable bigthink, arguing that the family, as the "nucleus of tomorrow," should forsake "the use of force, fear, and coercion to achieve anything . . ."

Craig cuts in. "Don't beat our guns into plowshares," he barks, "nor our children into goody two-shoes. . . . Our children . . . must be trained in self-defense and the use of weapons, ready to join us in protecting our freedom as individuals."

"Do you suppose we're survivalists?" asks Terry, his daughter-in-law.

"A survivalist is one who survives," Craig answers. "You don't know until after."

Craig's answer struck me as awfully cold, but as I found out during my second pod pilgrimage—to Maggie Valley, North Carolina—a philosophy of "I'm going to be OK, you're probably screwed" is one of Earth Changes' unfortunate by-products.

Maggie Valley sits at 3,000 feet, near the Great Smoky Mountain National Park in western North Carolina, in a region where the

Smokies and the Blue Ridge Mountains come together in a beautiful geological scrum. The town developed an underground reputation in the eighties as a safe spot for Earth Changes settlers, and by 1992 Matthew "Mooncloud" Stenger had moved there with his love-lady, Veronica. I called him one day and arranged to go down for a visit, squeezing him, as usual, for information about "others."

"Well, there's Greta Woodrew. She's a big reason people feel drawn to be here. She runs a foundation called STAR that is mainly about prophecy connected with the Earth Changes. There's also Hans Keller. He's somebody you should know about. He has a project called the North Carolina Biodome that is all about living lightly on the land."

"Like, Earth Changes lightly?"

"I believe you'll find that's the case."

I immediately called Hans and Greta. Hans said, sure, come on down, though he was confused about what I wanted to see. At Greta's house I got her husband, Dick Smolowe, who was also friendly if a bit touchy. Greta was well known in the New Age world for her 1981 book, *On a Slide of Light,* which related how super-intelligent entities from outer space had warned her of the Earth Changes. I mumbled that I'd heard she and Dick had formed a "very interesting group," the Space Technology and Research Foundation, to disseminate this knowledge. He barked back that "STAR is not a group, club, organization, or religion. It's a *foundation.*"

"Sorry, my mistake. Listen, can I come down tomorrow?"

"Well, hold on. Where are you calling from? Washington? That's ten hours from here!"

"I'll get an early start." And I did: I was white-knuckling the steering wheel by 5:00 A.M.

By now it was dawning on me that maybe I was the problem in these relationships. Instead of going slowly and nurturing trust, I was hectically calling strangers the moment I detected even the penumbra of pod. Pods are inherently personal—they're your womb when the planetary rebirthing begins—so this probably was a turnoff.

And yet, I couldn't help it. Earth Changes seemed so vague and wispy and hard to believe that I needed to experience something tangible to know that it was real. I needed to feel the physical reality of a shelter, to touch cool, underground walls. Preferably ones made of corrugated metal, braced by exposed 2 by 4s.

Not surprisingly, I didn't score in Maggie Valley. Matt and Veronica were living in a small rented house and had no pod, and their prospects didn't look good. He'd moved there in part to be around the Earth Changes elite, but, sadly, they didn't seem to want him. Greta and Dick later dismissed Stenger to me as a hanger-on, laughing at him and calling him "Matthew Moonbeam."

Hans, a dapper European who had made a pile in the hotel business, greeted me hospitably at the Biodome, which was basically a small, mountain-meadow farm featuring lots of A-frame cottages and an oversized hothouse. He was very polite and admitted that he originally came to Maggie Valley to "work with" Greta and Dick, but that they had split up because he resisted her attempt to "adopt" him spiritually and this "bruised her ego." He clammed up when I asked, with all the subtlety of someone tossing a live snapping turtle into his bathtub, "So, what sort of survival plans have you made for the Earth Changes?"

"Oh, I don't believe in all those dire scenarios," he laughed. "I am only trying to show people how to live off the land." OK . . . bye!

I jumped in my car and chugged higher up into the mountains to the STAR spread. After passing a few hokey country mailboxes I saw, in a large, sloping field on my right, the first sign that I was approaching Gretaland: a couple of dozen stumps arranged in a Druidy semicircle around a bonfire pile. Near that was a spiffy wood and stone building. This was the STAR House. Every year, STAR devotees convened for the "Slide of Light" conference, a weekend of

New Agery, healing, dance, and Earth Changes discussion. Greta and Dick were at the center of a sizable crowd of elite New Agers, and they made it known in their newsletter (the *Woodrew Update*) that they could service the needs of a select number of enlightenoids who might temporarily need help once the Earth Changes began. According to local buzz, every man, child, and stray dog in the area knew this, too. One story I heard in town, perhaps apocryphal, said that Greta once hired locals to unpack an entire tractor-trailer load of storable food.

Greta knew about the Changes because entities told her, and they told her to warn the world. Like Annie Kirkwood, Greta didn't request this role. It all started when she and Dick were living a "very active, fairly conventional, and utterly credible life in the Connecticut suburbs." The first contact occurred in 1976, when ESP and astral-projection experiments with a man named Dr. Andrija Puharich opened her mind to the existence of a group of ETs "from another civilization in another solar system."

It was called Ogatta, and in the years since, representatives of the Ogatta group—fourteen different beings, with names like Hshames and Tauri—had interacted remarkably with Greta and Dick. Greta, in spirit, was periodically beamed to Ogatta, leaving behind her physical body, which the astral Greta derided as the "middle-aged vehicle." When this happened, the entities spoke through Greta's form, puppet-style. Dick received the code name Ezra, in honor of the Old Testament figure, and he rapped regularly with Tauri, an entity who once warned him to use his tape recorder less and instead to *listen* deeply. Tauri threatened to blow up the machine, but contented herself with jamming the mechanism when it annoyed her.

After turning off the main road and negotiating a long, lushly landscaped lane that led to Greta and Dick's perky, upscale mountain chalet, I parked and knocked on their door. They greeted me with a smile and placed me on an overstuffed couch in a large, light-bathed living room. In person Greta was hefty and smiling, her gray hair kept short in a tightly wound frizz cap. Dick was the trim Alan Cranston type. There was no anti-Semitism on display—Greta and Dick were Jewish—but Greta was rather smug as she spoke, with gravel-voiced intensity, about the higher purpose of STAR.

"We spent a large part of our lives doing well," she said, meaning financially well. "And we *did* do well. And now we can afford to do good, and we are."

Nice speech, but it rang hollow under the circumstances. At that moment Dick excused himself to walk onto the back patio and yell at a workman.

On the wipe-those-grins-off-your-face front, there was the tape-recorder . . . incident. Greta and Dick made it clear that they didn't want to be recorded—they preferred that I simply *listen*—but I rudely moaned until they gave in. I pressed the record button on my trusty Panasonic, which had worked glitchlessly for the previous ten years. Not this time. The record button wouldn't go down. The mechanism was . . . jammed.

"Hmmm," I said, as if reading from a bad script. "The record button won't go down." Silence from Greta and Dick. But they were smiling. I don't believe in telekinesis, but it *was* a very strange coincidence.

Unfortunately, that was it for theater, though the conversation was interesting. Greta and Dick told me more about the Ogattans' Earth Changes message. In keeping with Earth Changes' malleable-reality style, the wise ones didn't provide exact dates. Greta thought the changes could happen in the nineties or as late as 2012. But she said they were definitely coming: she was repeatedly told "the Scenario stands." Tauri said that if humans were to shift consciousness "in a golden moment, on a slide of light," the Scenario probably wouldn't happen. But since we're not shaping up, it probably will.

Hinting boldly, I asked if there were any additional, you know, *dwellings* they might let me see. Yeah, said Greta, the STAR house— I could look at it as long as I wanted . . . on my way out.

Groan. I would see no pod this day, so I decided to risk asking a few obnoxious questions. Weirdly, Greta anticipated the first one.

"People ask if we keep weapons to protect ourselves," she said. "We say that depends on who you're talking about us protecting ourselves *from*."

I pressed on, asking about the responsibility of receiving this kind of prophecy. If Greta was really supposed to "tell them," shouldn't she be out in the streets, clad in skins with twigs in her hair, spreading the word like John the Baptist?

Nope. The world would call her insane, and besides, only through the exercise of their own free will can people appreciate the coming Changes. Sounding downright heartless, Greta noted that, besides, she couldn't stand the sight of poverty. She could never travel to India, for example—a place she might want to visit to savor its "spiritual heritage"—because if she "walked those streets and absorbed that grief it would kill me."

At that I went over the top and asked about "inner-city kids." What about a child born in poverty who never got a chance to attend a New Age conference and hear about Earth Changes? Who intercedes for him?

"First of all, I don't buy the statement," Greta said.

"The major problem in the inner cities is the 'parent problem,'" said Dick.

"Maybe that child *chose* that incarnation," snapped Greta.

That wrapped it up for me. I loaded up and left, driving down the mountain with a firm grip on the wheel in case those pesky Ogattans decided to run me off the road. On the way out of town I cast an evil eye at my tape recorder, which sat broken on the passenger seat like a symbol of my fruitless quest. Feeling a little nervous, I said "heh heh" and hit the record button one more time.

Choonk. It worked.

∞

"These will be worth their weight in gold," said Bob Hieronimus as he pointed to several Sam's Club–size boxes of Tampons stacked in a shadowy corner of a cool basement. It was a bright and windy spring Saturday in 1997. Bob, his wife, Zoh, my wife, Susan, and I were all standing around in the recesses of Bob and Zoh's Earth Changes bunker, which was built deep under their home in . . .

Er, I can't say. The Hieronimuses are old fringe-world acquaintances who revealed over time that they, too, were Earth Changes believers. After years of listening to me wheedle and beg, they generously agreed to let me see their pod, under certain conditions. One of them was that the pod's location would be kept secret.

So let's just say it's in the Baltimore area. It was a spiffy subbasement space of several hundred square feet, all underground, fitted out with a large, bright kitchen (no natural lighting, however), modern toilet facilities, beds, many shelves containing canned goods, and, in case of emergency, an escape route—a cave that led to a hatch that opened up near their house. The main entrance was conventional: a door in the home's "real" basement that opened to a set of stairs leading down to the pod. The Hieronimuses hadn't built it yet, but they planned to install a door-hiding wall that would conceal the pod's entrance from, say, roving marauders. The entire space could run on the grid or on a generator.

All in all, not a bad set-up. It looked nicer than most basement apartments, with a few unique touches thrown in. For instance, it contained enough bunk beds to sleep forty.

"It's really cozy in here," Susan chirped as we inspected the bunks. "It's like a slumber party."

"Anybody could do this," said Zoh. "What we're really talking about are *safe basements*. Some bedding. Some supplies. Food and water. Just to be able to take care of yourself for a month, that's really the most essential point we can share with people. I'm not talking about surviving Armageddon or nuclear war. I'm just talking about a very simple formula for people to be self-sufficient. For average people like us it's a question of making where you live ready."

In truth, the Hieronimuses didn't have much in common with average people. They were independently wealthy—her father was rich and had left her a lot of money—so their ability to live this way was a distinct luxury. But they meant well. Though they shared certain traits with the Blackwells, the Woodrew-Smolowes, and the Richmond-Donahues (like money, and a slight discomfort with masses of humanity), I would never lump them in with those smug sourpusses.

And yes, I *would* say that since I'm beholden to them for the gift of pod, but I also mean it. Bob is a cheerful guy with an impish face and voice that reminds you of a wise-cracking ventriloquist's dummy. Zoh can be a little more withdrawn, but like Bob she has a sense of humor about herself—a rare attribute among Earth Changers. Drawing on their inexhaustible energy, they plow a lot of money and time into spreading the word that mankind needs to get its nest in order. They both produce alternative radio programs that deal with all aspects of the paranormal, including UFOs, free energy, alternative health, parapsychology, and Earth Changes. They expect the Earth Changes to get rough indeed, but believe they're survivable. From their perspective, all this work is about saving lives.

"It gets kind of boring doing this," Bob said with a sigh as we left the bunk area and walked up front toward the getaway cave. "But we've gotta keep doing it!"

Constant hyperactivity is pretty much their defining mode. During the day's tour we saw various work lairs, jumbled high and deep

with books, records, reel-to-reel tapes of old radio shows, and decades of other pack-rat Hieronimus accumulations. Bob collects tons
of stuff, mostly for fun, but partly because he believes that some cul-
tural outcroppings—like Bullwinkle—amount to "archetypes" that
should be preserved in the post–Earth Changes world. He has an
extensive collection of Beatles, baseball, and golf memorabilia,
including a Babe Ruth autograph baseball, valuable Beatles figurines,
and framed commemorative cards from the Negro baseball leagues.
Zoh's office upstairs is flooded with books and papers. In the basement they have walls and walls of esoteric books and their own
soundproofed recording room.

Before we went back upstairs I made a special request. There was
a thick steel door in one wall, covering the pod's escape hatch. Could
we open it up so I could crawl through it? They thought about it a
second and said OK. This was a big inconvenience—Zoh got pinched
badly removing a heavy metal bar that served as a dead bolt—but I
couldn't help it. As thrilling as the pod was, it wasn't quite raw
enough. I still needed something that "felt" survivalist.

After leaning the rod against a wall with a clang, Zoh opened the
vault-size door, and I squirmed through a large metal hole leading
into the tunnel. It was lined with culvert pipe. Water had collected
on the cement-paved bottom. I could smell raw dirt. There was an
overpowering odor of mildew.

I closed my eyes, felt the metal, took a deep whiff. "Ahhhhhhhh,"
I said. Closure achieved.

Back upstairs, we sat around a circular table and discussed the
future. When will things start happening?

"We work from a basis of knowing that these are significant
times," said Zoh, "and I think that anybody who refuses to admit the
potential collapse of this country in the not-so-distant future is really
living in a fantasy. In terms of time lines, we just know that we feel
a need to be finished by 1998 at the latest. We're already witnessing

the changes. The high winds are winds we haven't experienced. The colder colds. The warmer warms. The long flooding."

Outside it *was* quite rowdy; tall trees were whipping and dancing as the wind whooshed through the limbs.

"See all these trees around here?" said Bob. "I think they'll all be on top of this house and this place will take a hell of a beating. These wind storms ain't gonna stop, and we'll get winds of two hundred miles an hour, and super hurricanes, and super tornadoes."

"All we want," said Zoh, "is the ability, in a hostile environment, to choose whether to live or die."

∞

"If anybody out there meets Shirley MacLaine, tell her I'm dying to meet her," said Annie Kirkwood. "That's something I'd really like to do."

On Sunday afternoon at the Earth Festival, Annie closed things out with a rambling, intensely personal chatalogue, touching on her own fears about the future—one being that she's too tubby to survive in a lean, mean, post-apocalyptic world—and her personal woes, which included family dramas, economic worries, and agoraphobia. That last fear, obviously, made her reluctant to go into the world and talk about Earth Changes.

"I would stand at the sliding glass door of my house and look out and be terrified," she recalled, "so I know what fear is."

Her talk was one of those comfy celebrity-takes-five moments—like Frank Sinatra in concert, loosening the tie and raising a Scotch with a tired paw. And it worked. The crowd's familiar sounds of dread were replaced by a mass coo: they understood.

Or maybe they just needed humanist relief. Since this time yesterday, they had received a steady diet of blood and guts. At the celebratory banquet Saturday night, busy Byron held a gala raffle-ticket giveaway. Regrettably, he spiked the mood when some of his prizes turned out to be survival gear. That morning, Dolores Cannon, a New Ager from Huntsville, Arkansas, told us how she had established a direct connection with Nostradamus, who clarified his prophecies about the millennium through hypnotized intermediaries. One noteworthy update: the Antichrist is already alive, hiding out in Egypt and powering up to start World War III, "like a spider waiting for his time." (Cannon even had a sketch artist work up a likeness, which she showed on an overhead projector. Chillingly, John Doe no. 666 resembled a homelier kid brother of magician David Copperfield.)

Annie's riffs made everything seem tolerable, though. Her squarky, pause-filled words washed over the crowd like baptismal water, ending the event on an uplifting note that said a lot about why people are attracted to the intellectual terrors of Earth Changes. What it said was: they're not, entirely. The scary stuff is simply the thrilling part, the fire-and-brimstone that precedes the soft murmurs of salvation. As Annie's little sermonette made clear, Earth Changes is partly about transforming the big, bad millennium into something tiny and specific: therapy. Annie said as much during the climax of her speech.

"People talk about the thousand years of peace," she said. "I want to tell you that it's not going to start with the drop of a ball in Times Square bringing in the year 2000. For people who have done their healing work—Alcoholics Anonymous, Al-Anon, Gamblers Anonymous—they've already started their thousand years of peace." Later she talked about taking "12 steps" toward the aftertime.

That sounded awfully wee—the Four Horsemen of the Inner Child?—but it made sense. At its worst, Earth Changes is about digging in and aiming for the eyeballs, to Hell with everybody else. In its most benign form, it's a strange type of self-help. Maybe it's a silly type, but people don't want to give it up.

In fact, they *won't* give it up, which is why, when the Changes don't occur quite as dramatically as predicted, people will keep predicting them all the same. Long after the conference, in the June–July 1996 issue of *Mary's Message/Newsletter*, Annie herself recalibrated the future by announcing that she had received an "update" from Mary: the Earth Changes would be delayed by at least ten years. Mary gave credit for this development to the faithful, to the fact that "many are taking action and are praying."

∞

And what about Craig & Company? They do get their hair mussed a little, certainly. The ocean's plankton die, a paralytic flu called Para rips through the continents, earthquakes rattle even Craig and Lex's remote enclave, monster volcanoes and hurricanes roar and swoop, huge typhoons wreck the Philippines and Japan, and Craig has to do something not-so-nice to his fellow man. In the woods one day, he catches "crazed druggies" as they prepare to rape and kill his daughter-in-law, so he plugs two of them and chases off the third.

But after that things start looking up for the family and for tired old Mother Earth. At the end of *Blindsided* Craig has it all. A safe family, a safe place, a simmered-down planet, and the nice glow of satisfaction that comes from having preserved an enlightened human remnant to build a brighter, better, druggie-free tomorrow.

"It was over," the novel dramatically concludes. "The newborns were scattered across her surface, like a litter of pups, and would soon be ready to nurse at her widely separated teats. . . .

"The birthing was over. The new life could grow slowly to an independent maturity, under her care.

"Her body could return to the slow pulsing, the abundance, the vitality it would need in the warding of her children. . . .

"Thank you," Craig whispers. "To someone. To somewhere. Out there."

Ron Cole, angry young man extraordinaire, during his "new David Koresh" period.

USED BY PERMISSION OF JOEL B. DYER.

Dressed in Fire, Shrill of Screams

Once again the FEDERAL AND STATE GOVERNMENTS are flexing their
muscle against sovereign people. About 1 hr. ago I talked to Rick
McLaren, he informed me that the NATIONAL GUARD had arrive [sic]
and . . . were unloading 2 APCs [armored personnel carriers] *and*
TROOPS. I can no longer . . . stand idle while this happens.

   If you want to join us in stopping these actions you would be welcome
in the Texas Republic. . . . Signed by Major Blackmon. REMEMBER THE
ALAMO AND WACO.

—MILITIA E-MAIL, APRIL 1997

The last stand of the Republic of Texas—a headline-generating mini-revolt against the United States, mounted by a small band of Texas-based right wingers in the spring of 1997—started on a Sunday. I was working that afternoon, and at some point boredom prompted me to dip randomly into the on-line version of the Associated Press, where I saw the early, sparky bulletins. A violent standoff was taking shape in Fort Davis, a dusty mountain town in the desolate outback of west Texas. At its center was an antigovernment zealot named Richard McLaren, who led a fire-breathing militia that rejected the authority of the U.S. government.

I'd seen McLaren on TV months before. He was a wild-looking guy with long, sandy hair on the sides and back, a balding dome, and a recklessly addled expression, like somebody had slapped a shovel against the side of his head—and he liked it. McLaren ran a splinter faction of the Republic of Texas, an internally fractured statewide militia group that harbored doomed fantasies about reestablishing the national independence that the real Republic of Texas forfeited when it joined the Union in 1845. (According to ROT faithful, Texas was "illegally and unlawfully annexed" by the United States.) For months he'd been out there, fizzing like the bomb of a cartoon anarchist and making threats. The endgame started when one of McLaren's men, Robert Jonathan Scheidt, was arrested outside the compound for possession of illegal firearms. A young ROT hothead named Richard Keyes III and some other McLarenites, including a mystery man named "White Eagle," retaliated by invading the home of Joe Rowe and his wife, Margaret Ann, neighbors in a sprawling housing development that also contained the Republic.

The Rowes, it later emerged, had made a snoopy-neighbor call to tell the police that Scheidt was heading down the road, thus the perceived justification for the attack. Now the invaders were holed up with the hostages in the Rowe home, which stood an indeterminate distance from McLaren's trailer-style "embassy." Joe Rowe had been wounded. Lawmen were closing in. Additional bloodshed seemed inevitable.

∞

Fresh updates on the situation were slow in coming, and as I sat there blinking at my computer screen I tried to think of anyone who might know something new. I remembered Ron Cole, an angry twenty-seven-year-old from New York State, then living in Colorado, who ran his own militia unit, the Colorado 1st Light Infantry. I'd "met" Cole on the phone in 1995 while writing about how rage over the federal government's actions at the Branch Davidian compound in Waco helped inspire Timothy McVeigh to retaliate with the Oklahoma City bombing. Cole hadn't been at Waco during the 1993 siege—he was a college student at the time—but the episode helped radicalize him and set him on a seemingly permanent path of serious, dangerous antigovernment activism.

In terms of mobilized manpower, Cole was not a major force in the militia movement—he says the 1st Light Infantry was designed as a "4- to 10-man cell"—but he fascinated me because he seemed different from a lot of characters on the far right. Cole wasn't a racist or an anti-Semite or a skinhead, but he was vociferously antigovernment, and he'd thrown away any possibility of a normal life to fight his fight.

For him, as for so many others, Waco was the catalytic moment: Cole considered it a clear-cut case of the mass murder of innocent people by an out-of-control police state. And though he rejected the wildest conspiracy theories that emerged after the fire on April 19, 1993 (for instance, that a flame-throwing tank pumped flames into the Mt. Carmel compound), he had no doubt about two grave allegations. One, that federal agents intentionally started the blaze to cover up lies and blunders about the initial raid by the Bureau of Alcohol, Tobacco and Firearms. And two, that the government mercilessly gunned down men, women, and children as they tried to get out.

Cole dropped out of college in May of 1993, moved to Waco, and hung out with the survivors and conspiracy researchers who coalesced around what was left. When I first heard about him in 1995, just after the Oklahoma City bombing, he had relocated to Colorado after a flamboyant period of involvement with the surviving Branch Davidians. Cultivating a uniquely in-your-face style, Cole purchased a black 1968 Camaro—similar to the one David Koresh drove—and briefly tricked it out with a license plate that read KORESH. Somehow he got his hands on a spooky T-shirt that survived the Mt. Carmel blaze. A gift from Koresh to Branch Davidian Michael Schroeder, who was shot and killed while trying to get into the compound after the ATF raid, it was silk-screened with a profile of Koresh playing the guitar, a five-color illustration of a serpent described in Isaiah 14, and the words "God Rocks." Cole, who had long dark hair, a slender build, and the cool stare of a heavy-metal fan, adopted much of the Branch Davidian ideology, wrote a book, *Sinister Twilight*, challenging the government's version of events at Waco, and set out to provide sufficient leadership to rebuild the movement, possibly with a new headquarters somewhere for the surviving Branch Davidians.

He didn't pull that off, but he did generate some heat. For one thing, he had an indirect influence on the mind of Timothy McVeigh. During McVeigh's trial, prosecutors described several works of fiction and fact that had helped shape McVeigh's thinking. One was *The Turner Diaries,* an apocalyptic novel that celebrates antigovernment terrorist acts by right-wing commandos. Other cited materials were a videotape called *Day 51: The True Story of Waco,* a documentary that starred Ron Cole and his allegations about the government's lies and murderous ways; and Cole's book *God Rocks,* which McVeigh reportedly had in his car when arrested. After the bomb went off in 1995, Cole didn't endorse McVeigh's horrible act, but he did make it clear he understood the source of McVeigh's rage. Mainly, he chided his fellow militia members for getting defensive and weak-kneed about what McVeigh had done.

"Up until now, militia members and federal authorities have been staring at each other across an open field, through binoculars, waiting for something to happen," Cole told the *Boulder Weekly,* an alternative newspaper in Colorado. "On April 19, 1995, someone within our ranks chucked a grenade. . . . The government killed innocent children at Waco, and, in retaliation, innocent victims died in Oklahoma City."

I called Cole again in 1997, hoping to fill in the blanks on his career. By then he was living near Denver, where he was leading both the 1st Light and a new antigovernment group called the North

American Liberation Army, complete with a Web site, whose aim was to broaden the sweep of the militia movement by connecting it with "internationalist" anti-American forces like Shining Path and the Zapatistas. That spring he started popping up in a high-profile setting, outside the McVeigh trial, where he positioned himself as a public advocate for McVeigh's right to a fair hearing.

Now, still sitting in my office around 6:00 P.M., I took a deep breath—Cole was always rather . . . intense—and dialed his number to see what he knew.

Plenty. "I've been on the phone with Richard McLaren," he said, obviously excited but sounding monotone and military.

"When?"

"Earlier today. After the shots were fired."

"What did he say?" Cole started to answer but he had to take another call. He was networking, too—unlike me, with results. When we spoke again, around eight, he proudly announced, "I just got off the phone with Richard Keyes."

That *was* impressive. I'd kept watching the wires, and I saw no sign that anybody had done that.

"The guy who took over the Rowes' house? What did he say?"

"I taped it. You want me to play it for you?"

"Uh . . . yeah." Cole fumbled around a minute, then two voices came over the line. One, his. The other, a gruff man who sounded very, very stressed.

"Hello?"

"Hello."

"Richard Keyes, please."

"This is Lieutenant Keyes."

"This is Ron Cole."

"Yessir."

"How you doing?"

"Pretty good."

"You're a little worried."

"Yeah, yeah. That would be a fair assessment. *Yeah.* That's a fair assessment of the situation."

"What's the situation down there?"

Keyes recapped, explaining that "Lt. Commander Bo Scheidt" was "being held as a prisoner of the State of Texas." The Rowes were "prisoners of war." Keyes asked that friendlies on the outside "pass the word accurately about what's going on, and, if possible, move reinforcements our way."

"Are you guys all right?" Cole asked.

"Yeah, everybody is OK right now. The next move is up to Jeff Davis County or the State of Texas. If they want to end this violently we're prepared for that possibility. If they want to walk away with no lives lost, we're very willing to work with them."

"What can I do to bring this to a peaceful conclusion?"

"If anybody is able to move in our direction," Keyes said, in a formulation that didn't sound just-so for peace, "tell them to pack up and move asap."

The tape ended. Cole offered a crisp assessment. The ROT guys had a "right" to secede; on the other hand, "You just can't go invading neighbors' houses." Mostly he worried that the ROT soldiers' "paranoia" would lead to desperate acts, by them or by violent supporters. He said he sincerely wanted to play a peacemaking role, as other right-wing figures had done—for instance, James "Bo" Gritz, who mediated at the Ruby Ridge standoff in Idaho. He'd already talked with both the Federal Bureau of Investigation and Keyes, offering his services.

"Tell me the truth," I said. "You're going down there, aren't you?" I was envious. I wanted to go, too, but saw no way it would happen.

"Only if asked. If people were to say, hey, this guy Ron Cole, let's bring him in, then I'll be there—boom."

"'Boom' maybe isn't the best word, Ron."

He laughed. "I mean I'll have my bags packed. I'm not going in with any rifles." We said good-bye.

Well, things do change. A week later I was in Fort Davis, having jetted down on impulse for an ROT-themed long weekend, and Cole wasn't. He didn't miss much, but I'm sure he would have swapped places with me in a jiffy. On May 1, a Thursday, Special Agent Bill Clifford, an FBI man who talked to Cole occasionally, asked Cole to meet him at an International House of Pancakes in Aurora, supposedly to talk about his mediating at Fort Davis.

Alas, it was a set-up. An informant had told the FBI that Cole's rented house in Aurora was full of guns, ammo, and explosives. Cole and two other members of the 1st Light, Wally Kennett and Kevin Terry, were lured to separate locations and arrested. Inside the house, according to the indictment, law enforcement officials found several machine guns, piles of ammo, a grenade attached to the front door, a pipe bomb, and a fragmentation grenade sitting near "cans of black powder in close proximity to one another."

Not a good development for my telephone pal. By the time the government finished adding up the charges, Cole, if convicted of everything, was looking at a possible sentence that would keep him in prison until his hair turned gray.

∞

On Sunday night, Cole's live-action tape recording got my juices flowing, so I banged away on the phone and the Internet, trying to find out how militia people would react to the ROT's predicament. There's an article of faith on the far right—I think it's a utopian fantasy—that says, post-Waco, all it will take is one more clearly outrageous affront by the government to touch off a mass militia revolt that will, in turn, be joined by a silent majority of Americans who agree with the cause.

Would this be the event?

Not likely, but that didn't mean something violent couldn't happen. For me, the permanent lesson of Oklahoma City was simple: it doesn't take an army. It only takes one or two people. And while the ever-present, usually overwrought rhetoric from the far right can sound ridiculous, it has a way of becoming unfunny very quickly.

I absorbed that the hard way a few months before the Oklahoma City bombing when, strictly by coincidence, I happened onto the subculture of independent researchers and conspiracy theorists who were challenging the government's version of events at Waco. The best of these people were putting oomph behind valid arguments that deserved (and later got) a wider hearing, and have lately been mainstreamed in books and films like *Waco: The Rules of Engagement,* a documentary that was nominated for an Academy Award in 1998. (One argument, for example, is that the initial bloodshed could have been avoided by arresting Koresh in town rather than sending in the troops.) The worst were outright kooks, fueled by apocalyptic levels of anger that helped inspire McVeigh to murder scores of innocent people.

A leading figure in the hothead camp was Linda Thompson, an Indianapolis-based attorney and conspiracy theorist whose videos (*Waco, The Big Lie* and *Waco, The Big Lie Continues*) were popular fare in the gun-show world in which McVeigh drifted. An irresponsible demagogue who made even her fellow radicals cringe—Ron Cole called her an "out-of-control maniac"—Thompson traveled to Waco during the siege and organized a group of marchers who strutted around outside the security perimeter brandishing unloaded weapons. She went way over the top in her videos; it was she who claimed that the Mt. Carmel blaze was intentionally set by government tanks that pumped flames into the interior.

Regarding Fort Davis, my poking around turned up plenty of cause for worry about random, senseless acts by Thompsonian wingnuts. Some militia people were disinclined to rush to the scene because the Rowe kidnapping seemed cowardly, which turned them off. (One faction of the much-factionalized Republic of Texas, headed by a man named Archie Lowe, was spinning this angle hard, denouncing McLaren's "blatantly unlawful act" on its Web site.) Some thought McLaren, warts and all, was worth fighting for simply because he was under attack by the *federales*. A typical figure here was Norman Olson, commander of the Northern Michigan Regional Militia, which had settled on a public strategy of nonviolent watchfulness. "A rational soldier doesn't rush into battle," he told me. "We need to put our own intelligence people on the ground in the area. We have to determine what our operational necessities are to respond to the threat."

None-too-discreetly I asked, "Do you know of anybody who's already heading down there with guns?"

"Some people I have heard from had that initial response, but whether or not they are still at Defcom One"—that is, marching off to battle—"I don't know."

Some sounded like they were halfway there. As the first week of the siege played out, I watched for signs that militia guys were hitting the road. They weren't long in coming.

On Monday, the Rowes were released in a swap for Bo Scheidt, who was not charged with a felony. This was a wise P.R. move by McLaren; many e-mail patriots took note and began to characterize the standoff as a classic Good Patriots versus Bad Feds situation. On Tuesday, an on-line right-wing news service calling itself "SAFAN ALERT" sent out a saber-rattling call, because it decided that too much federal presence had already washed up in Fort Davis: "The forces surrounding the Embassy consists [*sic*] of Local, State, Federal (FBI, BATF, Border Patrol, and MJTF) and the National Guard (military) with full equipment. Armored personnel carriers are also there."

On Wednesday, real action: Texas authorities detained seven armed men at a truck stop in Pecos, about seventy miles from Fort

Davis. The group reportedly was traveling with five semi-automatic rifles, one shotgun, a .45, several hunting knives, ammo, military rations, medical supplies, and fatigues, and each man was carrying a Republic of Texas identification card. That same day, promising negotiations with McLaren appeared to break down.

On Thursday, Ron Cole was busted. Duly noted by the e-mail patriots, his arrest was seen as a warning that a wider preemptive crackdown might start soon.

On Friday, Scheidt walked out and gave himself up, saying that the weird intensity inside the compound was just too much. McLaren didn't budge, and the e-mails continued to steam and hiss. Norman Olson's "man in the middle" posture about going on the warpath— "Wrestle with your own spirit and with your conscience," he wrote, "and having made a decision either way, rest in it and seek not others who may convince you of the rightness of that decision"—started to strike some patriots as wimpy mush.

"You and others who will bow down to the current Terrorists we have in Washington don't seem to understand," wrote Drew Rayner of the Mississippi Militia. "WE HAVE HAD A BELLY FULL OF THE FBI, BATF, DEA, ETC. ETC. AND THEIR GESTAPO TYPE ACTIVITIES AND WE ARE READY TO FIGHT!!!! So go ahead and kiss their *ss. WE WON'T!!! . . . Lock and Load, prepare to Rock and Roll."

Saturday saw two significant occurrences. First, McLaren dug in for what sounded like a bloody last stand. Saturday morning, as lawmen tightened their perimeter, he issued a "shoot to kill" order and a desperate short-wave-radio plea for help: "Mayday! Mayday! . . . Hostiles are invading the Republic of Texas. . . . This is a Mayday call for any nation in the world. . . . We are being invaded!"

Second, capping a five-day stretch of whining and wheedling, I finally convinced a publication to fly me to Fort Davis for the weekend, though its editor forced me to share the expenses. Wasting no time, I bought a short-notice plane ticket ($1,300! Mayday! May-day!) and packed up to go.

∞

After Ron Cole's arrest I decided to make a special project of decod-ing his motivations, an effort that continued long after my fly-in to observe the rise (and speedy fall) of the Republic of Texas. Why? Partly it was simple curiosity about the workaday existence of a typ-ical militia activist. What do you *do* every day if that's your role in life? How do you get by financially if your only "job" is insurrection?

But I was also interested because, strange to admit, I felt an unex-pected sense of big-brotherly concern about the guy, and about what he might do. To me he didn't seem evil, just stupidly, dangerously misguided, in that he was breaking the law to express political views that he should have expressed through normal political means, like joining the Young Americans for Freedom. Cole rejected that advice when I floated it to him, and he certainly resisted my bland efforts to nudge him toward the conventional right. During his time in jail, I occasionally mailed him a book on libertarianism or the violent life and times of revolutionaries like Che Guevera, suggesting that he'd be happier and healthier if he dropped all this stuff and found a girl-friend.

No go. Cole said that anticompromisers like himself played a cru-cial role—telling it like it *really* is, and thus bringing the "middle" closer to his radical position. As for girlfriends, he'd had one in Waco, but he told me melodramatically that he'd chosen to "sacri-fice" any hopes for love until his mission was accomplished.

Which was, of course, Cole's business, up to a point. Yakking about government overthrow is a protected right. Trying to do it, or committing acts of disruptive terrorism, is not. Cole hadn't done the latter, but as I found out, he existed in a shadowy gray area where there was ample cause for the FBI (and the rest of us) to get a little nervous. Cole was busted when the McVeigh trial was in progress, and there was a lot of concern that the trial would inspire terrorism. The FBI had an informant, an ex-Marine named Dan McNasby, who had briefly trained with Cole's mini-militia. He said the trio did not intend to go "proactive"—that is, to bomb anything or shoot anybody—but still, would you have wanted the mini-militia as neighbors?

Not likely. According to McNasby, the boys seemed certain they would eventually be attacked by the government, and judging by the affidavit they were primed to go out in a blaze of glory. "McNasby said each of them has a cache of ammunition in their bedroom with other resupply points throughout the house," the government's affidavit said. "The roommates have all told McNasby that they won't hesitate to open fire if confronted by law enforcement officers. McNasby has seen the roommates carry their rifles with them throughout the house and even take them into the bathroom when they relieve themselves."

McNasby reported the existence of alarming stockpiles, such as "six .50 caliber ammunition cans in the basement which the roommates have told him are full of explosives." He once asked Wally Kennett if he wasn't afraid to keep this stuff in the house. Kennett said yes, he was, adding that he didn't worry about it, though. Why?

Because if it went off, he wouldn't be alive to feel it.

∞

"The people writing the note said they regretted what they had done, but they had to resort to this," said an agitated woman on a radio call-in show I'd tuned in. "They took his kidney, left him in a bathtub full of ice, and left him $1,000 in an envelope and directions to get a taxicab. He managed to get home and is now back in Dallas. Now to me, the fact that somebody could kidnap you and take you to a hotel room and take out whatever organ they wanted is just *bizarre*."

"There's not many stories I swear by anymore," the host said, "but there's not many I doubt either."

"I've heard it said that, a lot of time, organs you donate regular at the hospital go to Arabs," the woman said.

"Whoa."

It was a bleak, moonless predawn in central Texas, about five on a Sunday morning. I was driving from El Paso, the westernmost city in the state, to Kilgore, way back east, almost to Louisiana, a distance of 760 miles. I had to get to Kilgore in time for an early afternoon meeting that I couldn't afford to miss—although, by any rational measure, the meeting was meaningless and *should* have been missed.

But I was in a "different place" from rationality by then, because absolutely everything had gone wrong with my plans. My first act after landing in El Paso was to call a militia contact who had agreed to ask around about where right-wing troops might bivouac in the Fort Davis vicinity as the siege approached its climax. That's when I found out the siege had had its climax.

"Hey!" said the contact. "Guess you heard. It's over."

"What? No! But McLaren was talking so tough this morning."

"Well, he came out."

I groaned as he described the final hours. While I was in the air, McLaren had gulped the old negotiator's bait of "surrender with honor." He was allowed to lower his flag (a lone gold star on a dark blue background) with full pomp. He would be allowed to speak his piece in court that the Republic of Texas was illegally annexed by the United States. Then he would be allowed to go to jail for a very long time. (Which he did. In late 1997 McLaren and White Eagle—better known as Robert Otto—were convicted on felony charges of organized criminal activity. They received ninety-nine years and fifty years, respectively.)

Not the best deal, but he obviously preferred it to Plan B: getting shot.

After staring blankly at the linoleum for a minute, I procured my rental car and putted around El Paso, morosely listening to the radio and evaluating options. Texas officials were deservedly bragging about the happy, no-bloodbath outcome. Granted, there was one teensy glitch—two ROT fightin' men had somehow slipped away, no names given yet—but that supposedly was no big problem. A drawling Texas Ranger said the fugitives were not experienced in the west Texas backcountry, so they would be easy pickings for posses or mountain lions. In any event, there was nothing for voyeurs to see. The militia would "stand down" and stay home. McLaren's trailer compound, which had been rigged up with potentially hazardous self-defense gizmos, was still off-limits to reporters.

There was one notable event left, however. On Sunday afternoon, members of the two other main splinter groups of the feud-riven Republic of Texas, including the Archie Lowe faction, were holding a "Rally & Summit" in Kilgore, to make it clear to the world that the movement would live on. I uncrinkled a Texas map and eyed the grim realities: the interstate stretch looked as long as the Amazon. Was driving that far worth it? No, but what else was I going to do, go see Carlsbad Caverns? So I strapped in and hit the road, keeping my mind occupied and eyes open with one of my favorite free commodities: Texas radio.

You may have experienced its many-faceted glories yourself. As you scoot across the state, flipping past the blare-horn mariachi stations or "contemporary country," you keep hitting these eerie all-news and talk-radio stations that, cumulatively, provide a steady, low-wattage reminder of why Texas produces way more than its share of premillennial excitement. Texas is a noble state, but her "peoples" seem to include a disproportionately large, fidgety rank-

and-file who gaze into the future with a perpetual squint, a look of startled suspicion, apocalyptic longing, hoodoo expectation. I was scarcely surprised, therefore, that post-game analysis of the McLaren incident contained plenty of instant, armchair conspiracy theory. One caller to a show broadcast out of Midland/Odessa pondered the escape of the two ROT soldiers, suggesting that this was . . . fishy.

"It's strange, isn't it," he said, "that them guys got out of there with so much concentration of law enforcement and media around."

"How so?" said the host.

"It's just strange is alls I'm sayin'."

Aside from the conspiracy froth, the big theme was McLaren himself, and the consensus did not support the idea that "the people" were out there waiting to embrace a militia uprising. Most callers were pro-Union and in favor of a quick lynching, a theme that had been voiced in Fort Davis all week. McLaren had alienated the townsfolk by filing dozens of bogus liens against other people's property, and they wanted him dead. "I'd like to see [McLaren] come out in a body bag," one Fort Davis woman told the *Los Angeles Times*. "I've already got a margarita party planned for when he's gone."

I heard this theme so often that it must have hypnotized me, like a cat staring at a dripping faucet. At daybreak, east of Abilene, I almost dropped off and weaved dangerously far onto the shoulder. Snapping my head up, slurping a line of drool, I woke up for good, vowing to keep the "seek" function on my radio busy at all times.

Fortunately, there were plenty of lively doings. (Thanks, Texans!) *Mash, seek, find.* I heard a woman describing how an old codger at a state fishing lake had been dragged off in handcuffs for catching more than his limit of crappie. "They shouldn't have done it that way," she said, adding darkly that some bystanders saw it as another example of government-out-of-control.

Mash, seek. A news report. The two escapees were identified as

Richard Keyes—the same Lt. Keyes whom Ron Cole had talked to, the alleged invader—and a man named Mike Matson. White Eagle was in custody. At daybreak the manhunt for Keyes and Matson would resume in earnest; both men were considered "armed and very dangerous."

Mash, seek.

"Brothers and sisters, we are now only a few *shart* years from the twenty-first century!" said a preacher with a thick southern accent. He was talking hard-core End-Times prophecy; his voice was barely coming in from who-knows-where, ghostly and spooky and ringing as he crooned softly about the Last Days. I turned it up, thrilling to the chilling effect of his words, with their timeless, superstitious delight in the coming tribulations.

"Years ago, I can remember, I was sitting in my home in North Carolina and the earth begin to shake, and I ran outside and I said, 'The Lord's coming.' And I got outside and the earth stopped trembling, but this was an indication that there's coming a tiiime when the earth is going to reel to and fro like a drunk-ert."

I heard him swallow some air, recharging.

"The Bible tells us that no man can know the arrr, but we know there's gonna be famines and pestilences and earthquakes in di-verse places. If we're going to meet our Lord, we can step outside and look up and our redemption draws nigh.

"And this . . . this is something *wonderful*."

∞

During the early weeks of Cole's incarceration it was impossible to reach him by phone. His lawyer stiff-armed me, saying it was not in Cole's best interest to blab to outsiders. I'd heard from another journalist, one who'd visited Cole, that Cole was taking things hard— sobbing uncontrollably, despairing that he would sit in jail indefinitely. That changed soon enough. As time passed, his chances for a tolerable sentence or a plea-bargain increased (some of the charges, including possession of a pipe bomb, were later dropped), and he started churning out the old saucy rhetoric on his Web site, with help from people on the outside. In one typical offering, "We're in solitary confinement; How did we get here?" Cole scotched any hopes I had that he might be "scared straight."

"[I]n spite of it all, I regret nothing," he wrote. "We still believe as strongly as ever that civil rights and constitutional groups from the left and the right will stand together against the enemy."

I wrote Cole, and he obtained permission to call me collect. We worked out a system. On the phone I'd request details about specific episodes in his life; he'd follow up with a letter. He also forwarded excerpts from his autobiography-in-progress, *What Wars Are Made Of: From Waco, Texas, to Oklahoma City,* which had been seized during the FBI raid.

Together, this material filled in the gaps on the political and philosophical makeup of Ron Cole, a unique blend of sincere idealism, actual bravery, and other, stranger attributes. Among them: crippling guilt about the limits of his bravery, a sense of premillennial urgency about the need to defeat the U.S. power structure, an alarming taste for at least the idea of violence, malformed notions about American history, and a terrific yearning, crossing over into narcissism, for personal notoriety.

What motivates such behavior, which the historian Richard Hofstadter so famously labeled the "paranoid style"? There are no scientific formulas to explain it, but there are theories. In their 1992 book on right-wing and left-wing political extremism in America, *Nazis, Communists, Klansmen and Others on the Fringe,* John George (a political scientist and sociologist) and Laird Wilcox (an independent student of extremism) offered a useful summary of what social psychologists have to say about fringe joiners, right or left. One obvious but powerful motive is conviction, which Cole obviously had. Another is a desire for purpose. Extremist groups provide it in bulk, in settings whose high drama generates what Arthur Koestler, that famous ex-Communist, called "the mental rapture which only the convert knows."

But George and Wilcox also pointed to another crucial factor, a desire for "recognition and favorable regard by others. . . . If what is desired is to be noticed . . . then 'bad' attention will serve the function equally as well as 'good' attention."

In *Harvest of Rage,* a 1997 book on the far right, a journalist named Joel Dyer examined various paths that, in general, lead people to the contemporary rightist fringe. Many activists, he argued, are farmers who lost out in an economic system that has been hard on rural Americans in recent years, especially during the wave of farm foreclosures that marked the eighties. Some are angriest about Waco and Ruby Ridge. Others are motivated by race hatred, anti-Semitism, or conspiracy theory and harbor deranged fantasies that America is under the control of evil supergroups like the Zionist Occupation Government. Farthest out are the adherents of an apocalyptic mutation of Christianity called Christian Identity, which in its most extreme form has it that white Anglo-Saxons are the Lost Tribe of Israel (the white man's real "identity") and that Identity believers are fated to fight a race war against Jews, blacks, and other minorities who are sometimes seen, literally, as the "seed" of Satan.

Dyer and other observers of the far right—like the Southern Poverty Law Center in Montgomery, Alabama, which tracks hate groups—believe that Identity followers are the most likely to do something violent before the millennium's end, inspired by the looming "significance" of the year 2000. The Southern Poverty Law Center's publications and Web site display a fairly staggering list of captured or wanted right-wingers who, after Oklahoma City, have already done something desperate. Among the more sprightly groups or individuals have been the Aryan Peoples Republic (alleged Christian Identity believers who were indicted in Arkansas in 1997 for murder and conspiring to revolt against the government, assassinate public officials, and create a whites-only nation); the Phineas Priesthood (alleged Identity believers who in 1996 were arrested and charged with robberies and a bombing in Washington State, supposedly as part of a campaign to help impose "God's law" on Earth); and Eric Robert Rudolph (the alleged bomber of an abortion clinic in Birmingham, Alabama, and reportedly an Identity adherent, who was still at large in the summer of 1998).

In this roiling world, where did Ron Cole fit in? It's fair to say he was simultaneously of it, not of it, and, in his unique Ron-ian way, out there spiraling in his own orbit. Cole was not a displaced farmer or an Identity believer or a racist, otherwise he never would have gone near the Branch Davidians, who are racially mixed. He was acidly antigovernment, and maintained that his ideology grew out of a principled opposition to the strong exploiting the weak. As suggested by George and Wilcox, I also think that an unsettling element of "Hey, lookit me!" was at work in his personality.

Cole told me, for example, that during his schoolboy days in upstate New York, he was "bullied" because he was different. He claimed he took proactive measures to show the school toughs that he would not be beaten down or silenced, organizing victimized kids into a strength-through-numbers cooperative that outmanned the big guys. "Sometimes we would surround bullies while they were alone, in an ambush, and suggest to them that they had better leave so-and-so alone," Cole wrote. "If that failed, we started our own harassment, glued shut lockers, pretty silly stuff, but it worked. They got the hint."

Starting at sixteen, Cole says he published a revisionist history magazine, called the *Asahi* [Rising Sun] *Journal,* featuring the type of radically distorted analysis of American history that has long been a staple on the fringe, and expanding it into a vast U.S.-as-bully-among-nations theory. Cole's special interest was "the history of the Pacific War as written by the victors," the United States.

"I learned very early on that the history I was being taught in school was B.S.," he wrote in a letter, "and I wanted the truth; the truth about Americans slaughtering Japanese P.O.W.'s by the thousands (over 20,000 executed in Borneo after Aug. '45), the truth about F.D.R. wanting an excuse to enter the war and using Japan as his trump card, the truth behind the unnecessary bombing of Hiroshima and Nagisaki [*sic*]. To make a long story short, I never 'believed in' the U.S. government of the past or the present."

For Cole, the end of the cold war was the turning point: it meant there was no longer any check on the horror of horrors, the final hegemony of the United States. His paramilitary activism began in the summer of 1992, the summer of the Ruby Ridge standoff, during which federal agents killed the wife and son of Randy Weaver, a white separatist. A student at the Rochester Institute of Technology, Cole spent those months in Fairplay, Colorado, where he fell in with a militia leader, supposedly a former Navy SEAL, whom he only calls "Jim." Cole put off his return to RIT; in January of 1993 he moved to Melbourne, Florida, where he hung around at gun shows and continued his training as a militia operative. When Waco started in February, Cole, like most everyone else, didn't know much about the Branch Davidians, but the turn of events sounded all too familiar.

"They were being made out as inhuman monsters. . . . I knew better, and the entire thing sounded like a textbook WWII era propaganda and demonization campaign."

Communicating by phone, Cole and Jim decided to organize

drastic action. They would hit an ATF checkpoint, seize an armored personnel carrier, and crash into Mt. Carmel. As they prepared for what Cole figured was a suicide mission, Cole's sense of anticipation and fear tore him up inside. "Jim was a veteran, but I was untested," he wrote. "For brief instances I'd chicken out, then I'd get hold of myself and feel ashamed."

Was there really any chance of this happening? Impossible to say, but I doubt it. As one militia activist who knows Cole put it to me, "That's not a *fabrication* lie, but it isn't true either. It's an understandable rationalization for guilt—guilt that people all over the country felt because they didn't do something to prevent Waco."

The important thing is that Cole believed it would have happened. Why didn't it? He says the Mt. Carmel siege ended just days before he planned to head for Waco—so he'd waited too long. In a darkened room, Cole sat staring for hours at a backpack he'd stuffed for the trip.

"[I]t was as if it was looking back at me saying, 'You stupid, useless, cowardly bastard!'" Cole wrote. "I diverted my gaze and stared blankly at the carpet. My hands were cold and shook, I clenched them into tight fists. My cheek twitched uncontrollably as my vision blurred, I closed my eyes and swallowed hard. Anger, rage, bitterness, a hateful kind of intense sorrow. 'Turn it into something else!' I croaked aloud to myself. 'Turn it into something else damn you!'"

∞

I pulled into Kilgore just before 1:00 P.M. on Sunday and located the site of the ROT rally, a dilapidated old motor lodge near a cluster of civic buildings and "your nicer stores" that makes up the city's tidy downtown. Outside the motel, all the trappings of a major public event were on display, baking under the midday sun: news trucks from Dallas, Fort Worth, and Houston; cars, pickups, and sport-utility vehicles from all over the state; and crafty-eyed stand-around guys in cowboy hats and western-cut suits who had the take-no-crap bearing of Texas Rangers. But they were, in fact, Republic of Texas security men—"ROT Rangers."

On display inside: all the trappings of the rumpus room at a state mental hospital. That sounds harsh, I know, but the ROT people just flat-out *looked* crazy. The first person I saw was a dotty, frizzy-haired little man waving a tiny flag and cackling, and I didn't see much else that day to counter the stereotype.

Nor did I witness any shame and embarrassment. ROT "ideas" had just cost taxpayers a fortune and easily could have cost several lives, but the meeting was characterized by self-righteousness, defiance, even a smug sense that the lawmen had lucked out, in that McLaren's dicey particulars had kept the militias from stampeding to his rescue and kicking butt.

The absurdity of ROT's posturing was entertaining . . . up to a point, but it was obvious that the Republic's hazardous enthusiasms would not soon disappear. About two hundred boisterous anti-Texans filled a big, cramped meeting room inside the motel, and the place was vaporously hot and musky with their excitement. The crowd was mostly men, middle-aged or above, with a fair sprinkling of angry young rednecks, graying wives, and cranky solo females. There weren't many young women around, which suggested the presence "back home" of fuming wives or girlfriends. I've often believed that for a lot of the younger militia guys, the movement is really just a forlorn hobby that they pursue to get out of the house.

This isn't to say that all the ROT members were hicks. Indeed, the first person I talked to was a dapper middle-aged man from Houston who looked like George Bush. He was smart, articulate, and college-educated, and he explained the whys and whats of the ROT schisms with careful precision. Those details are too arcane to bother with, but you should know this: the chasms were formed partially along class lines, not a good sign for a utopian Republic. This man was involved in the faction led by one David Johnson of Odessa, whose followers looked (overall) to be older, better-educated, and more prosperous than the followers of middle-brow Archie Lowe. There were also some McLarenites scattered about. They seemed the stupidest. Some were downright unhinged.

At the front of the big meeting room a long dais was set up on a raised platform. One side, nearly empty, was occupied only by a tall, youngish, dark-haired man with a mustache and a knobby old leathery guy in a western-cut suit. They weren't speaking, and I found out later that the younger man was an Archie, the older a McLarenite. The other side was crowded with a dozen more frowning representatives, most of them Johnson men. Johnson himself didn't show up, but some of his council members did—they were gray, natty, and stern, like Baptist deacons. Lowe was present on that side of the dais. A sleepy-faced longhair, he looked like an amiable, slightly zonked biker. His agenda that day included a quest for "international recognition" and the convening that summer of a Constitutional Convention for the ROT.

As TV reporters lining both walls aimed their cameras and giggled, the meeting was called to order by Daniel Miller, the balding young chairman of a group called the Gregg County Constitutional Committee. "This meeting is about unity!" he brayed. Negating his point, he gestured with pride at the men on the lopsided dais. As applause dribbled over them, they just glowered.

"This meeting is a little different format," Miller continued. "The guest speaker is gonna be you, the people. These gentlemen up here from various provisional governments of the Republic of Texas will get an opportunity to hear what you have to say and this is, uh, a fantastic opportunity. Before we begin I want to remind you that inflammatory or personal attacks will *not* be tolerated. If you violate the spirit of the meeting you *will* be escorted out." Grunts from the crowd.

After the intro, we were treated to an alternate-universe lecture on Texas constitutional history by Randy Miller, a self-described "journalist" who (I was told) was actually an ROT sympathizer. Miller had the droopy-dog features of Mr. Haney from *Green Acres,* but he sounded more like Hank Kimball, the addled county-extension agent. Laying out the basics of the "illegal" 1845 annexation, he closed with this ringing call for a new constitutional convention.

"It is your last opportunity in this millennium to say with an honest face . . . well, not my face but speaking for the face of William Barrett Travis at the Alamo, by whom I am inspired when he said, 'Give me liberty—'"

"Patrick Henry," heckled an audience grouch.

"What?"

"*Patrick Henry.*"

"OK. He may not have said this but he meant it. 'Give me liberty or give me death.' And that, from my perspective, is the foundation of the Republic of Texas."

Watery claps. After that the floor was opened to the people. The moderator, still controlling the tempo, told the audience to line up behind a floor microphone and address the softball question, "Why do you think we need to have the Republic of Texas?" Most obeyed him and stuck to the subject. Others . . . didn't. Among the highlights:

A woman in a hat and a shirt decorated with tiny cartoons of hats said that some of the Republic of Texas's proposed reforms—"Like not having a judicial system that exists *only* to cost people money"— would erase a lot of jobs. Possible solution: Republic-sponsored growth of industrial hemp, which she pronounced "hemp-uh."

A rattled old lady yelped that the federal government is "getting boxcars prepared with some kind of leg irons in 'em to fasten you into place to ship you to concentration camps!" This drew both winces and frightened hoots.

A very pale young man stood and said Judgment Day was coming soon unless the Republic of Texas took power. "This country needs to repent so bad. There's so much stuff. And . . . I hope I don't cry here . . . but Judgment's coming." Then he started crying.

After he staggered off, shoulders shaking, a stocky guy in a red shirt and a Republic of Texas cap stood and dramatically announced that he had been the victim of a gross government injustice. Yes, it was true, he went on, he and some ROT colleagues *were* traveling with full packs, semi-automatic weapons, pistols, radios, and plenty of ammo, but they were framed. They were simply driving to Kermit, Texas, to "hunt wild hogs." And furthermore—

The crowd shifted and gasped, suddenly realizing the significance: this man was one of the Pecos Seven!

∞

After the Mt. Carmel fire Ron Cole moved to Waco to live out what he calls, with a good sense of humor about how it sounds, "my 'new David Koresh' period." He lived there for various stretches in 1993, 1994, and 1995, with the overall goal of "keeping the old Mt. Carmel ideas and traditions alive."

Mostly that just meant trying to be the Branch Davidians' buddy, though Cole waded into deeper waters. I've heard it said that he hoped to "become" Koresh, but I doubt it. As he surely knew, the Davidians didn't want a new Koresh: they believed that the real one was a divine personage who would rise again someday. Even so, Cole assumed a leadership role among the survivors that for various reasons came to an end in early 1995. He's not entirely forthcoming about why, saying only that he grew weary of the role, especially since the survivors could be vague about their goals. As he told me in a letter, he loved the Davidians, but he was often baffled by their seeming lack of will in the absence of Koresh.

"[D]uring late 1994 I was taking care of so much that I can honestly say that I do know what things must have been like for David Koresh," he wrote. "Quite honestly, I found many of the survivors then in Waco to be completely dependent. When I'd take everybody to Mario's Pizza in Waco, for example, everyone looked to *me* to decide what was going to be on the pizza. If I did not proclaim the toppings, then we would have sat there all day. I found this disturbing."

Some people found Cole disturbing. In particular, he didn't mix well with Clive Doyle, a survivor of the Mt. Carmel blaze who emerged as the de facto spokesman for the sect as the survivors shuffled forward with various matters, including a huge cluster of civil suits filed against the federal government for wrongful death and other offenses. Doyle, a low-profile sort, thought Cole's overwhelming urge to "do" something wasn't especially helpful; in particular, he was made nervous by Cole's infamous battle with Amo Bishop Roden, an absurd but dangerous 1994 incident that paralleled a conflict in the life of David Koresh.

As recounted in *The Ashes of Waco*, Dick Reavis's 1995 book on Waco, in 1987 Koresh literally shot it out with George Roden, the mentally disturbed son of Lois Roden, the prophetess who ran the Mt. Carmel church until her death in 1986. Hoping to cement his shaky chances of inheriting leadership, George Roden dug up the body of a long-deceased Mt. Carmel believer and challenged Koresh (who was then encamped with his followers in Palestine, Texas) to raise the woman from the dead. Koresh ignored the taunt; instead he showed up with a small platoon of armed men, hoping to snap a picture of the open casket and thereby convince the local sheriff that Roden should be arrested for illegally molesting a corpse. In November 1987 Koresh and his men invaded the property and exchanged gunfire with Roden. The cops rolled in and everybody was arrested. Much later, after various legal proceedings, Koresh ended up with the property, mainly because he rounded up enough money to pay an outstanding tax bill.

George Roden ended up in a Texas mental institution, where he still remained as of 1998. After the Mt. Carmel fire, Amo Bishop Roden, his estranged common-law wife, squatted on the Branch Davidian property in a shack, displaying a tendency to wave guns at unwelcome "trespassers" on land she didn't own. Cole says the survivors wanted her out, and to that end he and Wally Kennett tested the waters by providing armed escort for a friend, Andrew Hood, who needed access to a shed that sat on the property.

The episode was stupid, but it was also quite dangerous. Cole and Kennett were armed with 9-mm pistols; Hood was unarmed; Amo was armed and angry. On November 23, 1994, the boys drove out, screeched to a halt, and immediately started ducking around for suitable cover as they made their way to the shed. Amo jumped out of her shack and allegedly fired a shot from a .22 pistol. Then she started to scream and wave her gun. Judging by Cole's account of what happened next, it's a miracle no one was killed.

"I stood up from behind the car, and attempted to talk to her," Cole wrote. "She cocked the hammer back on her weapon and pointed it straight at my forehead! . . . I had my hand on my gun, ready to draw and fire if she pulled the trigger, but I knew I'd most likely be dead before I hit the ground if she did. Amo screamed, 'God told me to kill you Ron Cole! If anyone is going to die here today it's going to be you.'"

It was almost her. "Wally, I discovered later, had his gun trained on her head all the time from behind Andrew's building," Cole wrote. "He nearly killed her at that crucial moment . . . but he restrained himself."

Before too long the cops came and arrested everybody except Hood. In jail, Cole was interrogated by two ATF agents. With horror he realized that they "were very likely at Mt. Carmel on February 28!" After calming down, Cole decided to get a few things off his chest as the interview ground on. He answered questions with surly vagueness, prompting one agent to say, "So you refuse to talk to us then?"

"I straightened myself up in my chair," Cole wrote, "made eye contact with each of them and said, 'I am who I am, you are who you are, and we are enemies.' The agents seemed bewildered at first, then one grumbled something inaudible to me, and they both walked out of the room."

Score one for the skinny guy in the GOD ROCKS T-shirt. Unfortunately for Cole, small moral victories were never enough.

∞

"We had nothing illegal in my vehicle," said the increasingly agitated member of the Pecos Seven, laying out his tale of oppression as the Republic of Texas crowd stirred and buzzed. "We were never arrested. We were 'detained' is what they called it. We had begged for phone calls to try to get ahold of people that were worried about where we were and what we were doing. They never arrested us. I asked the Texas Ranger that questioned me, I asked the deputies, I asked the police, I asked the ATF: *Am* I under arrest? They said no every time. When they fingerprinted me and put me in lockup, I said: Am I under arrest? They said no, you are not. They said you are a material witness. I said a material witness to what? Well, we don't know. The U.S. marshal told us to put you in here."

He paused to let this sink in, as if he'd delivered a white-hot account of life inside the gulag. No one seemed to grasp the obvious irony. Truly evil officials—Stalinists, for example—would have taken him to the nearest ditch and shot him through the head. He was relatively lucky: he only lost a few toys.

"Later, when they released us, I went out to my truck and got in. All of our backpacks and most of our food and everything we had in there was gone. Of course our weapons were gone. Any ammunition we had was gone. . . . They also had taken personal property of mine. They took C.B. radios out of there. They took a personal pager, a work pager. . . . Um, OK, I understand the ammunition. . . . I would have given them the ammunition, but a lot of that gear in there had no violent content in it. I need that to *work*. I had a pair of Danner boots. They're gone. I guess they just went through there and took what they wanted."

Roars and applause. The man sat down, but in short order a number of reporters hustled over and coaxed him into the hallway for more questions. Under direct interrogation, he didn't hold up too well as a civil-liberties victim. His name was Robert Summitt, he was from Garland, Texas, he looked overfed and pouty, he was a card-carrying member of the Republic of Texas (Lowe faction), and the fact was, he got caught with a Suburban full of weapons at a place he should not have gone anywhere near. What did he expect? Directions and free coffee refills? The local reporters, who were weary of ROT nonsense, gave him a hard time.

Was he handled brutally by the government? "No. Most of them were relatively nice to us."

Did they kick his ass and throw him in a dark hole? "We were put in a large classroom. We had to sleep on the desks. We had blankets. No pillows. Some of the men slept on chairs that had been pushed together."

Somebody pointed out that Pecos is not on the way to Kermit (his supposed destination to go "hog hunting") from Garland. So why was he in Pecos? "I was curious about what was going on," he admitted, "on a personal level."

I wandered off in search of additional "real people" testimony. I found Judgment Day Man, who looked alarmed when I spoke to him but agreed to follow me to a quieter interview spot. We stopped in a clatteringly noisy service hallway by the motel's kitchen, where I asked him to elaborate on his apocalyptic rant about the soon-to-come end for the United States.

"A country or empire has four phases," he explained, staring with disc-like eyes at a spot on the wall above my right shoulder. "Beginning, growing, decline, and then the fourth, which is called 'the end and it falls apart.' This country for many years has been deep into number three."

What did he think of the standoff? He paused a long time and stared at me. I was sure he was about to shriek and run, but in fact he said something completely sensible. "It would have been best if it never happened in the first place. Even if your next-door neighbor is like Mrs. Kravitz on *Bewitched,* you know, you don't go over and do nothing to them."

I wrote this down, and then looked up, pen poised. "Are you a fan of *Bewitched*?"

The tense face again. "I don't watch television."

We parted ways. I waded back into the foyer and killed time until a break was called and the crowd flooded out of the main room. Bouncing around amid the noise, elbows, and bellies, I introduced myself to the dais character in the western-cut suit. His name was Jim Warmke and he was a wiry, sun-burnished old man who had been a TV repairman prior to retirement. Honorable work. But now he was doing addled work: serving as "Secretary of Commerce and Trade" for the Branch McLarenian remnant of the ROT.

He extended a huge sandpapery hand and said, "Howdy! Jim Warmke. W-A-R-M-K-E. Hot lock, warm key." Speaking with dramatic emphasis on every fifth word or so, he started to explain why he was antigovernment, relating a tale of tragedy and sadness that involved his granddaughter's losing custody of her child to the State of Texas.

"It all came to fruition when I had to watch a great-grandchild being *destroyed* by an out-of-control protective-service agency that has all but brought about the *destruction* of that little girl. And today she has absolutely no protection against the forces that almost killed her once."

I was confused. What happened? "When she was six months old . . . Wait, back up. My granddaughter was fifteen years old when *she* had the child. Her husband and she *shook* that baby and caused a problem in her brain."

Yikes.

Jim seemed like a friendly guy, and yet there was that old, familiar problem: he was a hothead, and an unfunny one at that. He talked about McLaren—"The man is *not* out of control, he is a genius, he has a 160 I.Q."—and I raised the question of violence. Given that the federal government would always and forever prevail in U.S.-versus-Republic confrontations, what would it take to make a patriot like Jim pick up a gun and go charging into battle?

And with such overwhelming odds, *why* would he do that?

"You will not know how close some came," he said, preacherlike. "I can tell you that the militias have but *one* methodology in mind. They do not intend to assemble 10, 20, 50 thousand armed men in one spot and allow napalm to destroy them! There is a tactic called 'targets of availability.' What that means is . . . well, *your* interpretation would be terrorism. There is no one that can control that. There is no government could control that."

Bomb talk! Did he hear about specific targeted sites?

"I have suspicions, but I'll *not* answer that based on suspicions."

After Jim left, two Archie-faction ROT men scurried over and nervously said I should pay no attention to him. He didn't know what he was talking about, they conveyed, because . . . you know, he was a nut.

Great. Why didn't that make me feel better?

∞

As I learned by reading *What Wars Are Made Of,* Ron Cole lived through one other paramilitary adventure of note: the Gunnison Incident, a 1994 episode that took place prior to the Battle of Amo. The Gunnison fracas perfectly captured the essence of Cole's career prior to his 1997 arrest: once again, nothing happened, but it easily could have. What's most interesting is the intensity Cole brought to the situation, which can be interpreted in mutually exclusive ways. One, suggested to me by several right-wing figures who've encountered Cole, is that he's a poser, Barney Fife in cammos, a trust-fund kid (one widespread rumor was that Cole received money from prosperous parents), and a media junkie who becomes overwrought about meaningless encounters as a substitute for his ability to do anything.

Another is that Cole just might "do" something someday, that his guilt about not interfering at Waco is so great that he won't feel cleansed until he's been baptized in blood.

My opinion is: Who knows? But just to be on the safe side, let's all tamp down the Barney Fife talk. We don't want the kid to think he has something to prove.

The "incident" occurred in June of '94. Cole, Wally Kennett, and Kevin Terry were living in a rented farmhouse a half-hour from Gunnison, Colorado, where they hoped to establish another safe haven for the Davidians. Right away, though, Cole began to fret about security.

"We figured that we presented a juicy target, and Wally and I were still very jumpy after the Waco tragedy," he wrote in his autobiography. "Jumpy, in fact, is an understatement."

Soon they began receiving "information" that a nearby ranch, visible from their house, had been seized by the Drug Enforcement Administration about the same time they arrived. So? Cole and the boys decided it didn't smell right, and circumstantial evidence started piling up. A gun-store owner in town told Cole that DEA agents had come in asking about his purchases. Cole says he was tailed by a government-issue vehicle—an unmarked white Jeep with government plates—and got involved in a high-speed chase that ended only when he approached his property line. The "Mighty Men," as they called themselves (after some beings mentioned in Genesis), discussed matters and decided the government might be preparing to close in for the kill.

"'What do we do . . . if that undercover house across the valley is a prelude to a government raid against us here?' Wally [said]. 'We can't just ignore that possibility, it happened in Waco, and it could happen here. This is just like the kind of harassment David had to deal with, I mean, you can't forget that we're Branch Davidians.'

"'I have no intention of slackening our security!' [Cole] yelled. 'I just hoped that we would be able to live in peace.'"

The Mighty Men started preparing for mini-Armageddon. On their after-dark patrols, complete with loaded AK-47s and night-vision goggles, the guys would peek into the void, see lights, and wonder how long it would be before the attack began. The house's living room was well suited for conversion to a solid military redoubt—its walls were built with foot-thick logs chinked with cement—so it was here that the men positioned a command center for a "home under threat of imminent attack." They tuned their police scanners to search "local, state or federal frequencies." They stacked ammo and weapons near the windows, put steel bars on windows, booby-trapped the doors, covered the windows in black plastic, and cut sniper slits. Cole figured the logs would stop 9-mm bullets, but not "the more powerful .223 NATO rounds," so the men dressed accordingly: "I wore two level-three bulletproof vests under my camouflaged shirt and tactical vest. All three of us had brand-new bullet-proof helmets."

"Our situation here is critical," Cole wrote in his diary on June 15. "We have chosen, after a long meeting, to stay here and defend ourselves. There are no women or children here, only us 'Mighty Men.' . . . I hope we are being paranoid, but I fear we are not. God help us. . . .

"'Banzai!' I said under my breath. Never surrender. I won't ever surrender. . . . I'll fight you arrogant bully scumbags to the bitter end."

There was no bitter end. The government, if it really was "there," never attacked, and the guys eventually moved on to the next stage in their odd journey.

And how did they interpret all this? As a victory. During the incident, Cole sent out McLaren-style Maydays to militia units all over the country, and received ample assurance that troops were on the way. "It sounds to me like we'd better get down there!" Randy L. Trochmann, of the Militia of Montana, told Cole on the phone. "We've got 20,000 members you know!" When the attack didn't happen, Cole concluded it was because media reports of the incident (it was well publicized; Cole also called up lots of reporters) convinced the government that an unsinkable horde was coming to the rescue, so it slinked back into the shadows.

"Have you guys ever heard of a time in the history of the United States, when Federal law enforcement agencies were thrown to the matt [sic] by pressure from a home-grown paramilitary force?" Cole asked.

"Not that I've ever heard of," said Kevin.

"As of this moment, every ATF and FBI agent in this nation has, for the first time, had his authority challenged," Cole concluded.

"You might say that the Militias just won their first real battle," Kevin said.

Either that, or the Mighty Men were living out a pathetic fantasy. In 1998 I called the sheriff of Gunnison County, Rick Murdie, and asked for his take on the Gunnison Incident. He started laughing. When he stopped laughing he assured me that there was never a stakeout, a car chase, or any other kind of official interest in Cole.

"I didn't even know he was out there until I got a call in the office; it was them wanting me to come out and 'inspect their weapons.' I declined. I figured they wanted to get a picture of me looking over their guns."

"The next thing I know," he continued, "I'm getting calls in my office from Reuters, the *London Times*, telling me the Branch Davidians are moving to Gunnison, and my fax started filling up with every fringe group sending me information about the Great Russian Takeover."

"What did you do about it?"

"Nothing. Unless Mr. Cole broke a law, he was of no interest to me."

∞

After the ROT rally reached its blaring climax, I set out for El Paso ready to roll, hawkeyeing the road with a twelve-hour stare as I took deep, purposeful breaths to keep my brain well oxygenated. About a half hour later I started drooling and weaving again. Time to give it up. I steered my pokey rental car toward a cheap hotel, got a mildewed room, called to change my flight time, and "chewed pillow" from 6:00 P.M. to 4:00 A.M.

Predawn I took off again, heading for El Paso by way of Fort Davis. About 9:00 A.M., the situation started sounding deadly. Radio reports said that a posse had made contact with at least one of the ROT fugitives, who had opened fire and killed a bloodhound. The noose was tightening, and the fugitives weren't getting much sympathy anywhere, especially after the dog got shot. On his syndicated talk show out of Washington, D.C., G. Gordon Liddy—who'd once advised shooting ATF agents in the groin if they came through your door—dismissed all the ROT rebels as morons. Citing the dead dog, he said they deserved whatever befell them.

I arrived in Fort Davis about 2:00 P.M. and roosted for a while by the police roadblock at the entrance to the Davis Mountain Resort subdivision. In the distance rose the stark, rocky, mesquite-covered peaks where the ROT guys were trying to hide. A couple of dozen sunburned, siege-weary reporters were hanging around in cars, and one explained that the neighborhood itself was miles and miles away. Whatever was happening, we wouldn't be able to see it or hear it.

No need to hang around, then. I took off and stopped for gas in the nearby town of Valentine. Inside I met an old codger named Clifford Beare, who said he had recently retired from the Jefferson Davis County sheriff's department. I asked him if it would be hard for runaways to hide in treeless mountains.

"Well, I guess, but yeah, you could hide. There's a lot of caves and stuff."

Did he think these guys would get caught?

"I think they will," he said, rubbing his face and squinting. "Yes, I do."

He was right, too, though it took a while. About that time one fugitive, Mike Matson, was getting shot to death by law enforcement agents, an event that some on the right instantly transformed into conspiracy: the line emerged that Matson tried to surrender but was murdered.

Richard Keyes escaped, and on Tuesday the authorities scaled back the search for him, making vague noises about the terrain and wild animals finishing him off. "He . . . can only have a finite amount of food and water," said Mike Cox, the state's spokesman throughout the siege.

Those words didn't soothe me much. Keyes scrambled his way to freedom with a knife in his teeth. He *demanded* to be taken seriously, an impression that was underscored a few weeks later when, making national news, Keyes telephoned Joel Dyer and said he was alive and angry, and that he planned vengeful and violent payback for the death of Mike Matson.

Fortunately, the government kept on quietly searching—Keyes was arrested near Houston on September 19, 1997, and was later convicted of burglary and sentenced to ninety years. Unfortunately, this stuff isn't over yet. One thing about the year 2000 that I find scary—nightmare scary—is that the spirit of Richard Keyes is still out there, galloping throughout the land.

∞

I once asked Joel Dyer, the author of *Harvest of Rage* and an old acquaintance of Ron Cole's, if Cole frightened him. Not really, he said. For one thing, Cole's craving for publicity was not the normal style of a real terrorist. "The people who scare me," he says, "are the ones I *haven't* heard of." For another, he just didn't believe Cole had it in him to kill unless he was defending his life.

If I had to wager on it, I'd agree, but Cole is frightening in his own way. While he doesn't seem to be "proactive," he does live by the belief that violent tactical action is a legitimate political tool. "I did . . . support hit and run tactics against widely spread targets across the country," he wrote me. "The political advantage would be reversed against us, however, if people were killed during these hit and run strikes. So, I advocated unmanned targets in rural areas. That was in 1993. I also gave this lecture to Timothy McVeigh in Florida, but he ignored the last part!"

Cole's vision now is to broaden the antigovernment movement, excluding the far-right racists and forming a new ecumenical super-army that includes the radical right and left—"the Nation of Islam, the Malcolm X Grassroots Movement, the American Indian Movement, the Mohawk Warriors Society, the Militias . . . the Zapatistas, Hamas, the mujahideen, the Tupac Amaru . . ."

In short, if Cole had his way, it would be business as usual: he would resume his quest to transform the world, starting with a three-man army. As uphill battles go, that's as uphill as it gets, but don't look for Cole's fervency to simply go away. He seems forever scarred by Waco. During his time there, Cole's guilt chewed him up so much that he had recurring nightmares about "the screams, the gunshots, my friends, over and over and over."

He even wrote a poem about it, "The Calling." It goes, in part:

Someone take these dreams away,
that draw me to another day
These dreams replay a genocide,
faces in pain they mesmerize
They are calling me
Dressed in fire and shrill of screams,
features are plain their names I see . . .
The names of the innocent become
faces of death,
burned into my mind until justice is met . . .
My destiny's been set you see, if
death awaits then so it be
Then in your dreams I'll come to you,
I shall not rest 'till all is true
I'll be calling you!

And perhaps Cole will be calling us, whatever it is he intends to say or do. In early 1998, Cole's lawyer worked out a plea-bargain agreement. Cole pleaded guilty to possession of four machine guns, but all the explosives charges were dropped. He got a sentence of twenty-seven months. (Kennett and Terry also plea-bargained.) Counting time served, Cole was slated to hit the streets again in early 1999, just in time for the big countdown year to the millennium.

Don't be surprised if you hear the name again.

Dr. Steven Greer lecturing on the pending arrival of wise, friendly extraterrestrials.
USED BY PERMISSION OF *UFO* MAGAZINE.

5

Somebody Up There Likes Me

If . . . the extraterrestrial origin of the Saucers should be confirmed, this would prove the existence of intelligent interplanetary communication. What such a fact might mean for humanity cannot be imagined. . . . The reins of power would be wrenched from our hands, and, as an old witch doctor once told me with tears in his eyes, we would have "no dreams any more"—the lofty flights of our spirit would have been checked and crippled forever.

Naturally, the first thing to be consigned to the rubbish heap would be our science and technology.

—FROM *FLYING SAUCERS: A MODERN MYTH OF THINGS SEEN IN THE SKIES*, BY C. G. JUNG (1959)

It was dusk on a cool May evening in 1994, a Sunday, and I was cruising northwest out of Minneapolis in a five-vehicle caravan en route to a nighttime "skywatch" for UFOs. The sun was a plummeting blob but was still high enough to shoot pesky glare beams into my eyes. Suddenly, something strange happened—a chrome-sided object flashed into view just ahead, zigzagging through space at a terrifying speed.

Unfortunately, the object was a car I had to keep up with, a road-hungry Mercury Sable. The outing's leader, Dr. Steven M. Greer, an emergency-room physician from Asheville, North Carolina, had run late finishing his dinner, so our convoy was late getting started. We were supposed to be in place in a rural field by nightfall, and as darkness came on, a man named Martin Keller, a Twin Cities UFO buff and Greer's publicist and driver, hurried it up with an 80-mile-an-hour clip and aggressive, chassis-wobbling passes. After exiting I-94 to get on a smaller four-lane, Keller made a wrong turn that necessitated a five-minute roadside rethink and a U-turn. Whizzing back toward the tiny town of Big Lake on the dangerously dippy road, we maxed out at 85.

Eventually we skidded to a safe stop at our destination, a place called Sand Dunes State Forest. In a small parking lot that fronted a thick stand of woods, a dozen men and women gathered flashlights, daypacks, folding chairs, and ground sheets, and then trudged a half-mile down a sandy service road, walking past a pond that throbbed with nighttime critter noises. Before long we arrived at an open field littered with dead scrub and dropped our stuff. The night swooped in like a cape.

Greer was a well-built man in his late thirties whose sturdy neck supported a large, blocky head decorated with reddish-blond hair, a beard, and glasses—the overall look was of a bookwormy, well-groomed sasquatch. He's not a household name, but he's famous in a shadowy American subculture where the outré, conspiracy-tinged themes of *The X Files* play out in real life. In 1990 he created a group called the Center for the Study of Extraterrestrial Intelligence, or CSETI, which announced a wildly offbeat goal: to solicit contact with aliens in hopes of scoring an "on board" experience by the year 2000. Greer called this type of contact—our beckoning them, and succeeding—a "close encounter of the fifth kind," or CE-5. He made that term up, but it was built on existing UFO lingo devised by the late astronomer J. Allen Hynek, a leading UFO researcher from the fifties and sixties who had worked on the Air Force's investigation of the UFO phenomenon, and who became a believer after he decided the government was predisposed to dismiss flying saucers from the start. (In Hynek's formulation, for example, a close encounter of the third kind meant reports of "beings, usually humanoid," in connection with a UFO sighting. A CE-4, a term minted by subsequent Hynek imitators, refers to forced abductions by aliens.)

In the long history of alleged UFO encounters, alien contact has occurred when *they* want it to, and the results usually don't sound appealing. A typical, early example of an abduction story—a once-rare type of tale that became quite common in the eighties and nineties —was the Betty Andreasson case. On the evening of January 25, 1967, Andreasson, a housewife, was at home with

A vivid alien depiction by artist Jim D. Dallmeier.

her elderly parents and seven children in South Ashburnham, Massachusetts, when all hands noticed a pink light coming through a window. Andreasson's dad peeked outside and saw a group of tiny "Halloween freaks" hopping toward the house. At that point, everybody passed out except Andreasson, who recalled (years later, under hypnosis) that she'd been abducted. Fitting the now-classic profile, the intruders had big heads, gray skin, large slanted eyes, and small slits in place of normal noses and mouths. Through telepathy, they told Andreasson they were here to help the world, which they believed was "trying to destroy itself." She said she was then whisked aboard a UFO, put on a slab, and examined. The ETs pierced her belly and nasal passages with a long needle and removed something from behind her nose with a thin, flexible instrument. When she protested, the aliens conveyed that their experiments meant no harm. They had something to do with "procreation," and there were "some missing parts."

What could it all mean? One theory among contemporary UFO believers is that alien abductors need us as cross-breeding stock. In his controversial 1994 book, *Abduction*—which recounts the experiences of dozens of people who believe aliens captured them—John E. Mack, a Pulitzer Prize–winning Harvard psychiatrist, presented the astonishing argument that the abduction phenomenon involves actual events that are about "some sort of genetic or quasi-genetic engineering for the purpose of creating human/alien hybrid offspring." Why? That remains mysterious, but one theory is that the aliens are dying out, so they need our robust genes to physically replenish their species.

Another theory is that they're trying to help us somehow, which is Andreasson's view. As often happens with alleged abductees, she went on to become a spokesperson for an openly religious notion, that a group of aliens called "the watchers" are here now, keeping a close, benevolent eye on mankind. One entity, named Quazgaa, told her, "We have come to help the human race. We do not want to hurt anybody, but because of great love we cannot let man continue in the footsteps he is going."

Greer held similar views: whatever the "experiments" were about, he was sure the aliens had come to do good, to teach us peaceful lessons of millennial consequence. He also believed—and this marked him as *very* different from most modern UFO buffs, who are usually scared of ETs—that we can and should wave them in, regardless of the risk. So, armed with a hardware cornucopia (high-power halogen lights, radar detectors, walkie-talkies, still and video cameras), Greer and his followers did exactly that, gathering at darkness-swaddled mountains, fields, and woods, where they beamed photons and positive thoughts into the inky infinite. Throughout the nineties, Greer barnstormed all over the place teaching his beliefs and methods, and he boasted of an astonishing success rate at calling in UFOs. By 1994, when I hooked up with him, he and his "CSETI teams" claimed more than a dozen close sightings in the United States, Mexico, and England. The grand prize, physical contact, hadn't happened yet, but Greer confidently said it would before century's end.

Greer was an assertive person, used to taking charge, and as we settled in at the Minnesota nightwatch field he glanced around and frowned thoughtfully, like a diligent platoon leader. He squinted. He took a deep breath. He nodded. Yep, he decided, this would do.

Indeed, what Greer considered promising data whistled in shortly. From a large sprawl of tall pines about a quarter-mile to the north came the call of a whippoorwill and a weird, lonely tone I'd never heard before: *dewp, dewp, dewp.* Greer turned an ear to the trees. Body alert, he announced that the tone was "almost identical" to a sound recorded a few years back by a different UFO skywatch group in Canada, whose audiotapes Greer owned. Significantly, the tones were recorded near a field where crop circles—patterns and lines that for years have been mysteriously turning up on British and North American farms—had recently appeared. Greer said a technical analysis of the Canadian tone showed that "it did not match any sound known on the planet."

Which, if you think about it, is a strange thing for a doctor to say in the middle of nowhere at dusk. (And yes, Greer really is an M.D.; I checked.) Physicians are technical, scientific people, and the scientific verdict about crop circles is that they're hoaxes. Greer didn't buy that. He was sure UFOs played a role in their formation, and in his mind anyone who said otherwise was wrong. Or lying. One of Greer's main themes was that various interests, primarily the federal government, conspire to prevent citizens from learning the truth

about aliens. Once, on the Art Bell radio show—a nationally syndicated talk program about the paranormal—Greer said the UFO subject was wrapped up in a burrito of "covert management and extra-
extra-secret supersecret management."

"We are hearing beeping sounds off on the near horizon," one of
Greer's assistants said crisply into a microcassette recorder. Greer had
told each of us to carry one and to log reactions as events unfolded.
Ignoring the helper, he continued his evaluation, speaking hush-
voiced to his own machine.

"We assess this site as . . . pretty good," he said in a soft southern
accent, ticking off its attributes.

"It is in a known active area." He was referring to the nearby
town of Elk River, which had undergone a flurry of reported UFO
sightings in 1992.

"It's not too far from a nuclear site." Many UFO researchers
believe aliens are worried that we're too stupid to handle nukes
responsibly, so they zip around monitoring them and us.

"We have a good horizon-to-horizon view and a high cloud ceiling—"

Dewp. Dewp. Dewp. The sound again . . .

"And it's doing a pretty good imitation of a crop-circle noise!" the
assistant said.

Whatever the sound's source, it *was* spooky: metallic, ringing,
metronomic. Soon it stopped. I peered at the treeline. By the failing
light it looked like a dark, blurry smear on an inept watercolor. Later
that night, Greer would theorize that a "blacked out" UFO might be
hovering among the limbs.

I stared at the *dewp*-ing woods. I figured we had a better chance
of seeing a leprechaun hop out of there than an extraterrestrial, but
you never know, so to get in the spirit I tried to establish a recep-
tively spooky mindset by imagining "contact." What would I do if a

rubbery, potbellied imp with a head the size of a butt roast came skittering and chittering in our direction?

Mulling it over, I remembered something Greer had said earlier in the day, during a six-hour workshop on contact etiquette. "This is a mutual dance," he advised, "but let them be the leading partners. Don't rush up and give them a hug. For all you know, you'll crush them."

∞

"The evidence is now clear to some of us that we are being visited by technologically superior beings whose agendas are complex and currently difficult to fathom," writes Brian O'Leary, a former Apollo astronaut turned New Age theorist, in his 1996 book, *Miracle in the Void.* "It is also apparent that our UFO visitors have mastered free energy and antigravity effects, as well as the ability to transfer abductees through walls and to pop in and out of our limited space-time dimensions."

"Apparent" may be a stretch, but for now let's focus on O'Leary's broader argument. Like Greer, he's a prominent player in an easy-to-overlook area of the millennial and utopian style—fringe science—and his book makes helpful connections between what, on first hearing, sound like unrelated subjects: UFOs and "free energy."

UFOs you know about. Free energy, probably not. The term is the modern label for what historically has been called "perpetual motion," which refers to the centuries-old quest to invent a machine that somehow produces more energy than it takes to run it, or produces energy from free "sources" like magnetism or gyroscopes. While belief in UFOs is not synonymous with belief in free energy (or vice versa), the subcultures often cross-pollinate, and their partisans share an important basic belief: the idea that mainstream science is heading for a fall that will reshape our world in the next millennium. The most fervent zealots are convinced that the scientific establishment is turning a blind eye to—or suppressing—knowledge about UFOs and free energy that would make much of what science now accepts as "truth" look like a pathetic joke.

The overwhelming majority of scientists, of course, say UFOs and free energy are the jokes. They rule out UFOs because the distances between stars are so great—other than the sun, the nearest star, Alpha Centauri, is more than four light years away—that they can't accept that aliens from another solar system could get here. To do so, they would need to have discovered suspended animation and/or a means to travel at speeds that we can't imagine with current technology. UFO believers like O'Leary and Greer are sure aliens have done so, and assume aliens have produced spacecraft that travel at or near the speed of light using some type of infinite power source.

Scientists have trouble accepting that one, too, at least in the terms O'Leary is talking about. Aliens might be able to chug along very efficiently if they had, say, a working on-board nuclear fusion reactor, which would take them a long way on little fuel. But O'Leary assumes they've discovered something even more magical: perpetual motion, "free" energy. He also believes various inventors here on Earth are pushing forward with a "new physics" that is rapidly taking us where the aliens already are. One such device he cites is the "unipolar generator" produced by a maverick Indian free-energy inventor named Paramahamsa Tewari, whom O'Leary has visited, and who supposedly uses "corotating magnetic disks" to produce "electrical outputs that exceed the inputs with efficiencies ranging from about 200 to 400 percent."

That really would be something—in simplest terms, O'Leary is saying that Tewari can put fifty cents into his gizmo and get several dollars back. Physicists scoff at such claims, because they violate immutable physical laws, namely the first two laws of thermodynamics. Among other things, these laws dictate that you can't get more energy out of a machine than you put in it, and that energy cannot be created from magnetism, which is a force, not an energy source.

Of course, as a layman, I have to say: Gee, I don't understand any of this. But if I'm forced to place a bet, I'll wager that the scientists know what they're talking about. After all, they created rockets and A-bombs and computers.

The UFO and free-energy partisans would argue that this is the attitude of a blind sheep. They sincerely believe that the government (and corporations) will do anything to prevent us from finding out that aliens are here, and that tiny bands of frontier-seeking scientists are starting to learn what they already know, despite the obstacles and dangers.

The dangers? Yes, because according to the drama-packed UFO and free-energy mythology, funny things happen to maverick inventors and researchers. They suddenly, mysteriously develop cancer. Or they get an emphatic visit from CIA agents, Men in Black, or oil-company goons, who convince them that now would be a fine time to shut up about their alien encounter, or to sledgehammer their machines and move to Uruguay.

This is a bizarre world view. What's even stranger is that for today's fringe scientists, it's ultimately a source not of black pessimism but of utopian optimism. Carl Jung, who became interested in UFOs soon after the first reported sightings in 1947, argued that if UFOs were real—he didn't come down either way, but he didn't rule it out—the superiority of alien technology would make us feel like stunned aborigines in the face of a superior culture. O'Leary and Greer see it just the opposite. To them, science itself is the dream-killer. Having dominated this century, it has also left us marooned in a very cold and lonely place, where many forms of "magic"—like the limitless possibilities of alternative science, not to mention the likely reality of higher powers and an afterlife—are declared to be scientifically unorthodox and therefore impossible. In this myth, aliens and their technology represent a liberating force: if they're real, the joke is on the scientists. And if they do come down, a New Age would begin, marked by spectacular technological leaps and an accompanying expansion of human consciousness.

Greer therefore considers himself a warrior battling the stonewall tactics of dangerous authorities. He also believes the government has recovered alien technology during episodes like the Roswell Incident—the alleged 1947 crash of an alien spacecraft and its occupants near Roswell, New Mexico—and has successfully "reverse engineered" the aliens' techno-secrets.

Many fringies feel the same way. In a 1997 book called *Alien Agenda*, Jim Marrs (a veteran of the JFK conspiracy-theory scene) connects all the dots, maintaining that a global cabal of the "wealthy elite" and the "energy monopoly" has a vested interest in quashing the free-energy secrets of the extraterrestrials, in order to "suppress any uncontrolled energy source, whether from UFOs or innovative human inventors."

This conspiracy theme is not brand-new—it's been a staple among fringe-scientists for at least a century, especially since World War II, and it must be said that the government sometimes helps create the climate of paranoia. For example, as the fringies know, the authorities did lie for years about the Roswell Incident, which began on July 8, 1947, when the Roswell Army Air Field—home to the Air Force's nuclear-equipped 509th Bomb Group—issued a news release about the nighttime crash of an unidentified flying object on July 4. Relying on the military's release, the *Roswell Daily Record,* the local newspaper, published an astonishing story headlined, "RAAF Captures Flying Saucer on Ranch in Roswell Region." The next day the military retracted that, saying that the crash was merely a weather balloon, a line that officialdom used for the next forty-seven years. Roswell became a hot topic in the seventies and eighties, and in 1994, under mounting pressure from UFO buffs and members of Congress, the General Accounting Office—Congress's investigative arm—revisited the Roswell story and reported that, yes, the government had lied all along. The silvery wreckage was not from a weather balloon, but from a top-secret balloon-ferried sensor designed to detect high-altitude residue from Soviet nuclear tests. In 1997, as the hullabaloo about the fiftieth anniversary of the Roswell Incident approached, the government released still more reports. These elaborated in great detail on the general line that fifty years of sightings were easily explained: people had intersected with secret government military operations, which had to be denied at the time.

All of which may be true, probably *is* true, but by then the hardcore buffs weren't listening. They saw the latter-day alibis as just another whitewash.

It's also a fact that the government has oppressed free-energy crusaders in the past. The classic case involves Wilhelm Reich, an Austrian-born Freudian psychiatrist who in the forties and fifties theorized that the planet and the cosmos are filled with a universal form of helpful free energy called "orgone." To harness it, he built devices like the Orgone Energy Accumulator, a large box that was supposed to collect and store ambient orgone for therapeutic delivery to patients who could benefit from a blast of orgone healing. His "cloudbuster" devices manipulated orgone content in the sky—to break up smog or produce rain.

The government took issue with Reich's claim that orgone had legitimate applications in the treatment of disease. In 1954, after a long investigation, the Food and Drug Administration obtained a court injunction against the manufacture and distribution of the boxes and any printed matter that ascribed curative powers to orgone. Reich famously defied this and was jailed in 1957. He died that year of a heart attack, still shaking his fist at the world.

"We have lost, *technically only,* to an incomprehensible procedure treadmill," Reich railed when he was sentenced in 1956. "I and my fellow workers have, however, won our case in the true, historical sense. We may be destroyed physically tomorrow; we shall live in human memory as long as this planet is afloat in the endless Cosmic Energy Ocean as the Fathers of the cosmic, technological age. . . .

". . . I have won the battle against evil."

Actually, "evil" bashed Reich into the turnbuckle, but it's an inspiring image anyway. He saw himself as the New Prometheus, the bringer of free energy and justice. In this ongoing drama, the role of today's fringe-science believers is clear: they must keep the faith and fight the power.

Or as O'Leary puts it, the looming apocalypse isn't about destruction, but about the unveiling of previously hidden truths.

"Apocalypse does not point to a fiery Armageddon," he writes, quoting Joseph Campbell, "but to the fact that our ignorance and complacence have come to an end."

∞

Heroic talk, but to those of us who doubt that UFOs and free energy exist, there are obvious questions: If the aliens love us so much, why don't they just drop from the sky and fix our world? For that matter, if the free-energy inventors have succeeded, why are we still paying so dearly for gasoline?

This is where evil comes into play, the essential millennial and dystopian narrative that sees a dark force blocking our path to enlightenment. Many fringe scientists insist that the aliens won't come because mankind's consciousness is still too debased, and that free energy inventors are forced underground out of fear. This belief often plays out in obscure mini-dramas that most of us never hear about, but which can be surprisingly operatic—tragically *and* comically.

Among the heroic warblers, nobody fights the fight harder than Steve Greer. On a raw, dribbly Saturday night in Minnesota, the night before the rural skywatch outing, I watched him explain it all to an audience of about two hundred people, whom he chilled with tales of "high strangeness"—accounts of his alleged UFO-sighting adventures, crashed flying saucers, government cover-ups, and "disinformation" plots to destroy CSETI's work.

"What we're going to be talking about tonight is admittedly a controversial area," Greer said, standing on the amber-washed stage of the World Theater in downtown St. Paul, "but we at CSETI have determined that we are not alone." He asked for a show of hands. Who felt the same way? Several arms shot up. No surprise there: polls have shown that most Americans believe in the possibility of extraterrestrial life. Then he lobbed another shocker. "We can document that in the fifties, UFOs were classified at least two levels higher than the H-bomb experiment." That caused a murmur—what is "two levels higher"?—and apparently some people were turned off. A few walked out.

I'd become interested in Greer because he seemed like a perfect case study for a question that had long nagged me about fringe scientists: What was really going on in their minds? By then I'd spent my share of time studying the UFO-buff taxonomy. At one extreme were the nuts-and-bolts people, what I called the "hardware" crowd, who tried to bring classic methods of investigation to bear on the subjects of crashed saucers and abductions—eyewitness interviews, photo analysis, archival research, Freedom of Information Act requests, and so on. At the other were loopy "contactees" who, like the people in the Unarius Academy of Science, simply assumed that UFOs are out there and that they're piloted by beautiful, angelic beings.

Where did Greer fit in? More important, how did he fit his hard-edged medical side and UFO beliefs into the same brain? At first, I tried to break the mystery down to elemental choices. They seemed clear enough:

1. Greer was right. The aliens are here and there's a cover-up going on.
2. He was wrong, but he meant well.
3. He was wrong and cynically lying—either for profit, ego gratification, or perceived "power" over others.
4. Or (an *X Files*-y alternative that I'd actually heard suggested about Greer) he was serving as a "disinformation" agent for the government—the idea being that his public goofiness would discredit UFO people everywhere.

Susan, who had come along on this trip, said the truth was probably a combination. Greer might be a little right, a lot wrong, a little rational, a little well meaning, and a big ol' jerk all at once. As she'd done before when we met fringe characters together, she suggested using a pie chart. I should analyze the different traits at work in Greer's m.o., label them, assign relative proportions, and fit the pieces together.

As Greer talked, I sat there charting him out. I hadn't met him yet—that would all happen tomorrow, the workshop-and-skywatch day—and he'd been a hard man to pin down. I'd first heard about him in early 1993 on the UFO grapevine, where a buzz was growing about a big, pushy guy from North Carolina who had started showing up at UFO hotspots with a "team" of trained seekers. Reportedly, they used flashlights and platoon telepathy to urge space pilots to land.

The buzz also had it that Greer was rapidly becoming unpopular. UFO buffs are turf-conscious, and Greer had annoyed quite a few of them with his tendency to arrive at a UFO scene and start marking territory. According to some buffs, that's exactly what happened in 1992 in Gulf Breeze, Florida, a coastal town that is a world-famous setting for nighttime UFO sightings. One night in March, a thirty-nine-person CSETI squad descended on the beach, ran the CSETI drill under Greer's tutelage, and shot videos of what looked like nothing more than distant lights passing over the water—that is, ordinary aircraft. The way Greer told it in a subsequent self-published report, the group had, in a snap, done what dozens of other Gulf Breeze skywatchers had failed to do for years: scored "a confirmed, close range, multi-witness . . . interactive encounter" with five UFOs that responded in kind when he signaled "with a 500,000 candle power light in intelligent sequences."

To put it mildly, unaffiliated witnesses didn't support Greer's version of events. "The sad part," grumbled Bruce Morrison, a local skywatcher whom Greer listed as a "witness" to his sighting, "is that we were standing right next to him and we have everything on videotape and voice tape. Regarding his claims, let's just say he has a very, very bad habit of embellishing what he sees."

Such sniping might be nothing more than intra-buff sour grapes, so I was eager to talk to the man himself. That was difficult. Greer surrounded himself with officious helpers like Martin Keller, and I got nowhere trying to interview him on the phone. If I wanted to meet him, Keller said, I'd have to sign up for a workshop like everybody else. Keller even made me fax in a letter describing my motives and goals.

Why the star treatment? I decided early on that it involved the nature of Greer's mission. I assumed he believed deeply in what he was preaching, and my tentative theory was that, because he was sincere, he truly was convinced that he was in danger. Given that, proper security was crucial. For all Greer and Keller knew, I was a government agent.

Greer was also avowedly idealistic. "What does it all mean?" he asked the St. Paul audience late in the lecture. He speculated, like O'Leary, that we're on the verge of a paradigm shift—the ETs are about to make themselves known, so we're getting a slow, gentle introduction to what will be a remarkable future. Greer said we're being thrown into "a schoolhouse for the Earth."

And the lesson plan? "We're being taught to empower ourselves," Greer said. "In my opinion, the most important science of the next millennium is the science of consciousness. It is likely that any star-reaching civilization has reached the point where they have, to a large extent, mastered that science." What followed echoed Jung. "It's been said," Greer went on, "that if you encountered a civilization with 100,000 years of advance in technology over us, what we would see would seem to us like magic."

During a Q & A session that followed, people focused on less lofty issues, but Greer kept bapping the shuttlecock back up into the ether. One man asked him when the UFO phenomenon started and why.

"There are two schools on that," Greer said. "Some think it's been going on since the beginning of time—that's my view, but there's no way to prove or disprove that. I think the intensity of activity did increase after the explosion of the atomic bomb. I think there was a big cosmic red flag that went up and they said, 'Hey, this bunch of primates is about to blow up the planet!' And they decided that with this ability, coupled with space exploration technology, we may at some point in the not-too-distant future be dangerous to not only ourselves but to others."

The audience chuckled nervously. "Hey, take a look. A hundred million people were exterminated in this century alone through genocide, warfare, and craziness. I don't think it's a coincidence that a large number of the highest quality sightings have occurred in and around high technology and nuclear facilities."

Next, a skeptical shopper asked Greer how he could be so sure extraterrestrials mean no harm.

Playing his M.D. card adroitly—Greer often liked to remind people that he was a doctor, which lent credibility—he replied with a grisly medical analogy, that of a critically wounded "accident victim" who is brought into the emergency room and mistakes rescue procedures for torture. Strapped down, with bloody, rubber-handed strangers manipulating his pain-wracked body, the victim may perceive that he's being violated when in fact he's being saved.

So it is, said Greer, with mankind, which is in dire need of help from Trapper John, E.T.

"Any computer projected into the year 2100 will tell you that we're not going to be around if current trends of environmental disaster and other things hold," he declared. Then he got spine-tingly again. "If the *Titanic* is sinking and you're plucked off the bow, were you abducted or rescued?"

∞

The pie-chart technique started during my forays into the world of free energy, which predated meeting Greer and which yielded very complicated pies. The people involved in it were even more secretive than the doc—they really, really believed enemies were out to get them—but, like medieval priests swatting at unseen devils with a crucifix, they also tended to hurt innocent bystanders.

I began dabbling in the subject after the Gulf War—a terrible, apocalyptic reminder that the oil monkey was still screeching on our backs—figuring that it would invigorate the free-energy underground. As I knew from reading up on the topic, the seventies had been a golden age for the cause thanks to the Arab oil embargo, which created an alternative-energy hunger that helped give the inventors a boost. The star of that era was Joseph Newman, a garage inventor from Mississippi who emerged with his "Energy Machine," a D.C. motor that he claimed produced more electrical juice than it consumed. After a long struggle, he obtained a court order forcing the National Bureau of Standards, which tries to ignore perpetual-motion inventors, to give it a serious evaluation. In 1986 the Bureau concluded that his machine was less efficient than an ordinary D.C. motor, but Newman had a bracing run. Along the way, he won support for his right to a hearing from two dozen scientists and engineers, several congressmen, and Dan Rather, who in 1984 introduced a CBS News report on the machine that lauded Newman's brilliance.

Free energy dwindled after Newman's defeat, but it never went away. The first buff I found was a Texan named Jerry Decker, who maintained a computer bulletin board, "KeelyNet," dedicated to the memory of John Keely, a nineteenth-century inventor of a perpetual-motion machine, eventually exposed as a fraud, called the "Hydro Pneumatic Pulsating Vacuo Engine." Decker, a friendly, generous man, didn't think it was a fraud. In his version of reality, Keely was a mental giant whose findings were suppressed by big coal. The quest now was to rediscover what he had learned and, as usual, to tap into the larger universe of extraterrestrial know-how. Decker spoke soaringly of building a multimillion-dollar free-energy academy and lab in Texas, but he was also pessimistic and fidgety about his chances of getting it done. He soon stopped returning my calls.

I ran into this shrinking-violet trait again and again. A man in Colorado Springs knew of "someone" who had reconstructed the Keely Engine, but he wouldn't say who. A man named Bruce de Palma had produced a free-energy-generating "N Machine" but declined to speak to the media. Dan Davidson, author of *Breakthrough to New Free Energy Sources,* a history of the quest published in 1977, was chattier but cautious all the same. He told me about lamented lost devices like Viktor Schauerberger's "Zokwendle," a World War II–era machine that used revolutionary water-turbine principles to generate 100,000 watts out of nothing, but which was eventually captured and destroyed by the Allies.

I asked Davidson why the inventors were so jumpy.

Simple, he said: they get roughed up. That's what happened to Schauerberger, who died penniless, a broken man, all his discoveries scattered and lost. "A sad tribute," Davidson eulogized in his book, "to another tireless worker in nature's deep arcanum."

In time I hooked up with a talkative, above-ground pair: Bob and Zoh Hieronimus, a husband-and-wife team in Baltimore whose talk show, "21st Century Radio," was devoted to fringe and paranormal topics. The Hieronimuses were well-meaning, gentle people—they were the folks, you'll recall, who eventually showed me their Earth Changes pod—and they were shocked by the pointless brutality of the Gulf War. In 1990 they were inspired to produce a lengthy series on "energy alternatives," which really meant free energy. They talked to a couple dozen inventors, including Joe Newman and two men who said they'd invented engines that ran on ordinary tap water, Yoshiro NakaMats and Stanley Meyer.

"Alex," Bob told me with lovable conviction, "we don't have to be slaves to fossil fuels anymore if we would just pay attention to these remarkable inventors!"

I had just missed the big event during Bob and Zoh's intensive focus on free energy: a U.S. visit, which the Hieronimuses helped pay for, by NakaMats, a Japanese inventor. Fortunately, I was able to reconstruct what happened after the fact, and noticed that Naka-Mats received respectful treatment—nay, bootlicking—from the media, corporate types, and government officials. This sort of gave the lie to the "suppression" myth. If an inventor really did produce a free-energy machine, the establishment wouldn't kill him. It would line up to suck his toes.

NakaMats rolled into Baltimore in November of 1990, boasting that he held 2,360 patents, twice as many as Thomas Edison. He said he'd been offered $7 billion in cash for his water fuel cell, called the

Enerex, and that he might be ready to cut a deal while in Maryland . . . or so he led people to believe. Excited, the Maryland Department of Economic and Employment Development hosted a ceremony in honor of "Dr. NakaMats Day," November 13, proclaimed by Maryland's governor. Local media also pitched in, saying that, while free-energy claims obviously sounded too good to be true, this one had to be taken seriously because of NakaMats's staggering number of patents.

Judging by NakaMats's resume, I wasn't so sure about that. Written in fractured English, it was a minor comic masterpiece that listed pages and pages of tiny-type accomplishments and honors, many of them meaningless: "Professor St. Louis University and other 10 U.S. Universities. . . . The Japan Praise Association (similar to the Nobel Prize Award) awarded Dr. NakaMats the 'Socially Distinguished Prize for Invention'. . ."

As I learned easily enough, back home in Japan, NakaMats was well known as a zany public figure, a novelty inventor. Old newspaper clips showed him walking around Tokyo in a T-shirt that proclaimed I AM GENIUS. One of his inventions was a golf club that for some reason doubled as a tuning fork. Another was the Cerebrex Chair, an electrically powered seat that increased brain function by stimulating the sitter's butt with "far infrared rays." Another "invention" was NakaMats's act of changing his name from Nakamatsu to NakaMats.

During NakaMats's visit, all this went unquestioned by industry representatives and dignitaries who lined up to meet the great man at the Hieronimuses' home in suburban Baltimore. According to the usual plotline of the free-energy suppression drama, these "forces" should have been waiting with sapper clubs and handguns. Not quite. On hand for a Sunday brunch, their tongues lolling, were, among others, representatives of Westinghouse, the University of Maryland, the governor's office, and Baltimore Gas and Electric. On the Friday previous, Ron Williams, chief engineer for the House Committee on Space, Science and Technology, and Frank Murray, staff director of the Subcommittee on Energy, had come out for a private look.

But alas, they were all in for a disappointment, which the Hieronimuses captured on videotape. As people milled around before the presentation started, the Enerex—a plastic cylinder with wires, about the size of a tennis-ball can—sat on a pedestal, sealed in a plastic display case. Bob, emceeing, got everybody's attention and said proudly, "We don't need to go to war! If Dr. NakaMats is correct, oil will no longer be the . . . god that it is in our society."

When NakaMats's turn came, he stood and smiled. He was a compact, dapper Japanese with wire-rim glasses and a well-tailored suit. For a while he yakked about his inventions. Then, suddenly, he announced that he was very, very, very sorry, but because of security fears, he wouldn't be able to run the Enerex after all.

Or to provide any meaningful details on how it worked. Then he talked some more and yielded the floor to Bob and Zoh. Looking like they'd swallowed fish hooks, they tried to pretend that they were taking this in stride. Later they explained that NakaMats decided "the moment wasn't right." The promotional expenses for the visit, which they helped raise, came to $8,000.

What did NakaMats gain from this charade? It was hard to "pie chart" that accurately since I'd never talked to him, but I think he was less of an edge-seeking frontier scientist than a tireless self-promoter. His wife videotaped every event, and Williams and Murray, the congressional men, were captured on tape when they came calling. So, aside from some amusing home movies of baffled Americans, the tapes no doubt provided the type of priceless, marketable publicity that helped NakaMats sell a few more Cerebrex Chairs back home.

∞

In Minnesota, Greer had a harder time selling his product. Turnout for his UFO workshop, held on Sunday in a downtown Minneapolis performance space, was low, and there were no dignitaries. About a dozen men and women showed up, along with various CSETI assistants, including Martin Keller—decked out casually in anticipation of the field trip—and a few anxious, anonymous aides-de-Steve, who flitted around like mosquitoes as they tended to his many needs. I walked up, introduced myself to The Man, got a few very stiff replies, and left him alone. Susan and I took our seats in a circle of green plastic chairs and studied Greer, who had on elastic-waist chinos, a sports shirt, and running shoes. He was fidgeting with a bulky light as an old "Sightings" episode about CSETI flickered on a monitor behind him. Soon he cleared his throat, arranged his papers, and talked in a steady gale through the morning and afternoon.

This was supposed to be a workshop, but it was mostly lecture. Greer didn't like giving up the floor, a fact that created tension, because the class was full of throbbing New Age types who had feelings they wanted to express. But whenever somebody chipped in, Greer's body language shifted to highly impatient until the affront mercifully stopped. The most annoying pair was a fortyish couple of old hippies—a big, loud, bearded guy named Elias and his smiling wife, Lisa—who kept challenging Greer's view that aliens were inherently good. Greer slapped them down by pointing out that it's in the government's interest to promote such "paranoia."

"The Red Scare has been replaced by the Gray Scare," he said, referring to the widely held notion that many aliens have ashen skin. "Personally," he added, "I consider the term 'grays' a racist appellation."

Elias and Lisa piped down. Temporarily.

Between such crackling high moments we got a reprise of the night before, but with an increased level of detail that took us one layer closer to the inner sanctum. Completing this class was a pre-requisite for becoming a member of CSETI's Rapid Mobilization Investigative Team—RMIT, a specially trained corps that flew off to UFO hotspots on short notice—an enticing prospect, given that Greer said this elite squad had a "batting average of one thousand." After a review of the basics (the importance of higher consciousness, the need for an "open mind"), Greer walked us through the Contact Trilogy, his three-component, argot-rich method of ET-calling.

As he launched into an extended wheeze, Greer sternly empha-sized that these were serious protocols, developed "through trial and error, experimental research."

"This is not a loose skywatch collective, but a team," he stressed, eyeballing Elias and Lisa. "It is not a support group. People who are looking for 'support' on their fears should try another group. Our goal is clear: to achieve an off-planet experience."

The techniques sounded fun but silly. First you waggled lights. Greer hoisted his, a black-plastic-encased halogen baby whose beam was visible ten miles away, available for $40 from Sears. "These are used for primary vectoring," Greer jargoned. "This lets 'em know where a team is. We can't assume they know that. They need sig-nals." Then he talked about "secondary vectoring," more commu-nicative signaling used once you got a "confirmed lock-on."

Next, sounds. CSETI teams played recordings of crop-circle tones to signal to the ETs that they were hip to the tones' secret signifi-cance. To demonstrate, Greer played a tape recorded during a July 1992 CSETI vigil held in an active crop-circle region near Wiltshire, England. To me the noises sounded like tree frogs. An ebullient New Agey woman commented that the sounds were "animal-like."

Greer stiffened. "These tones have been analyzed—"

She added a soothing corrective. She meant only that the aliens "may be coming in using the sound of animals to protect themselves from . . . whatever."

"Could be," Greer said stiffly. "We just don't know."

Finally we got the how-tos of "coherent thought sequencing," which was analogous to what golf-instruction manuals call "visualizing success." Greer called this the "ultimate networking," a "new science."

The new science worked like so: essentially, you closed your eyes and tried to use remote viewing or telepathy to establish a conscious connection with a UFO pilot (or crew) and then imagine the flight path that he, she, they, it, or its would take to find you. We shut our peeps and performed a twenty-minute test run. "It's not effective unless you try to experience a nonlocality of mind," Greer advised. He suggested visualizing macro-scale landmarks—like the finger-shaped western edge of Lake Superior—to give the pilots direction. Afterward he asked who saw what, and it became clear that this group was hair-trigger ready.

"The craft is round," Lisa said. "A ball. With many different lights around it. They communicate telepathically. If you say, 'Come in peace,' they'll come. If you think negatively, they won't come."

"Right, right," said Greer, cutting her off. "That's very true."

∞

After the NakaMats near-miss I grew desperate to meet a free-energy tinkerer in the flesh, so I phoned Stan Meyer (the other water-as-fuel guy) at his home in Grove City, Ohio, just south of Columbus. Meyer was loud and friendly and, unlike the other buffs, eager to share materials. He mailed me a pile of stuff that I found incomprehensible. (To me, fringe physics looks a lot like regular physics on the page.) Photos in his newsletter showed him to be a tall, barrel-chested guy with graying hair and a big grin, hard at work on his favorite demonstration project, a water-powered dune buggy. Despite his outward sunniness, though, Meyer turned out to be an altogether darker figure than NakaMats.

With help from some physics experts, I got busy trying to absorb the basics of Meyer's claim. His cell used electrical current to separate water into its constituent elements, hydrogen and oxygen. (No big deal there: that process is called electrolysis, and high-school science students do it all the time.) He then enhanced the hydrogen with lasers and other wizardry and produced "energized . . . gas atoms." When exposed to a spark, this mojohydrogen supposedly combusted with "thermal explosive energy up to and beyond 2.5 million barrels of oil per gallon of water." Wow. With an engine like that, you could fly to Mars and back several times on a big tank of H_2O.

That sounded impossible, but what did I know? So I visited George Lewett, an expert on energy-related inventions at the National Institute of Standards and Technology in Gaithersburg, Maryland (formerly the Bureau of Standards). He glanced at the brief, laughed, agreed to give it a thorough look, and (a while later) declared it bogus. He explained that it was fine for Meyer to run his dune buggy on hydrogen. But nothing he did could "add" energy to the hydrogen, so he was really running a car on batteries with extra steps thrown in—that is, isolating the hydrogen from the water using electricity—that actually made his car less efficient than a car run solely on batteries.

A strange gift to the world, but Meyer pursued it with an evangelist's fervor. Once a month he held an investor-seeking "Dealership Seminar" in a meeting room of a vast, lonely resort hotel, the Deer Creek State Park Lodge, which sat about forty miles south of Columbus. In April 1991 I drove out to one with Susan and caught his act.

The lodge was a cozy-looking place in the middle of nowhere, with lots of richly burnished, exposed timbers inside and a creepy silence broken only by—this will sound contrived, but it's true—the *Twin Peaks* theme, which wafted over the sound system.

Meyer and his entourage were late arriving, so several people stood waiting and talking outside the designated room. Not to be mean, but they struck me as sad rubes who seemed to believe in Meyer in large part because he was a Christian. An old lady with a Dr. Zorba hairdo and a beige arm cast announced that she was a longtime investor in the Cell. Her nephew Basil, a missionary student, had told her about Stan and said he was a good, faithful man.

"That was all I needed to hear to know he's all right," she declared.

Meyer finally arrived with several men and set up a demo model of the Cell. It was a tall, hollow plastic cylinder that housed numerous metal rods and was filled with water. About thirty people—mostly men—listened, rapt, as he launched into a four-hour spiel on his struggle to bring his invention to the world in defiance of the odds. Before long he dragged Jesus into it. The Lord himself, Meyer said, gave him the Cell's secrets in 1975, in response to the Arab oil embargo.

"I did ask the Lord to help me write a perfect patent," he said, speaking in oddly biblical syntax. "And when I had filed this patent the powers that be came to me, and they foamed at the mouth, and they pounded on the table, and they vowed unto death that we would never get the patent on this technology."

This bluntness seemed crazy: I expected everybody to get up and walk out. Nobody walked. Apparently they were all comfortable with revelation physics. I then realized that this was, in fact, an interesting move by Meyer. If people left, fine. Anyone who stayed had accepted an astonishing premise ("God Is My Lab Partner") that made them likelier to invest.

Meyer pressed on, giving frequent cues that the nonsense he spouted was deep science. "Therefore, the electrical attraction force set up between unlike atoms q and q-prime is equivalent to the two shared negative-charged electrons, and for every action there is a what? An equal and opposite reaction. Isn't that right?"

The audience murmured, like high-school physics students faking comprehension.

Finally came the pitch. Meyer said the Cell would soon generate a cool $330 *trillion* in profits—he just had to work out a few bugs. He was selling right-to-do-business shares for $5,000 down, plus $45,000 to be paid off when the complete line of applications was ready. These shares allowed investors to sell auto, home, or industrial "retrofits" in their geographic area once they became available. To get on board, you had to sign a contract stating that you were "sophisticated in financial and business matters" and could afford the risk of losing your initial investment.

One obstacle to success was the familiar conspiracy specter: Meyer might be murdered at any moment. That day he told several stories about secret meetings with Pentagon and Patent Office "brass" and dangerous foreigners who were tripping him up or trying to steal his "prototype retrofits," which included the dune buggy and a jet.

Fortunately, Meyer's best friend, Jesus, made sure that evil forces didn't destroy him. He meant this literally. After the lecture, Susan and I went to dinner at a Spaghetti Garden in Columbus with Meyer, his crew, and a youngish married couple from Richmond, Virginia, who were thinking seriously about gulping the bait. As we settled in at a long table and raised mason-jar glasses full of Coke in a toast to the future, I asked Meyer how he protected himself from unseen enemies.

"You know what a guardian angel is?" he said.

The Richmond man cut in. "You mean like those gang members in New York?"

"No. I mean like that big mother over there. That big-chested fella." Meyer pointed across the room, but we only saw a waitress balancing a tray of beers. "Watch, I'll call him over." Waving his beefy hands like Doug Henning, he said, "Hbdldlbldd." According to Meyer, the big-chested fella scurried over and stood right beside our table, huffing and puffing like a Disney cartoon character.

Once, Meyer explained as our food arrived, he was in Egypt showing the Cell to "top officials in the government." Afterward, en route to the airport, the driver took a wrong turn. Meyer protested, but the driver said, in perfect English, "I only speak Arabic." Meyer peered out the back window and saw "a car full of the biggest, meanest, most hook-nosed Arabs you ever saw, armed to the teeth!" He looked toward the heavens and cried out, "Lord, unless you do something now, I'm a goner, and the technology you've showed me is, too."

The Lord responded. He caused the driver's burnoose to "spin around on his head," blinding him. Then he sent the bad guys' car hurtling off the road and "directed" Meyer's car to the airport.

I checked out the Richmond couple. According to my theory about the inverse power of Jesus physics, they should find this comforting. And so they did. They smiled serenely and nodded. Later in the meal, to be sociable, Susan confessed to the Richmond woman that she hadn't understood most of Stan's lecture. The woman looked at her patronizingly, lifted a jar of water, held it beside her head, jiggled it, and said, "Hey, it's as simple as this."

So, pie-chart-wise, was Meyer a deluded believer or just a con man? I think there was a little of both bouncing around inside his big body. In the years that followed he ran into serious problems. Angry investors sued him, and a judge ordered him to stop what he was doing. But he never did, and like Wilhelm Reich he came to a defiant end. In March 1998, he was coming out of a Grove City restaurant with his brother and some potential investors when he suffered a ruptured brain aneurysm and died on the spot. According to subsequent reports, his last act was to grasp his brother's shirt and weakly croak something along the lines of: "They finally did it! They . . . poisoned me."

∞

"Marc, could you get on the line? This guy has some questions about Steven Greer."

That was Tracy Tormé talking, producer of *Fire in the Sky,* a Hollywood feature film about the 1975 UFO-abduction case involving an Arizona man named Travis Walton. Marc Friedlander was a colleague who, with Tormé, had met Greer at a small UFO confab in Crestone, Colorado.

I could hear Marc in the background. "Oh, shit, you mean David Koresh?" Various getting-on-the-line clunks ensued, then Marc joined us on three-way.

"Now why do you say that?" Tracy laughed.

"Because he seemed to have these goofy followers. And he was kind of leading the way to this awakening, this Shirley MacLaine shit."

"Didn't he also say to you that every time he goes out you're guaranteed to see a UFO?"

"Yeah, especially when the Royal Order of CSETI Knights or whatever goes out."

"I usually find anytime anybody in Ufology says 'Here is the answer, here is what's happening,' they don't know shit," said Tormé. "I had never heard of this guy and I went to this sort of semiformal meeting in Crestone in November of 1993. Crestone is this

sort of mountain conferencing center, and maybe thirty or forty people were brought together by Tom Adams, who's a UFO researcher
from Paris, Texas. From the second Greer and his flunkies walked in
the room, he took over the entire thing. First thing he does is tell
about all the sightings he had just *driving* to Crestone. Said he'd seen
three or four UFOs, and at one point they maneuvered into the logo
of CSETI in the sky. Just for him."

He drew a breath. "There are certain guys who live in a world of
lies and can't separate their bullshit from reality. To me this guy has
such an ego that he's built up this following, this *thing.* I would divide
his followers into two groups. Some have to be aware that he's full
of shit, at least partially. Some would be shaken to the core of their
being to even have him challenged."

"Yeah. OK. That sounds right," said Marc.

As I absorbed these opinions, I figured they would require some
creative new labels (Full of Shit? Cultic Pretensions?), but overall the
analysis seemed sound. I didn't learn much more about Greer in Minnesota—though he did lead me on a remarkable sightings adventure—so after the weekend was over I started calling around looking
for answers, which was how I found Tormé. At first things settled
into an irksome ping-pong pattern. Some thought Greer was a nut, a
goof, sometimes an evil nut-goof, and they had nothing kind to say
about him. Others absolutely adored the man and saw no flaws at
all. To my surprise he'd attracted some notable followers. Among
those who had either joined, made donations, or attended a CSETI
meeting were the folk singer Burl Ives (who has since died) and his
wife, Dorothy; Horst Rechelbacher, founder of Aveda Corporation
(who bought a "lifetime gift membership" in CSETI for $10,300);
Marie "Bootsie" Galbraith, wife of Evan Galbraith, President Ronald
Reagan's ambassador to France; and the philanthropist Laurance
Rockefeller, who gave CSETI $20,000. Most of them declined to talk
to me about Greer, but Dorothy Ives was happy to shout his praises.

"The first time Burl met Steve," she said, "he looked at me and said, 'This man is *eminently* sane.'"

Maybe so, but I eventually hooked up with some disgruntled followers who told juicy tales. Greer's imperious ways, over time, turned many people off, including three individuals who worked for him on the road or at the home headquarters in Asheville: Janice Williams, who managed the CSETI office for a while, and another woman who wants to remain anonymous—call her Mrs. X—who had also worked for Greer, videotaping workshops and helping at the office. They helped me assemble a pie that came out like so:

> One slice of Sincerity.
> One large slice of Delusions of Grandeur.
> A smallish slice labeled Greedy.
> And a slightly bigger one, still skinny, labeled Cultic.

There was room left for one hefty slice that had to do with Greer's moral and ethical status, but I didn't know what to call it. Evil?

No, that seemed way too strong. I settled on Naughty. Then I topped the whole thing off with a generous dollop of Jerk.

This breakdown seemed fair, because the tattletales painted a picture of an egotistical fraternity president, the type of guy who believed mawkishly in the values he represented, but who didn't much care about his pledges except as dues-payers. Basically, Greer had decided he'd been anointed by fate to be the one who initiates contact. To that end, he spent a large amount of time, energy, and money (mostly other people's money) scurrying around playing the Hegelian role of World Historical Individual.

Granted, the tattlers *would* trash him, since they were disaffected, but fortunately they had taken the time to make photocopies that backed up almost everything they said. The lapsed duo told tales of behind-the-scenes tantrums, expensive globe-trotting to spread the word, and rampant chintziness. What Greer got out of CSETI was, of course, self-gratification and an ability to gallivant in style. A typical year included a couple dozen first-class jet trips in the United States and abroad. Usually these involved either fund raising or RMIT missions. In a representative one-month spree, Greer went on a vast circuit from Asheville to Los Angeles, Phoenix, New York, London, back to New York, and back to Asheville.

All of which is between Greer and his troops. Of more general interest was his declaration, recalled by Mrs. X, that he was something of a divine personage. According to her, Greer believed that he was fated "to be martyred for the cause—which he says is his destined mission to be the one who represents humanity when the ETs come." That sounds pretty wild, but it fits the pattern of a paranoid "contactee" personality. Greer told Mrs. X that he'd marshaled a psychic power known among paranormalists as "remote viewing"—that is, an ability to "see" distant events that are taking place simultaneously. And though he shied away from saying that he received direct mental feeds from outer space—which would make him undeniably a "contactee," a label he shunned—Mrs. X said that Greer used to have her transcribe his taped recollections of "lucid dreams" in which he communicated with a "female entity" from outer space who informed him that he was destined for greatness.

Greer hotly denied all of this when I asked him about it, but if true it helps explain certain grandiose themes in a 1993 CSETI white paper titled "Project Starlight Overview." This internal document, written by Greer, was an action plan for spreading the truth about extraterrestrials to a global power elite, but it read more like the journal of an overly imaginative egomaniac. Greer assigned numerical values to the "disinformation" threat posed by various hostile forces and exhaustively listed a grab bag of people who must be cultivated. The targets for the plan included the White House, Pope John Paul II, Bhoutros Bhoutros Ghali, the Dalai Lama, the Aga

Khan, Pat Robertson, Carl Sagan, Walter Cronkite, Michael Eisner, King Juan Carlos, C-Span's Brian Lamb, Robert Redford, Barbra Streisand, and, yes, Steven Spielberg.

∞

That was then. In the years since, Greer has continued with more of the same, always upping the volume of his claims, and continuing to anger his colleagues. In early 1997, Greer appeared on the Art Bell show to brag about a top-secret UFO meeting he was about to hold in Washington, one that would introduce reporters and officials to witnesses from inside the military who knew the truth. Bell introduced Greer by saying he had met with "senior CIA officials, Joint Chiefs of Staff, White House staff, senior members of Congress, and congressional committees," and so on. But during the interview, Greer trumped all that:

> **Greer:** I'll say this with some confidence, I'm quite sure that I'm the only UFO researcher in the world who has had a nearly three-hour meeting with a sitting and empowered director of Central Intelligence. And I have.
> **Bell:** On this subject?
> **Greer:** On this subject. Specifically for this subject, and I know that this is an extraordinary statement. I have the bonafide [sic] to back this up and someday it should all come out in a very interesting book and movie.

That's very ripe talk, but there may be some freaky reality behind part of it. Greer's big meeting in Washington didn't help his reputation among the other buffs—he was accused of swiping his document, "Best Available Evidence," from another UFO group—but as of 1998 he was still bragging about his extensive contacts in the government, finally naming the CIA official he met: James Woolsey, who ran the agency from 1993 to early 1995. Whether that happened or not may be unknowable, but it's not inconceivable that Greer enjoyed his official moment.

That's because President Bill Clinton may be something of a UFO buff himself. In his book, *Friends in High Places,* Webster Hubbell, the President's former assistant attorney general, wrote that Clinton was fascinated by UFOs and wanted to know if they really existed. Hubbell emphasized that Clinton was "dead serious. I . . . looked into both, but wasn't satisfied with the answers I was getting." Reporting on this little-noticed, oddball revelation, White House correspondent Sarah McLendon reported that Greer really did meet with Woolsey. Unfortunately, Greer was her only source.

All of which made me wonder: Could it be? Hubbell declined to discuss it. In a hurry-up phone conversation, Woolsey told me, "I *did* talk to somebody once, briefly, about UFOs, but I talk to a lot of people, and I don't remember who it was."

Could it have been Greer?

"That does not ring a bell."

Whatever took place, Greer's story will probably just keep getting stranger. He likes to say that he's living on the razor's edge with his daring defiance of the secret government, and he later announced on his Web site that he and his research director, a woman named Shari Adamiak, had been diagnosed with cancer.

Was this simply bad luck? No way. "Both have appeared, rather enigmatically, at the same time," Greer wrote, "a fact which seems like a rather strange coincidence."

Yikes. Perhaps the martyrdom is getting under way.

∞

If *The Steven Greer Story* is ever filmed, I hope the director includes the climactic scene from the skywatch in Sand Dunes State Forest, because it was special. After the initial thrills of the "crop-circle noises," the truth set in: we were going to sit out there all night, and it was cold. Greer seemed distracted, only half with us. My theory, strictly a guess, was that he was sulking about our lackluster team. Or it might have just been Elias, who sat on a blanket to my left, braying about things like a "suit" he'd invented that would somehow protect the wearer from the shifts in air pressure, temperature, and gravitational force experienced during an abduction.

Greer reviewed the "boarding party" details as our team fussed with sleeping bags and squeaked rusty lawn chairs into position. Each member recorded a brief message on the official team microcassette. That way, if we were all snatched up, whoever came along and found all our stuff would know whom to notify.

Greer kicked it off. "This is CSETI team leader Dr. Steven Greer, boarding party member number one. My wife is Emily. Her phone number is . . ."

When Elias's turn came, he was stumped. His wife, Lisa, was sitting next to him, fingering a piece of lapis lazuli jewelry that she planned to present to our alien guests. "My wife is here. I have no one I can notify," he said dolefully. Then he passed the shiny plastic lozenge to me. "This is Alex," I said, "boarding party member eleven. My wife is Susan. She decided not to come tonight, but she's staying at the Red Roof Inn—the, um, the one south of Minneapolis."

I should have added: "She's the smart one in our family."

Greer told everybody to choose a buddy, just like at camp. I exchanged a silent look of complicity with Bob, a sixtyish guy stretched out on a folding chaise longue. Like an all-business camp counselor, Greer said that if anyone found himself or herself overcome with terror in the event of a landing, he should go to his buddy—his "buddy for life"—and ask for an escort to the "safe place," a designated circle of grass a short distance away.

We began. Greer narrated a coherent thought sequence that

sounded like unedited Hallmark copy. "Send a thought of love to a loved one; now see whereby you are able to perceive these thoughts, and ask yourself, 'What is that awareness?'" He positioned flashlight-wavers in various spots around our circle; pulling duty with touching resolve, they silently and diligently high-beamed the universe. Fortunately, though chilly, it was a beautiful night. The stars were out, the sky was bright but partly overcast. At one point a high, ragged cloud dragged underneath a triangle of stars, briefly creating the illusion that the stars, not the clouds, were moving. Elias was fooled.

"There they are! There they are! Three UFOs, flying in formation!"

Nobody said anything. Curiously, Elias didn't recant so much as lose interest, telling Lisa that he just saw three craft "straight over us" and then dropping the subject. I took a break, duly notifying my buddy.

"Going to the bathroom in the safe place, Bob."

"Check."

After that, all was quiet for a while. Then the tones, which had faded in and out a few times, resumed, so Greer and Keller decided to mount a formal search-and-confirm operation. I tagged along, and the three of us crunched purposefully toward the woods, jiggling our flashlights. Greer had bragged that he was "part Cherokee," but part Tonka truck was more like it. Our crashings would have scared off anything that wasn't wearing moss. Surprisingly, though, the tones continued. And grew louder.

At the edge of the woods, before we ducked in to meet our destiny, Greer told Keller in an excited whisper that he wouldn't be surprised to see a UFO hovering in a clearing inside the copse. We marched in. Crunch, snap. After a few minutes of pinpointing and failed triangulation, we lucked out: suddenly the tone was directly overhead. Keller pointed his light. Sitting in the trees, looking down, was an easily identifiable object: a perched owl. And not just any owl, but an especially grumpy-looking one whose glare seem to say, "What the hell are you doing?" I turned to Greer to watch how he handled this particular CE-zero.

"Interesting," he said. "The tone was similar to a crop-circle sound, but it was aurally distinct enough to not quite match it." He turned to the expressionless Keller and said, "Well, that's what field-work is all about."

This is how perfection looks: scenes from Marshall Savage's plans for a utopian island colony.

6

Let Freedominium Ring!

Most people came to the United States to escape tyranny in their native lands.

With totalitarianism gaining the upper hand and internal revolution almost a certainty, has the time now come to start a new country, so that those who love life and liberty can escape the evils which the collectivists have created all around us?

—FROM *A NEW CONSTITUTION FOR A NEW COUNTRY,* BY MICHAEL OLIVER (1968)

"We don't want to fail at an initial stage because we were stupid enough to let some dictator smile at us," Brock d'Avignon said, sounding sort of beepy, like Wally Cox after a snort of helium. "We have to be inde*pen*dent."

Time and place: a cool summer evening in 1992, in the living room of a modest, cozy home in Orange County, California, the pulsing philosophical heart of American libertarianism. The speaker: Brock, the pulsing philosophical heart of what I like to call "Brockianism," a grab bag of libertarian ideas, futuristic enthusiasms, data, convictions, theories, beeps, and bluster. And the agenda? Exactly what Michael Oliver had in mind when he wrote his frantic manifesto in '68: starting a new country from scratch and living in it, as a way to escape the social turmoil and oppressive big-government presence of the contemporary United States.

A short, energetic thirty-eight-year-old polymath from Lancaster, California, Brock was "Presider" (his lingo for "leader") of an outfit called the New Island Creation Consortium, or NICCO. This was one of the early meetings for the group, which had assigned itself the towering goal of creating a fully independent nation-state by the year 2000. It would be housed on an artificial floating island, one that NICCO planned to create with bold new technologies.

But that was all in the misty future. At the moment Brock was explaining the various political problems that could thwart this vision. First and foremost were Smiling Dictators, bad men who say they'll be happy to cut a deal and let you create a country in their neighborhood, but who always renege when it comes time to start writing constitutions and hammering nails.

"All the attempts by libertarians to start new countries have failed when they involved setting one up that, on paper, was a protectorate of an existing sovereignty," Brock said, rubbing his pant legs as a grin lighted up his face, a friendly slice of paleness topped by boyish brown hair. "Operation Atlantis in the sixties got a promise of protection from Papa Doc Duvalier, who said he was interested in getting help with economic development in Haiti."

Here Brock was speaking of a dark moment in the surprisingly active history of modern micronation-attempting. Operation Atlantis was the brainchild of Werner Stiefel, a wealthy New York State businessman who wanted to create a Caribbean country modeled on the super-capitalist philosophy of the late Ayn Rand. In her 1957 novel, *Atlas Shrugged*, Rand wrote of an America that was sliding into the corrupt malaise of communism and collectivism. She gleefully depicted the country's most productive citizens—bankers, industrialists, inventors, transportation magnates—checking out, ditching the commies and whiners, and holing up at a secret mountain retreat in the Colorado Rockies. There they created a utopia, varioulsy referred to as Gulf's Gulch or Atlantis, which was based on the Randian principle that the greatest good flows from "men of the mind" acting in their own self-interest.

Inspired, Stiefel and a few young followers built a reinforced-concrete ship, the *Atlantis II,* and embarked from New York for the Bahamas in 1969. The Atlanteans' plan was to percolate patiently in international waters until they found a home for their country. Details vary as to when and why it all swirled down the drain— the history of nations that never existed is, by nature, sketchy—but Brock's version rang with just the right cautionary note. He said Duvalier told the Atlanteans they were welcome to a patch of "enterprise zone" on Tortuga Island, then changed his mind, at which point things got ugly fast.

"The ship was forced into a hurricane by Haitian gunboats," said Brock, savoring the clash-and-splash drama of it. "All hands were rescued, but the ship foundered and sank. The project was an eleven-million-dollar loss."

Brock's audience for this was six youngish and middle-aged guys who looked like members of a 12-Step group for male-pattern addiction to *Popular Science.* Three were engineers, one an analytical chemist, and three (including Brock) were amateur techno-buffs. They weren't an especially emotive bunch, and their reaction to his tale basically consisted of a joint "hmmph."

Brock's reaction? Undaunted, he cranked up another one.

This time it was the sad history of the Republic of Minerva, whose prime mover was a famous figure in the new-nation subculture: Michael Oliver, a Lithuanian who emigrated to the United States after World War II and settled in Nevada. Oliver prospered by selling real estate and old coins, nursing an understandably deep loathing for the Soviet system that hounded him from his native land. Domestic social static in the sixties convinced him that America's ship of state was heading for similarly pinkish waters. In reaction, he published *A New Constitution for a New Country* in 1968 and conceived of a fresh-start nation on the Minerva Reefs, a pair of tidal atolls 260 miles northeast of the Kingdom of Tonga in the South Pacific. In 1972 he hired an Australian dredging ship to dump enough sand on the reefs to make them inhabitable. Half a year and some $200,000 later, he had amassed enough "land" to poke a flag into. He called it the Republic of Minerva, proclaimed its independence, even minted coins decorated with the profile of the eponymous goddess. Unfortunately, Tonga's 350-pound king, Taufa'ahau Tupou IV, smacked his lips and moved quickly to swallow up the reclaimed island, sending out the royal marching band and a boatload of convicts to capture it in his name. The party planted a Tongan flag, played the Tongan national anthem, and left. Satisfied, the king ignored the place again. Wind and surf soon erased what man had wrought.

"And that was pretty much the end of that deal," Brock said.

It would be poignant to report that the guys responded to this tragic saga with a sniffle. But to them the debacle was just an example (and an amusing one at that) of mistakes they would *not* be foolish enough to repeat.

"So," said Howard Hinman, a bright, talkative computer consultant, "with our own island, we won't have to worry about getting land from someone who will just turn on us later!"

"Right," said Brock. "And to make money we'll build fish farms, or get art grants, or make floating world maps that can serve as fishing-boat marinas."

"The bottom line to remember is this," said Hinman, staring at me with eyes that were gleaming visionary beads. "This planet is mostly covered by water, so the oceans are the next frontier."

Most of the T's on this deal weren't quite crossed yet, of course— like how the NICCOnauts would corral the several billion dollars needed to get the job done—but Brock did have a name, site, and basic design picked out. He would call it the Freedominium of Merica. "Merica" was from the French word *mer,* "sea." "Freedominium" was his label for the system of "nongoverning" he would adopt, one that placed the right to "own and sell personal property" at the peak of man's fundamental liberties, and that forever kept evil, swollen governments at bay.

The spot he had in mind was in the Pacific Ocean, south of the equator at 135 degrees west longitude. According to data compiled by the Tropical Ocean Global Atmosphere Project—which Brock, a heroic squirreler of info, stored in one of his sixteen file cabinets— the weather there is balmy and calm year-round.

"It's Earth's weather eye," he said, almost cooing.

I had to admit, the place sounded fetching. When Brock described the island, his voice soared, and you could hear in his words the animating power of a dream.

"I imagine a city," he said, "built on a floating structure that can rotate 360 degrees with the help of current-catching blades mounted on the bottom. We would avoid having pilings and other features of the typical ocean-platform look. Instead this would be a vast, buoyant structure made up of segments linked together in concentric rings. The architecture on top would be free-form, complemented by waterfalls, palm trees, and lagoons."

Because the surface of the island would be subject to cracking in the sun—its surfaces would be formed using a hard but vulnerable concrete-like substance called "coral accrete"—Brock said it would need to be doused regularly to keep it moist. This, too, would be handled with aesthetic care.

"This will be a city of fountains," Brock said. "Like Italy on the high seas."

∞

I came across Brock in a roundabout way after attending a 1992 conservative political-action conference in Washington, D.C. There, alongside the rock-ribbed anti-abortionists and the red-cheeked College Republicans, an intense little libertarian man—that is, a man who favored the least amount of government short of anarchy—was selling some old free-nation texts, including Oliver's manifesto and a sparky 1979 book called *How to Start Your Own Country: How You Can Profit from the Coming Decline of the Nation State.* It was written by Erwin Strauss, a computer consultant and part-time fringe-world historian who, it turned out, lived in nearby Fairfax City, Virginia. I'd never heard of such ideas, so I phoned Strauss one day and arranged to drive out for a visit. He said fine, come on.

Strauss lived in a tidy red-brick apartment complex full of singles and young families who must have regarded him as an eccentric. He was a hulking, dark-haired MIT graduate and student of libertarianism who had converted much of his apartment's interior into shelving for his gargantuan supply of arcane materials on his many interests, including free nations.

As we roamed his shadowy shelves, hunting for folders, Strauss grunted and fussed and made it clear that he was no longer a free-nation player, though he was still fond of the topic, which he'd discovered at the Massachusetts Institute of Technology in the late sixties. "C.B.s were new then," he explained, "and I got interested in the idea of taking gambling bets from my own offshore ship, under a flag of convenience, so I researched it to see what had been done."

By the time I met him, Strauss was lukewarm on free nations, though he still had a plan to set himself up in a well-equipped old bus—just to get away from it all. His exhaustive knowledge of the subject led him to the bleak realization that new countries, if they didn't fail simply through their founders' incompetence or silliness, were fatally vulnerable to attack from established nations, à la Brock's sad historical examples.

This put serious new-country builders in a geophilosophical hard place. If a country was too inconsequential it was, by definition, a joke. (One typical example: New Atlantis, founded in 1964 by Ernest Hemingway's eccentric younger brother, Leicester, on an 8-by-30-

foot platform off the west coast of Jamaica. He issued stamps, claimed "de facto" recognition from the "prestigious International Court of the United Nations"—a body that didn't exist—and was generally ignored until he called it quits.) Conversely, if a country did amount to something, dictators would gobble it up.

Mulling all this, Strauss decided that tiny nations would never stand a chance unless they were heavily armed, and a few popguns and cannons wouldn't cut it. They would need to try the strategy followed by the Duchy of Grand Fenwick, the wee nation in *The Mouse That Roared* that held the United States at bay by threatening to use a weapon of mass destruction.

Strauss went pretty far with this, flatly writing that having a nuke was essential to any start-up country. He explained the principles of do-it-yourself A-bombs in a 1980 book, *Basement Nukes*. In *How to Start,* he explored—with full Kissingerian pomp—the morality of small, new countries deploying "atomic and thermonuclear explosives, radioactive dust, germ warfare, and poison gases."

"[S]ome new-country organizers will recoil at the thought of inflicting large numbers of casualties," he philosophized. "This is a personal decision. But the fact is that war . . . lies at the heart of statecraft, and he who has no stomach for it needs to look for another line of work."

Strauss loaned me a stack of materials, cautioning that the action in free-nation building was stone-cold over—"The last real boom was the sixties and seventies, there was a sense then that anything could be done"—but I decided to verify that for myself. This was in the early nineties, before the era of easy access to the Internet; back then, locating fringe people was a slow process of scanning classified ads in magazines, posting messages on computer bulletin boards, and making many, many fruitless phone calls. Eventually, after weeks of wilting conversations, I heard about Brock, called him, and introduced myself.

"Greetings to ya'," he said.

Heart thumping, I told him I'd heard he was launching a new-nation project. Deep breath. Was he?

"Yep," he said, gliding into a long, pauseless boast about what he and his "team" had accomplished already. "We plan to build an island of coral, using the coral 'accrete' process. We can build an island the size of Kansas. We'll do fish-farming. We have a talent pool of thirty experts approaching this challenge, and we've achieved a 98-degree-strong structure, which means that it can handle almost anything the ocean can throw at it. The design is a double-suspension mathematics theorem called the pizzahedron mathemat. This summer we're making a proposal to a tourist submarine company that has need for a floating passenger terminal. We're also proposing doing a human-dolphin embassy. We're also planning on dealing with one or two refugee populations in the next five years as part of our PAYE plan—"

Pay?

"That stands for percentage-as-you-earn financing of capitalist refugee-resettlement," Brock explained.

Where did things stand with these projects?

"Wailll," he said. "We're pretty embryonic on the business end."

Meaning what?

"We don't have a whooole lot of nickels to rub together right now."

∞

I'll admit it right up front: I became a Brock fan from the moment I met him, which happened at a time when a few years of random browsing in the world of contemporary utopian futurism had left me bored and disappointed.

In my twenties, I'd been fascinated by the various utopian experiments that popped up in nineteenth-century America—like Fruitlands, the Transcendentalist commune founded in the 1840s by Bronson Alcott, Louisa May Alcott's dad, whose members expressed their idealism by subsisting on roots and bread and taking only cold-water baths—and by the gritty Italian futurists, who howled that anyone who denied the superiority of the machine over pitiful human flesh was a weepy sap.

What I wanted (and what Brock delivered, at least in his verbal cascades) was a futurism that combined these themes: the anything-is-possible communal urge along with old-style futurism's nifty visions, spiffy cars, pastel tints, and infinite belief in a world where life would be sleeker, faster, more sane, more just, more rewarding, and more fun. What I found was that this style of futurism had died.

Actually, to be more precise, it had been rubbed out. My fullest exposure to the crime scene occurred in 1989, at the Sixth General Assembly of the World Future Society in Washington.

Perched on the eve of the final decade of the twentieth century, the WFS gathering should have been as diverting as a miniature World's Fair, and its title certainly sounded ambitious: "Future View, the 1990s and Beyond." But in reality, the week consisted almost entirely of dull gusts about "possible reshaped societal outcomes" and "useful new meta-trend models." The WFS was founded in 1968—in Erwin Strauss's mind, the golden age of forward think-ing—but somewhere along the way it chickened out and began to shrink back from the idea that futurism should be about anything as audacious as imagining the future. *What Futurists Believe,* a WFS book published in '89, even denied that this was what futurists were sup-posed to do.

"The notion that futurists are mainly concerned with predicting the future," it harrumphed, "is one of the persistent myths that futur-ists have to live with."

Needless to say, it was not always so. In the 1930s, to cite another exciting time, futurism meant using beguiling images and words to make hopeful prognostications about tomorrow. A lot of these were wrong or stupid, but so what? They were also entertaining and inspiring, and the old-style futurists scored many hits along the way. With boldness and panache, the great 1939 New York World's Fair dared to imagine streamlined change on the grandest of scales. It featured a Town of Tomorrow, a spiffy burg called Democracity, and Norman Bel Geddes's Futurama exhibit, which placed viewers in moving chairs that whizzed them around above a three-dimensional map of the United States, interconnected with a new system of superhighways. The 1964 New York World's Fair featured such wonders as the Amphicar ("the car that swims"), the Runabout (a three-wheeled pod vehicle whose hood came to a point), and an appliance called the Dish Maker that ground up dirty plastic dishes and reformed them into new, clean tableware.

Granted, many of these displays were ridiculous—the 1939 fair featured a seven-foot-tall robot named Elektro and his dog, Sparko— and many were nothing more than corporate "visions" of consumer goods we ought to have. Indeed, one reason that futurism is winded as a "thoughtstyle" may be that we're now too sophisticated and canny to fall for it. And yet, as David Gelernter argued in his book *1939: The Lost World of the Fair,* our modern cynicism comes with a cost. To some extent it has taken away our ability to imagine a better world. The people who designed the fair, he wrote, shared a fundamental conviction that the public would find utopian prophecies to be worth a look, simply because they still believed in—and enjoyed—the quest for perfection.

"*Fundamental convictions, powerful prophetic messages* are words that came naturally to the New York World's Fair," he wrote. "It was the mountaintop: Fairgoers ascended and looked out at the promised land."

The World Future Society gathering was more like ascending the mountaintop and looking out at a carpet-and-tile showroom. The week-long "Future View" program broke down into dozens of null-thrill panel discussions under the headings Sociosphere, Biosphere, Technosphere, Econosphere, Politisphere, Futuresphere, and 21st Century Studies. As I stood in the frigidly air-conditioned lobby of the Sheraton Washington hotel, reading the program, I felt stymied—*nothing* looked interesting. I scanned the lobby and halls. Zipping to and fro were swarms of faceless academics, business people, and obscure government functionaries from all over the world. Playing a hunch, I decided to follow the first strange-looking person I saw. Before long a promising specimen shambled into view, a tall, balding man with a gray nimbus of mad-scientist hair. I tailed him.

This worked out . . . somewhat. He led me to a panel on "Future-tecture Communities" that was the only invigorating session I attended all week. Tellingly, though, it was a museum piece. The speaker, Roy E. Mason, was "architecture contributing editor for *The Futurist* magazine," and the session was devoted to homes of tomorrow—all of them conceived years and years before. Even so, he applied infectious energy to the task of showing off pod-shaped fiberglass houses that looked like giant larvae, an inflatable home that looked like a monstrous blister, a giant-crater municipality, and (this was more like it!) cities on the sea.

After that I focused on sessions that treated the convention's dominant theme: utopian political theory about human governance. In those days, with the cold war starting to thaw, many WFS-style futurists were pushing for an updated, touchy-feely version of that old, hopeless concept born during the world wars: One-World Government.

The marquee session was a roundtable on "New Thinking for a Globally Interdependent World," a packed four-hour yabberthon that, revealingly, dissolved into anarchy. I could tell we were heading for trouble early on, when Reinhart Ruge, president of the World Constitution and Parliament Association (not to be confused with the Preparatory Committee for the World Constituent Assembly, also present that week), began musing on the ethics of meat-eating as it related to global deforestation and got shouted down by a restless crank.

"If we kill animals we have to kill trees," he droned. "It becomes a vicious cycle all around. Oh, I wish it was possible that we could stop this cycle somehow—"

"MOSQUITOES!" the heckler yelled.

"Pardon?"

"Mosquitoes. We *have* to kill them."

The real collapse started somewhere during hour six or eight, when Barbara Marx Hubbard, an elderly, New Agey futurist who was helping emcee the panel, detected boredom in the crowd and invited audience members to come up and have their say. Big mistake. A burly man from Vermont immediately hustled to the mike and decried the "paradigm" that broke these meetings down into wise "speakers" and passive "listeners."

"It's ridiculous that after twenty years of this society we're still lined up in rows facing authorities behind a microphone!" he yelled. The audience roared, and many other people came up to rant in turn.

Among the highlights:

A sage, blinking professor from South Korea stood and explained that when "we in the West" speak about "new" we forget that what is "new" to us may be "quite ancient to thinkers in the East."

A woman, her eyes narrowing into intense philosophical slits, said, "I think our discussion is moving toward a meta-level."

A young, beard-faced guy said earnestly, "Hey, people? We are *still* caught up in existing paradigms here."

Bowing to crowd reaction, Hubbard promised that at that night's session on Supra-Sexuality, she would, instead of running the show from start to finish, let the audience take over and create the mechanics of a new structure for future conferences on newness in the future. More roars.

I went to that session, too. She ran the show from start to finish.

∞

You can see why I was drawn to Brock. No, I didn't believe he would single-handedly rehabilitate wing-finned futurism. In fact, I had a strong suspicion right from the start that he wouldn't accomplish much of anything. What interested me was the quest. Brock, full of passion and drive, was charging toward the ocean, waving a flapping battle flag that said "Utopia or Bust." Yeah, he could be a blowhard, too, and I knew he might never wiggle his toes in Liberty's brine, but at least he was going for it.

At the Friday night NICCO meeting in Irvine, I sat and listened quietly as the group chugged forward on the vapor of Brock's combustible ideas. The NICCOnauts were a fun bunch—smart, friendly, idealistic—but it was hard to visualize them striding purposefully across foamy, pitching decks. Brock had been raised in California and as a teenager was a member of the U.S. Naval Sea Cadet Corps, but he didn't look like he'd been near the beach since then—in late summer he was white as a fish belly. The other guys looked gung-ho yet somewhat shaky on the physical-fitness front, like they had spent a lot more time at Radio Shack or the Comic Dungeon than the gym. Still, if I concentrated hard enough, I could form mental pictures of a few of them barking orders, squirting around in outboard skiffs, diving for conch, lassoing dolphins. Claudio Scalisi, a civil engineer, and Rock Wylie, a salesman and technobuff, looked physically fit and squint-eyed capable, as did Etsuro Nagahisa, a structural engineer from Japan.

Alarmingly, Etsuro also looked rather wild. He wore a mustache and samurai mutton-chops that stopped at his chin, and he seemed to have dangerous ideas about performing renegade aviation stunts as a "hobby." During a break between Brock perorations, he told me in his thick Japanese accent that he was building a small plane, a single-engine Smyth Sidewinder, named *Iron Rod,* that he intended to fly around the world and into Japan as a libertarian protest against state restrictions on homemade aircraft.

"I will be a hero," he declared, "the Charles Lindbergh of Japan."

Most of the guys were excited about starting their new country, although the meeting revealed a sliding scale of belief in its feasibility. Brock and Howard bounced around at the super-psyched end; Claudio, a friendly, dark-haired man with a stern side, served as the voice of skepticism and moderation. The others landed somewhere in between. Claudio's role was necessary, because both Brock and Howard, in their enthusiasm for the project's conceptual splendor, tended to get carried away. Like a gruff sheep dog, he tensely mumble-growled them back into line when they went too far.

Case in point, Brock and Howard's beepy disquisition on one of their favorite topics, asteroid mining. Asteroids are known to contain billions of dollars in precious metals, and science-fiction writers have long pondered ways to exploit this resource. In one imagined sequence, spaceships would tractor small asteroids to refineries orbiting Earth, from which processed metal would be sent down to splash-land in the sea, in a form, such as hollow tubes, that floats. Busy-bee ocean-based entrepreneurs would haul the metal to port. Howard and Brock figured NICCO could serve as a bustling Marseilles for 'roid-mining's merchant marine.

"There is going to be major money in asteroid mining," Howard said. "Like, *major.*"

"I think . . . at the beginning," Claudio said, stiff-jawed, eyeing my notebook as I scribbled away, "that . . . um . . . it's gonna start out smaller, with commercial sea platforms."

Claudio was referring to NICCO's "phase one" idea for actually making money to support itself: using existing and new technologies to devise economical sea structures for use by oil companies, manufacturers desiring cheap offshore surfaces where they could build plants, residential developers, and submarine tourism outfits.

The NICCOnauts were serious about this and had even tried to attract seed money, but nothing was panning out. Etsuro had traveled to Japan to talk to representatives of Mitsui Zosen, which uses coral accrete for underwater fish-farm structures. His trip was designed as a skull-tapper, a way to sound out what real-life Japanese bigshots thought of NICCO's plan in its broad outline. The Etsuro Report, which he delivered at the meeting, underscored one strength the NICCO boys would need in abundance in the years ahead: a good sense of humor about themselves. Etsuro said things went very slowly because, to protect NICCO's intellectual property, he couldn't provide any technical details about the idea, only the generalities.

What did the big boys think of the generalities?

Not much. "They say to them the concept is bee-zuh," Etsuro said.

"It's what?" someone asked.

"Bee-zuh."

"What?"

"I think," Brock suggested, "that's he's saying 'berserk.'"

"Oh, berserk!" a couple of guys said at once. "Ha ha ha ha ha ha!"

∞

Actually, the concept wasn't all that bee-zuh. Claudio showed me a model of the structure that would make it possible—the so-called "pizzahedron mathemat," a geometric design jointly developed about eight years before by him, Brock, and NICCOnaut Ron Wroblewski. As they explained it, a pizzahedron was a floating platform made up of building blocks. These blocks could be made in any size or shape—imagine one that is, say, forty feet long and wedge-shaped, looking like a jumbo version of the game pieces used in "Trivial Pursuit." Each wedge would consist of a steel framework covered with a thick, waterproof shell of coral accrete. The interior of each wedge would remain hollow except for the structural supports, thus making it buoyant. The island would be composed of these individual slices, fitted together to make a circular platform. Another such platform, or two, or three, or more, could be stacked on top of and interlocked with the first. (In Brock's lingo, two pizzas stacked and locked together form a "mathemat.") To cover more surface area, this basic structure would be expanded outward in concentric additions.

In theory. In fact, the only part of this concept that had been field-tested yet was the basics of the coral-accrete technique, which was developed back in 1973 by Wolf H. Hilbertz, a professor of architecture at the University of Texas at Austin. Coral accrete involves running electrical current through metal dunked in sea water, which causes minerals in the water (calcium carbonate and magnesium hydrate) to affix to the metal. Over time this builds up a coating that, according to some tests, has a compression strength comparable to that of concrete.

But could NICCO simply start using Hilbertz's process for commercial purposes? Not a problem, said Brock. He said Hilbertz experimented with the process for several years before moving on to other projects; he had given it to the world, gratis, for anyone's use, like the Smiley Face.

He was wrong about that. I tracked down a business partner of Hilbertz's—Bill Wilson, an environmental planner in Texas—who said Hilbertz hadn't donated anything to anybody. Wilson was president of Marine Resources, a company devoted to commercial and scientific applications of the technology. It was involved in projects that used accrete for pier restoration, artificial reef formation, and underwater structures for fish farming, pollution control, and habitat development.

"We certainly encourage people to be creative," Wilson said, "but we have encountered a few people who are bent on doing their own things. The process is patented, and our applications are very thorough." Wilson hadn't heard of NICCO's plans, but said the group would have to make suitable arrangements with Marine Resources before proceeding.

I talked to Wilson after my NICCO visit. When I reported his warnings to Brock, he ran the bad news through his mind and squeezed out this conclusion: "That's great! I've said all along that I'd be glad to pay Hilbertz a royalty fee."

As for the larger goal of creating an artificial offshore island, the NICCOnauts were by no means alone in thinking about it. In fact, hundreds of "AOIs" exist all over the world, but only for industrial or macroengineering purposes. Ernst G. Frankel, a professor of ocean systems at MIT, told me that no city has made greater use of them than Tokyo, where AOIs make sense because the steep cost of land gives corporations and governments an incentive to build. Since 1970 the city had quadrupled the area of its waterfront with fake land masses.

Frankel was not a student of the new-nation subculture, but he knew a lot about futuristic plans for marvelous sea-based population centers. Probably the best known of these was one developed in the seventies (but never built) by England's Pilkington Glass Company for Sea City, a glass-domed concrete island perched on coastal shoals. More recently, Frank Davidson, director of MIT's Macroengineering Research Group, proposed Liberty Island, a fanciful structure two hundred miles out in the Atlantic that would be linked to America and Europe by a "multibed tunnel." Frankel also drew up a plan for a Gaza Peace Island, an industrial port facility off Israel's coast that could serve as an Arab enclave and help reduce tensions in Israel. Hilbertz and Wilson, with the designer Newton Fallis, devised a plan for a 50,000-person sea city that they called Ecopolis, which sounded a lot like what NICCO had in mind: "a marine, multilevel series of accrete concourses" protected from storms and hurricanes by "accreted barrier reefs covered with mangrove and coconut trees." In the early nineties, Japan's Shimizu Corporation produced plans for a city the size of Tokyo, some sixty miles out in the Pacific. Shimizu's blueprints called for construction of a circular, 140-foot-high wall rising from the ocean floor to a rim high above the waves. Water inside the wall would be expelled, forming a dry inner surface that could be landfilled.

Apparently, though, this was just another exercise. "It's feasible technically, but nothing is in the works," said Davidson, citing the gargantuan costs. "I guess they published the plans as a publicity stunt, but it could be done." In his opinion, AOIs would only happen when the market dictated that they were worth the trouble and cost. And if that happened, governments and corporations would certainly lead the way—not private citizens.

For Brock, obviously, "corporations" and "governments" weren't words he wanted to hear. He wanted an island on his terms, not as a consumer good.

Sadly, though, unlike Michael Oliver and Werner Stiefel, he was penniless, so his only chance was to strike it rich. That seemed very unlikely. As I gathered when I got to know him better, Brock didn't have an identifiable profession—he majored in communications in college—but he did have big, big ideas. Two typical examples of his get-rich-quick schemes: (1) he published a newsletter called *Bonanza Size Ranches Unlimited* that listed hot, huge properties for sale for which he was not the assigned broker; and (2) he had a plan, which I never understood even after multiple explanations, to sell underpriced "futures" for rights to mine asteroids that he also did not own.

These ideas netted him a grand total of $0 in 1992, and when I first visited him he was living with his dad in a motor home. After my visit I broke down and pressed him on the financial realities. How did he keep going?

"Right now I'm making ends meet by managing a pizza restaurant in Temecula," he admitted.

I instantly felt bad for asking.

"No shame in that. Many great projects have started small."

"Yyyyyep," he said with a lilt.

∞

Big project on Saturday with the NICCOnauts: a road trip with Brock, Etsuro, Claudio, and Claudio's girlfriend, Teresa. We met early at Claudio's place in Irvine, site of the Friday night meeting. When I showed up, Claudio and Teresa were disposing of a couple of McDonald's breakfasts; between swallows she made crabby comments about spending the day driving around with Brock, whom she didn't especially like.

Brock ignored the jabs. Clad in shorts and a casual, buff-colored shirt, he was busy buzzing around, giving orders in military jargon.

"What's our E.T.D.?" he asked Claudio. "Let's do it to it," he added with glee as we piled into my rental car.

The trip started badly. Etsuro seemed slightly off his feed; he didn't speak unless spoken to, and then only in short bursts. Claudio was his same quiet, all-business self. Teresa was a grump most of the day, alternately napping and waking up to snipe at Brock about this or that. Brock chattered on merrily through it all, gamely leaning into her withering gusts of negativism with insights, theories, regional history, and half-hour lectures on anything I asked about and many things I didn't.

Significantly, we didn't go anywhere near water—Brock had bent the truth when he told me "we have achieved" a coral-accrete structure. I (stupidly) took that to mean NICCO had constructed experimental coral-accrete platforms that were bobbing around at a pier somewhere. Nope. All they had "achieved" were sketches and Claudio's tiny model.

Our itinerary, therefore, carried us not west to the ocean but on a painfully symbolic trek north into the desert around Lancaster and Palmdale, where we spent hours and hours driving long distances between destinations that weren't really destinations. Though there was nothing to see, Brock was determined to keep me busy "reporting," so he set up a useless-but-fun excursion to a sprawling power-generating windmill farm near the Mojave Desert town of Tehachapi. (Windmills? Yes: Brock wanted to use them to power the ongoing coral-accrete process once NICCO hit the ocean. Claudio favored solar panels.) That day, we also drove past a road leading to Edwards Air Force Base, stopped at a roadside exhibit of an out-of-service spy plane built by the famed Lockheed "Skunk Works," and drove into Palmdale to say hello to Steve Cervantes, NICCO's "merchant banker."

As we shoved off that morning from Irvine, spinning past Orange County's seemingly endless supply of half-mile-long, overly land-scaped blocks, I asked Brock why this area had given rise to so much liberty-minded dissatisfaction with the existing order. Orange County has long been famous as a breeding ground for extreme right-wing politicians. Conservative Congressmen William E. Dannemyer, Robert Dornan, and Dana Rohrabacher all hailed from here, as did several California state legislators who were part of a group collectively known as the Cave Men.

Brock came out of the same tradition as these guys. As a lad, he joined William F. Buckley's Young Americans for Freedom. But somewhere along the way he outgrew all that, deciding it was foolish to "even play the game." This has been the other persistent theme in Orange County politics: a desire not to control the system, but to dismantle it or escape it. On this topic Brock was a virtual Chatty Kathy, delivering a complete, off-the-cuff summary of Orange County political history.

"It all started early in this century when a man named R. C. Hoiles was approached by a number of businessmen who asked him to write an editorial on what he thought a 'fair tax' was," Brock said. "Wailll, he couldn't." Hoiles concluded that all taxes were immoral and unfair, so in 1912 he founded the *Orange County Register,* an "anarcho-capitalist libertarian newspaper" that became the most important libertarian organ in the country.

Brock said he caught freedom's bug while delivering the *Register* as a thirteen-year-old. "At the time," he said, "I was living in El Modena, an area that back then was full of illegal Mexican immigrants. Wail, I noticed I was able to triple my route in that neighborhood because the *Register* came out in favor of open borders and for the elimination of the government's border-patrol service. So that was a verrrry interesting example of the power of libertarian ideas."

Since that defining cub-libertarian moment Brock had more than earned his Eagle rank, with a life of club-joining and steady ingestion of essential texts. These ranged from obvious, popular reads like *Atlas Shrugged* to hard-core awakeness-snuffers like *Human Action,* a nine-hundred-pager by Ludwig von Mises, the twentieth-century Austrian-school economist who decried socialism and celebrated the principles of an unfettered free market.

Brock was quite serious about his disgust with government and his total trust of the marketplace as the final arbiter of good. Later, I asked him to send me a digestible book or tract that had directly influenced his desire to start a country. He mailed *FREELAND,* a 1983 screed by a California libertarian named L. K. Samuels, whose work grew out of a series of yearly conferences held on the new-nation idea in the early eighties. (Brock first heard about coral accrete at a Freeland gathering, where a pair of young libertarians had set up a demo booth, hailing it as a potential miracle spackle for free-nation founders.) Samuels took a hard line. He thundered that historians were fools to blame the collapse of great civilizations on anything but government: "[T]o the libertarian, it is the inner working of government which has victimized every major civilization in recorded history. It is this mistake—failing to recognize government as a slowly ticking doomsday bomb—that has condemned mankind to the inevitable crash of their civilization and the rise of tyrannical overlords."

Brock never rumbled and roared like that, though. He was more the calm, endless-monologue type, and he could discuss an amazing range of subjects. Give him a nod, and he would lecture on anything from Revolutionary War–era "naval privateering" to the "down side" of asteroids, that of course being the possibility that one could wallop Earth at any time, killing millions of people and perhaps triggering nuclear winter.

Shifting in the front seat and smiling, Brock explained that in 1989 two asteroids, "shaped like potatoes, a mile-and-a-half in diameter each, real civilization-busters," came within half a million miles of Earth, "the closest call in fifty years." He brooded about this and decided that the Defense Department wasn't doing enough to address the question of what, if anything, could be done to stop a 'roid on an obvious collision course with Earth. This has since become a hot topic in Hollywood and in real life, giving rise to furious debate among scientists about whether, as Edward Teller has suggested, nuclear warheads should be used to deflect the objects.

Brock was certainly ahead of the curve with his awareness of the issue, but in his mind he was more than a concerned citizen. He was a prime mover who influenced national policy. That's because, soon after the near miss, he sent Admiral William J. Crowe, Jr., then chairman of the Joint Chiefs of Staff, a blistering letter titled "A Demand for Earth Defense" that told the Defense Department to get off its ass and do something.

"And," he said, capping the twenty-minute story, "I *don't* think those guys were used to being dressed down like a bunch of shave-tail lieutenants."

"Hold it," I said. "Are you telling me it was your letter that got the Joint Chiefs of Staff to take action?"

"Wail, that appears to be the case." And that was the essential Brock: he could imagine his printed beep rocking the halls of the Pentagon.

A tragic flaw? Maybe, but to my mind it gave the little man a lovably heroic stature.

One surprising detail came out as we cruised past mile after mile of scruffy desert en route to the wind farm. I asked about religion, assuming that everybody on the good ship NICCO was a confirmed techno-atheist.

Not so. Brock, Etsuro, and Claudio were all members of the Church of Jesus Christ of Latter-day Saints. (Teresa, who was snoozing, was a lapsed or "Jack" Mormon.) The faith, which sprang from the fertile mind of a nineteenth-century New York State farmboy named Joseph Smith, is a mutation of conventional Christianity that nonetheless shares many of its spicier beliefs—including an ardent millennial awareness, and a sense that the faithful should prepare for what may be a rough period of Tribulation. Wondering if there was a hidden agenda here—were the NICCOnauts planning to float in isolation somewhere until the apocalypse ended?—I asked if Mormonism was an important theme in the NICCO plan.

Brock said no, pointing out that most NICCOnauts were not Mormons. All the same, the faith did play a networking role in NICCO's early days. Brock and Claudio both attended Brigham Young University, and Brock met Etsuro at the Santa Ana church ward for Mormon singles. Brock did think it was "neat" that NICCO might start a "New Zion"—that is, a holy city—in the Pacific, but assured me NICCO was secular.

With that, we analyzed the nuts and bolts of how Freedominium would turn out. Brock figured the optimum size would be 50,000 people max, formed into a loose confederation of individuals, each of whom could set his own agenda without any guff from Big Brother. The governing document remained to be written, but it would be influenced by *Drafting a Constitution for ORBIS,* a compact for a hypothetical space colony whose author, Spencer H. Mac-Callum, laid out a system founded on mutually supportive, profit-oriented, privately based provision of what we commonly think of as public services.

The result read like a lease agreement. *Drafting* described relations between Orbis's guiding corporate entity—Orbital Communities, Inc., or "O"—and Joe Doakes ("J"), a citizen. Pity the sixth-grade citizen of Orbis who might have to memorize this constitution for the school patriotism pageant someday: "Now therefore 'O,' for the consideration set forth below, does convey to 'J,' his heirs and assigns, until such time as terminated by any of the conditions of this lease . . . equal access with all other residents to the common areas and facilities of Orbis. . . ."

What about the big issue—defense? Brock said the debate on that was hot. Some theorists believed, à la Strauss, that apocalyptic firepower would be necessary. Brock said he favored a calmer approach. He was starting to explain what it was when something apocalyptic occurred in the car: Teresa snorted and *zzzrt*'ed awake.

"Brock," she asked, rubbing her eyes, "are you talking about starting your own country on an island?"

Whoa. Apparently Claudio hadn't gotten around to telling his love-lady that their future together might require deck shoes instead of fuzzy slippers. I checked her out in the rear-view mirror. She looked miffed. Her question caught Brock right between the eyes, prompting the shortest answer I ever heard him give.

"Waillll . . . yes."

Claudio swooped in—mumbling, soothing: "Actually that's just something that's possible to look at down the road." Etsuro kept his mouth shut.

Then, Teresa: "You can't do that! It wouldn't work!"

I clutched the wheel and seethed. *Go, Brock, go!* I thought, praying for him to open a can of whip-ass on behalf of dreamers everywhere. And so he did, sort of, hitting Teresa with a wave of precise refutation, analysis, and technical woof that so awed, intimidated, or bored her that she went back to sleep.

Crisis past, we drove into Lancaster, another sand-blown town, and met up with Bud Pickle, a big, boisterous guy who worked at the wind farm. We split into two vehicles and drove out of town for a final bounce over corrugated dirt roads. In the distance, hundreds of tower-mounted propeller turbines whirred and gleamed in the late-afternoon sun.

Etsuro rode with me, and I asked how he became a Mormon. He said he was converted at age sixteen in the classic manner, by a pamphlet-wielding Mormon missionary who cornered him outside his high school.

Missionary nostalgia got him thinking about my spiritual status. "Have *you* admitted Jesus Christ into your life as Lord and Savior?" he asked, looking very serious.

"Ummm, no. I'm still working all that out." He frowned, genuinely concerned that I was damning myself.

As I learned shortly, Etsuro was very serious about his beliefs, and for him, NICCO did have millennial meaning. He had worked out a complicated personal eschatology, combining Mormonism with his own unique prophetic ideas, that foresaw the Second Coming happening soon, possibly in 2025. He didn't think the usual Mormon survival preparations—a couple of years' worth of food in the basement—would be good enough. He figured Freedominium, if it ever got built, was the place to be.

"Mmm," I said generically, as we slowed to a stop at the wind farm's operating station. With nothing to add, I groped for a different topic.

"I've never heard the name Nagahisa before. What's the equivalent in English?"

"My name in Japanese," he said proudly, "means 'Eon.'"

We parked and got out. Brock was springing around excitedly in the shadow of a windmill, but everybody else looked bored. Deep down, I knew that Teresa's pessimism might be correct: the idealistic fella was probably deluded. But he was a happy dreamer—his take on the future brought him great pleasure. Could anything be wrong with that?

On Sunday, Brock and I tootled around some more in Irvine and then said our good-byes. He gave me his résumé, eight single-spaced pages of madcap schemes:

> ORION TRANSPORT, Placentia CA 1973–1974
> Invented wheel-chair locks, back-of-van air conditioning, & "as-the-crow-flies" charging system to merge taxi/bus/charter services occurring simultaneously. Researched and wrote venture capital proposal resulting in $3-million tendered offer from the MANUFACTURERS BANK OF BEVERLY HILLS to the first free-market van service for "shut-ins."

I snapped a picture of Brock standing beside the tailpipe of his dad's motor home and buckled up, wondering if he would ever even gain the Freedominium of his own bachelor pad. By now I knew how to fight off this despair: ask him something.

"Brock, you're going to need women, the can-do types who populate Ayn Rand novels. Where will you get them?"

"Wail, that's an interesting question," he said. "Unfortunately, in the United States, libertarian men outnumber libertarian women by about seven to one. Interestingly, that isn't the case in Europe. . . ."

He was still talking as I drove off.

∞

After I went home I wrote about Freedominium for a magazine . . . somewhat sarcastically . . . a treacherous act that opened a temporary rift with the NICCO men. Brock told me on the phone that he felt betrayed reading that he "beeped," and none of the 'Nauts appreciated my implication that they weren't getting anything done.

"But you do beep, and you guys aren't getting anything done," I said. "So what? I'm skinny. The important thing is to figure out how to improve on your deficiencies. Have you talked to Hilbertz's people yet about those patents?"

"Waill, I'd certainly be willing to discuss joint partnerships that could—"

"There's no partnership! *They* have the patents. You can't do anything to make money off them unless they give or sell permission. If you do, they'll sue."

I didn't really know that, but more to the point . . . why was I lecturing Brock?

I guess I'd gotten involved. Like a pushy older brother, I was worried me that he was thirty-eight, unmarried, and without serious prospects of a job or a love life, unless you counted the "Mormon singles" events.

Moreover, not long after I returned, I heard about a man with Brockian ideas who sounded much more capable than the original. His name was Marshall T. Savage, and he had recently published a book called *The Millennial Project: Colonizing the Galaxy—In Eight Easy Steps.* Judging by the confident wording of an ad I saw for the book, he was Super Brock, an impression that was bolstered when I phoned his office in Rifle, Colorado. Instead of getting him, I got an assistant.

Brock never had an assistant.

"What's this project trying to do?" I asked warily.

"Just read the book, man!" a young guy shouted. "It's all explained in there. Marshall is really, really, really, really brilliant."

The book arrived a few days later, and in one sense it was comforting. A self-published effort, it contained a picture of Savage that revealed him to be a big, bearded guy who looked slightly deranged, like a cross between Grizzly Adams and Mephistopheles. He wore a kooky vest with Buck Rogers epaulets; a lightning bolt crackled on the chest of his T-shirt. Judging by the eruption of nerdy references in the index ("Borg, the," "Arthur, King," "asteroids, mining") I was tempted to dismiss Savage as a *Star Wars* junkie who had attracted a few stoned believers.

And yet . . . the book was an impressive utopian document, revealing Brockian levels of information-gathering, serious amateur study of everything from astronomy to Wagner, and better organization. As I learned over time, Savage had cooked up an even more grandiose vision than Brock's. For him, establishing a working sea colony was simply step one in a plan for mankind's eventual colonization of the universe, which he considered the inevitable solution to Earth's population pressures. It was our destiny to "seed" the stars, which he figured were most likely devoid of life.

"To all appearances, the galaxy is entirely vacant," he wrote. "As far as we can tell, we are utterly alone."

"Now is the watershed of Cosmic history," he went on. "We stand at the threshold of the New Millennium. Behind us yawn the chasms of the primordial past, when this universe was a dead and silent place; before us rise the broad sunlit uplands of a living cosmos." We had a choice: we could spread life to the universe, engulfing "the star-clouds in a fire storm of children, trees, and butterfly wings," or let ourselves "fail, fizzle, and gutter out."

The eight easy steps were Foundation (that is: starting a group to get the ball rolling); Aquarius (the NICCO stage: "Grow floating cities at sea to feed the world and learn the lessons of space colonization"); Bifrost and Asgard (establishing "habitable ecospheres" in Earth's orbit); Avallon ("domed lunar craters with independent ecologies"); Elysium (terraforming Mars); Solaria (populate the solar system, and how: "In the year 3000 A.D., the population of the solar system could easily exceed five billion billion!"); and Galactia (taking our act to other stars).

And yes, I know none of these steps is "easy." As Savage realized, they would take centuries. The only step he had accomplished was Foundation—forming a club—which put him right where Brock was. Still, when I finally spoke to him on the phone, it was clear he'd formed a much better club.

"We're growing with terrifying rapidity," Savage said of his group, the First Millennial Foundation. "We're attracting a tremendously high level and quality of leadership: scientists, computer people, judges, etc. So it's not the kind of fringe aluminum-hat crowd you might expect, but serious, sober-minded, able, capable people."

Anybody could say that—Brock *had* said that—but Savage's booming hubris appeared to be (relatively) warranted. He was, like Brock, a science buff, not a real scientist, but he had moved in a world of heavier hitters. Born in 1955, he became obsessed with space exploration during the golden age of NASA, so he mapped out a career path that would make him a fit candidate for the Mars missions that he assumed would define his adulthood: Air Force training and a hard-science Ph.D., probably in geology. But that fizzled. Savage lost interest because the nation lost its interest in the space program—in "the future we were supposed to have"—so he shifted gears and majored in classics at Swarthmore College. Even so, the old stirrings remained. In an astronomy class one day, a Swarthmore alum named Gerard K. O'Neill—a Princeton physicist who is considered a godfather of space-colony theorizing—talked about space colonization and "all my hopes for the future were reborn."

Savage graduated on the seven-year plan with an English degree, and then migrated home to western Colorado in 1981, where his family was, he claims, on the brink of becoming billionaires. Major oil companies had come to the area to set up processing plants to convert oil shale to usable fuel, and the Savage family held mining patents on thousands of acres that contained "literally billions of barrels of oil."

Oil shale never happened—companies like Exxon pulled out, deciding that the production costs and environmental headaches were too much, so young Marshall had to deal with a new future. He did it by conceiving of a newer reality.

"The potential of that money being there caused my mind to develop a sort of reality-distortion field," he said. "I had the expectation that I'd be enormously wealthy, and that I'd at least be able to implement the first step, the creation of a sea-based colony, step one to building up to a space-based infrastructure."

Savage jumped into various family business enterprises and wrote *The Millennial Project* in his spare time. Seemingly doomed to obscurity, the edition I read received a significant boost when Arthur C. Clarke (the author of *2001: A Space Odyssey*) read it, liked it, and recommended it to his agent, who sold it to a major publisher. The publicity helped. By the mid-nineties, Savage was holding well-attended meetings that attracted buffs and futurists from all over. By 1995, his "Core Conclave" was a sizable gathering that pulled in citizen-in-space heavyweights like Robert Zubrin, a prominent engineer who has long pushed the notion of a private project to colonize Mars.

I didn't know most of this when I first ran into Savage, but his very existence was enough to make me worry that Brock had been outgunned. I even called Brock once with treason in mind: I was going to suggest he merge with the more powerful Other.

But that would have been fruitless. I phoned Brock to tell him about Savage, but Brock cut in, indicating that, surrrrre, he would be happy to show the kid the ropes.

∞

After that, I lost regular contact with Brock for a while, checking in occasionally—via his mom—to make sure I didn't lose him entirely. He tended to generate multiple phone numbers, as his various projects took him to different rented office spaces in the Lancaster and Palmdale area. Supposedly I was on the NICCO mailing list, but that hadn't yielded much aside from a sporadic black-and-white newsletter crowded with inscrutable Brockiana. I noticed that Brock and NICCO hadn't turned up on the World Wide Web—a bad omen, since the First Millennial Foundation put up a sophisticated site in no time, as did the aggressive, cocky creators of a new free-nation group called Oceania: The Atlantis Project.

Founded in 1993 by a disgruntled Nevada libertarian named Eric Klien, Oceania was to be a "free island" perched off the coast of Panama, made of concrete and steel and holding the same old disgruntled truths to be self-evident: "Ranging from the most vicious socialist wealth-redistribution schemes to the over-regulated, protectionist fascist economies," Klien wrote, "we are offered strangulation and enslavement at every turn."

The year 1995 saw other action, including publication of a book called *Free Space: Real Alternatives for Reaching Space,* which told of grandiose new visions like Luna Corp (goal: a private, self-sustaining lunar colony), Robert Zubrin's Mars Direct, the League of New Worlds (goal: a seafloor colony designed to accustom pioneers to the strange environments of future space colonies), and OUSPADEV, a proposed private space station that would offer "sleeping (and other after-dark activities) in weightlessness."

But where was Brock?

That year a newsletter—a *color* newsletter—arrived in my box with the answer: he was still at it. Its cover showed a gleaming white "Capitala fun ship" chugging merrily toward Freedominium, laden with "sea-homesteaders," "SCUBA-trained refugees," "surfer-welders," and other workers who would build fish farms, grow kelp, process information, and generally drive the island's thrumming futuristic economy.

I called Brock, who was friendly as always—"Howdy, stranger!"—and full of news. Claudio had dropped out of NICCO. He had married Teresa and moved to Utah, so that was that. Howard Hinman and Etsuro were still on board, and Etsuro was still tightening bolts on his Sidewinder. Biggest flash of all: Brock had a wife. He'd met a woman named Mary Anne Wallace at a Mormon mixer, and they'd married in 1994.

"You dog!" I said, thrilled by the news. But would that be it for NICCO?

Nope. The wife was a believer, and Brock still felt confident.

"I know 2000 is not far off," he said happily, "but we feel that things will move fast now that we've got all our applied-science ducks in a row."

How many green ducks were in a row?

"Wail, the thing is, we haven't tried to find an investor yet, because we didn't want to proceed until we felt we had something worth putting our own shekels into. Now we do."

∞

Wail, they didn't. In the summer of 1997 I happened to be in Los Angeles, so I called Brock, who gave me a set of complicated Brockian directions—"Pass 'R.' Fork to the right. Go up to 'M.' Go right. Go a quarter mile. You'll turn left on 10th Street West, the second street on your left is L-12. Go a half mile, we're at 1110 West Ave. L-12, #B1"—that led to a parched-looking office plaza between Palmdale and Lancaster.

I got lost, naturally, and ran late. As I parked, I could see Brock peeping out a window, fretting with worry like a clucking mom. He saw me pull up and bounded out, grinning and waving. He looked the same, except that he'd put on a small ring of marriage fat and his hair-cap was going gray. His "fifth cousin" Ron Wroblewski was with him; Ron was helping Brock with a new business that he figured would be the big moneymaker he'd always hoped for. It involved using the Web to relay fan messages to celebrities.

"Long time no see!" Brock said.

"It's great to see you again. How's it been going?"

Not so good. Once we settled down inside, Brock revealed something he'd failed to mention in 1995: in 1994, he had been wiped out financially by "real-estate pirates" and "bad guys" who cheated him in a venture involving "the most advanced digital studio in the world—which I put together."

I groaned. How bad was it?

"It was a hard hit," he confided. "Everything I had pretty much went down the tubes."

But there was good news too. He was on his feet again, developing a new business and teaching high-school social sciences and history to prisoners.

Best of all: Mrs. Brock was pregnant.

"That's great! If it's a boy, will you promise to name him Brock Jr.?"

"Wail, I dunno," he said.

"How about Little NICCO?" Ron said.

"I guess that's possible," Brock laughed.

Brock and Ron showed me the Web site and a depressing bank of phones in a windowless room where fans would supposedly call in their "orders" on 900 numbers. A sign on the wall admonished that attitude was crucial. "Remember," it said, "the person on the other end can tell if you're smiling."

"Did you know that in the entire seventy-five year history of Hollywood, nobody has known where to send a fan letter?" Brock told me. "We'll guarantee delivery. Or you won't be billed."

After that, Brock talked for two hours. I drifted into a blissful fugue, serenaded by fragments of chatter:

" . . . it's called cause marketing. In addition to NICCO, we're looking at a World War II film rescue operation . . ."

" . . . see these pontoons on the bottom of sea planes? Those are gas hogs. Wail, in the 1950s, they pioneered some skis . . ."

" . . . the Pakistani army is right now floating around a bunch of money in the international money market . . ."

At one point I asked, "Did you ever get any experiments done in the water?"

"We interested an investment banker who had a pool at his house. Five or six of us built a NICCO-style platform . . ."

"And?"

"We put it in the water and had him sit on it. And this impressed him."

"Did you coral accrete this platform?"

"No, that one we did quick and dirty with ferro-cement."

"You still believe you're going to do this, don't you?"

"Oh," he said, surprised I even had to ask, "yeah."

Brock led me out of town with a quick stop outside the studio—his Agincourt. Was he trying to show me that he symbolically could rise above defeat? I don't think so. He just thought the building was "neat" and wanted me to see it. Then he led me out of town and waved good-bye.

Back home, I checked in with the other strivers and found out that Brock was not alone in losing the good fight. Savage was still at it but sounded discouraged. "I don't expect to see ocean colonization in my lifetime," he said. Operation Atlantis had crashed on the shoals of cash flow, and its high-concept Web site was inert. Even Strauss had downgraded: he said his plan for a freedominium bus had been put off—at least until retirement.

Wondering if reality would ever cause Brock to formally lower Freedominium's flag, I called Brock's wife, Mary Anne, and asked her. With a baby on the way, did she think he should put all this nonsense behind him?

Not at all. "The thing you have to understand is this," she said of the NICCO men. "They're all geniuses. If it can be done, why yes, absolutely. We could start a whole new world!"

They want to live! Mr. and Mrs. Larry Wood believe supplements are the key to long, long lives.

PHOTOGRAPH BY GEORGE LANGE, USED WITH PERMISSION OF LARRY WOOD.

7

Death, Be Not in My Face

*[By 2062], scientists had firmly established that emotions of human sup-
pression, prejudice and hostility were life-threatening for the subjects as
well as the objects of these feelings. . . .*

*At the same time, there were feelings of devotion, spirituality and rev-
erence that were found to be greatly life-enhancing. The immortality
groups that now covered the globe found, however, that they did not need
a god or a sacred text to invoke those feelings. Haltingly at first, and
then with increasing abandon . . . people found they could feel holy
about themselves and other people. . . . [M]ore and more . . . became
converts to this new way of life. Immortality became the religion to end
all religions.*

—FROM *WHY DIE?: A BEGINNER'S GUIDE TO LIVING FOREVER,*
BY HERB BOWIE (1998)

"Obviously, I'm an optimist to some degree," said Larry Wood, an
amiable, muscular fifty-year-old with fashion-forward ideas
about the future of the human body, "but I really believe we
could be the first generation that's going to live forever. Either that,
or we'll be the last generation to die."

That's optimism, all right, though the second part might inspire
pretty bleak daydreams. Suppose you believe, as Wood does, that
technology has the potential to conquer aging someday, vastly
increasing human longevity, perhaps delivering the ultimate gift:
physical immortality. Now suppose you die a year before the technology rolls out. You wouldn't know what you'd missed, but for
Wood there's infinite agony in just knowing he *might* miss it. Extrap-

olating hopefully from real-world developments in aging research—which could, in theory, increase the maximum human lifespan by a few years or decades during the twenty-first century—he's convinced that scientists will deliver immortality within fifty years, so he's determined to hang on.

Through the slight fuzz of a long-distance connection he described his predicament. "The whole thing is this," he said. "You do whatever you can for the next ten years. Then the next ten years."

For Wood this has meant a longtime involvement with "life extension," a blanket term for a variegated pile of fringe health regimens and futuristic enthusiasms. His quest has taken him down some tangled paths—for a while he was interested in cryonics, or body freezing, in hopes that he could be thawed and brought back from the dead in the future—and once it even landed him in jail. In 1990 Wood, who holds an undergraduate degree in biochemistry from Cornell, started a company called Unlimited Longevity Research that sold life-extension products, mainly dietary supplements and drugs. That year agents from the Food and Drug Administration raided his offices in Thousand Oaks, California. After a complicated flurry of legal tussling, Wood was eventually charged with interstate commerce of a controversial body-enhancing substance called GHB. He served six months, though his conviction was later overturned on appeal.

When I first talked to Wood in the summer of 1997, he had given up on cryonics ("It doesn't work"), placing all his bets on exercise and supplements. His routine included regular exercise (he had $40,000 worth of fitness equipment in his garage), healthy habits (a balanced diet, not much red meat, no smoking or hard alcohol), and daily intake of dietary extras.

Lots and lots of extras. Wood faxed me his menu, which added up to roughly 140 grams of liquids, powders, and capsules that he swallowed or injected every day. Some items were typical enough, including a whopping 10 grams daily of Vitamin C. Some were things whose anti-aging properties or safety is highly debatable—like mela-tonin, a presumed "antioxidant," or dehydroepiandrosterone (DHEA), a naturally produced hormone whose manufacture in the body declines with age. Life extensionists believe that swallowing it can restore youthful vigor.

Most, whatever they're for, were exotic chemicals that to my lay-man's ear sounded like lawn-and-garden sprays: ornithine, virazide, glutathione.

Is it safe to mix all this stuff together?

Wood doesn't really know. He's his own lab rat, out there alone on the megadosing frontier, and he's aware that he might be hurting himself. "One person told me I'll probably die of liver cancer," he said cheerfully. As a safeguard, Wood makes regular visits to the doc-tor for blood tests that might reveal signs of "imbalance" that could lead to organ damage.

In the end, he feels certain he'll be fine, an opinion that is defi-nitely not shared by Dr. Victor Herbert, a physician and nutrition expert who (at my request) inspected Wood's intake, and who basi-cally shrieked that Wood was committing supplement suicide. "This *will* shorten his life," he said. "It may kill him of cancer—brain, pan-creas, testes, prostate, you name it. It *will* produce liver damage."

His advice for Wood? "Don't touch this stuff!"

∞

So there you have it. Physically, Wood is either saving himself or hastening his demise. But how about spiritually? What, if anything, is going on there?

Obviously, Wood's goals aren't cozy-puffy metaphysical. He's a rock-ribbed atheist, focused entirely on the material preservation of his body. Still, you could argue that he represents a new type of spir-itual seeker. At a time when science has robbed many people of their ability to believe in an afterlife, Wood is fantasizing about an immortalizing relationship with a newer, more accessible god: technology. In exchange for accepting the chilly scientific verdict that we are, in the end, little more than meat puppets, soulless life-support systems for our DNA, he just wants somebody, somehow, to keep the puppet dancing longer.

In a way, it isn't asking too much. Science hasn't been all that nice to our souls, but it has been very good for our "containers," so there's a natural human tendency to want more. The average lifespan in the United States has increased by twenty-six years since 1900 (it's now seventy-six), thanks mainly to advances in medicine and nutrition, and there are scientists, real ones, who think lifespans could be doubled again during the twenty-first century.

Wood isn't alone in his fidgety longing. He's joined by a fairly sizable subculture of Americans who clamor for a life-extending fix. Most aren't as intense as Wood, but some are, and some bring a surprising measure of spirituality to their immortalist dream. One of the more self-consciously "religious" buffs is Herb Bowie, forty-six, an Arizona-based life-extensionist and the author of *Why Die?*, an odd little book that pushes the unique notion that physical immortality is not only coming, but that people can make it happen by having faith that it's coming. It's a tricky idea that grows out of an old New Age practice called Rebirthing, which has it that what people believe influences their physical, spiritual, and emotional "reality" in tangible ways, at a fundamental level.

"An extension of that," Bowie explained, "is the idea that perhaps even death is something we create through a combination of social and mental conditioning." Bowie urges his readers to absorb the deep-soul conviction that immortality is their birthright and to stop feeling guilty about wanting it. If enough people do so, immortalizing faith would become immortalizing fact: with the majority of the world clamoring to live forever, the mighty engines of government and commerce would, by universal demand, be redirected toward the goal, and we would see a "war on aging" comparable to the golden age of the space race.

The believer's task is to . . . well, to believe this, and to live as if immortality were coming soon. "Immortality is something I already am," reads one of Bowie's good-news tenets, "something I am creating for myself on a daily basis."

That's a challenging faith commitment, but Bowie is firm about it. "If scientists are going to offer us the option of extending the human lifespan through technology," he told me, "we *have* to start resolving these conflicts in our psyche."

∞

Wood's and Bowie's hopes are obviously utopian. Both men fantasize about a shining time when science will provide a commodity that religion, and only religion, has offered in the past: a way to cheat death.

A different take—call it "dystopian"—comes courtesy of an old acquaintance of mine named Chet Fleming, whose name is a pseudonym for a real person, an engineer and patent attorney in his forties who lives in . . .

Let's just say the "United States." Fleming told me years ago that unless I promised to preserve his anonymity, he wouldn't talk. He's worried that people will think he's a creep, a nut, or a ghoul. He isn't—he's an intelligent, well-meaning person—but when you consider the nature of his work, it's easy to see why he's shy of publicity.

In 1987, Fleming self-published a bizarre book called *If We Can Keep a Severed Head Alive . . .* , a 461-page elaboration of a U. S. patent that he obtained that year, No. 4,666,425, for a gizmo and related procedures that he labeled "Device for Perfusing an Animal Head."

Translation?

"In simple and blunt terms," Fleming wrote, "this operation

involves cutting the head off an animal, or maybe even a human someday, and keeping the severed head alive. Now you know why it's going to cause controversy."

It did, but not in the way he imagined. A technically oriented man who strongly believes in the benefits of science, Fleming obtained the patent as part of a quite serious crusade to *halt* research in an area whose theoretical applications to life extension struck him as probably inevitable and most certainly horrible: keeping a head, and only a head, alive on a life-support system.

It sounds insane. Why even think about such a thing? Fleming said he couldn't help it. The idea came to him in a flash, uninvited, and when he researched the concept in the early eighties, he learned that grisly animal experiments had already been performed in the sixties and seventies that achieved primitive, short-term severed-head "viability" with lab monkeys.

Perhaps his fear was irrational, but the possibility that an operation like this might ever be done on a human filled him with foreboding, the same sort of future-shock dread that many people experienced when they first heard about the successful cloning of Dolly the sheep. He obtained the patent to put the brakes on. A patent allows the patent holder to block anyone else from doing what the patent claims, until the patent expires or unless the holder licenses the rights. Fleming didn't plan to license any rights; his intent was to block severed-head research until the human race could carefully debate the vexing questions this operation raised.

Like: Should it ever be allowed?

You wouldn't think so. In numbing detail, Fleming sketched out a procedure that resulted in a severed head being mounted on a life-support console that provided oxygen, glucose, and other essentials. A "discorporated" head, or "discorp," he wrote, would not necessarily be a freak-on-a-box cloistered in the dark recesses of a lab. It could speak with help from an electronic voicebox, it could move around on a voice-activated motorized wheelchair. Indeed, society might have to get accustomed to seeing discorps scooting around in public. "If the sight of a severed head being wheeled through a museum offends people," Fleming wrote helpfully, "museums might restrict discorps to visiting on one or two days a week."

Fleming made it clear that the operation would not lead to physical immortality, but he did assume it could extend lives, and he tried to imagine positive applications. (For instance, giving a great research genius extra time to complete his work.) On the dark side, he worried about the obvious potential for evil. In one scary vision, Fleming imagined a dictator severing an enemy's head and keeping it alive on a cabinet. Why? So that the discorp could be tortured year after year, and forced to watch as its family and friends were tortured, too.

Fleming fretted that the risk of such horrors might outweigh any possible benefit, but left this for society to resolve. He wrote that the ethical debate about severed heads was "coming at everybody, like a high-speed train roaring through the night. Whether anyone wants it or not, this technology will soon be here."

That was in 1987. The technology isn't here, though at this point nothing is stopping it. Fleming lost his patent in 1989, thanks to a Patent Office "reexamination" that he believes was motivated, at least partly, by patent officials' fears that animal-rights activists, among others, would raise hell that such a "device" had been recognized. I first wrote him in 1991—*Severed* contained a post office box number—asking him to call me up and tell his story.

Alas, he wasn't at all interested in going public, even with his name changed, so I left him alone, trying him again in 1995. By then he'd loosened up a little. He told me about himself, including these scattershot facts. He was born in Alaska and raised in the South and Midwest. He held an engineering degree from a good state university and a law degree from a top Ivy League school. At eighteen months, he was disfigured in an accident, one that shaped his overriding desire to do something useful with his life: he chewed through a live electrical cord, suffering severe burns to his face that, over the years, required half a dozen reconstructive operations. As an adult he'd prospered, married, divorced, and was now married again, to a woman he adored. He had children. He was happy working as a patent lawyer and wanted to make good on idealistic urges that had long been part of his mindset. As an outgrowth of this, he'd made an unsuccessful bid for political office in 1994. He lost decisively, and the experience left him doubtful that serious ideas could be aired in the current political marketplace.

And now he was polishing up a novel he'd started several years earlier.

Its subject? Research on severed heads. In the manuscript, a governor with the combined virtues of Robert Kennedy, Gandhi, and Martin Luther King is stricken with Lou Gehrig's disease, a degenerative disorder of the nervous system for which there's no cure or treatment, and which always results in paralysis and death. But then a ray of hope appears—a weird and flickering ray, to be sure, but one possessing a certain Faustian power. The governor's technical advisor (also the novel's narrator) hears rumors about research into a strange new surgical procedure that involves severing the human head. . . .

Fleming mailed me the novel and asked my opinion. I said that it was well written (true), but that the plot "might turn some people off" (very true) and that his narrator was a little too preachy (very, very true). This last trait turned up all through *Severed,* which was full of seemingly unrelated essays, diatribes, and gee-whiz opinions on everything from Christianity ("to the best of my knowledge, the leaders of Christian nations have started more wars than the wars started by the people of any other religion") to the pressing need for a universal language, called "Simplish."

Fleming took the criticism like a man, but then we lost touch again until 1997, when I called him to see what he made of the epochal Dolly cloning. In one sense, the event made Fleming look quite prescient, because it remarkably paralleled his Cassandra prophecy in *Severed.* The world had long known that cloning of animals and humans was theoretically possible, but it had failed to prepare for the ethical challenges. Now the genie was out of the bottle, cackling and beating its chest, and everyone was struggling to get a grip on it.

In another sense, Dolly was a downer. Put simply, cloning was poised to become the attention-demanding issue that Fleming had only dreamed severed heads would become, and that's exactly how it worked out. In early 1998, when the renegade Chicago physicist Richard Seed announced that he intended to clone humans, he drew international headlines, even though it quickly emerged that he lacked the know-how to pull it off. In the wake of Seed's announcement, Jeremy Rifkin, the maverick science watchdog, and a New York State cellular biologist named Stuart A. Newman applied for a patent that proposed using cloning technology to produce a horrible ape-human "chimera." As the men made clear, though, their real intent was to jump-start a debate about the ethics of such projects, and to position themselves to block any such attempts.

Severed heads and cloning are not the same thing—a head would still be "you"; a clone would only be a copy of you—but I still had to wonder if all the cloning excitement might depress Fleming. Not really. When I called, he sounded happy, and both clones and heads were far from his mind. He said he'd invested in a successful over-the-counter medication and was doing very well financially. He was also writing a new novel on a new subject: mankind's colonization of space. He offered to send the first few chapters, and the lilt in his voice made it clear that he'd picked up and moved on.

These reports revived my long-dormant desire to meet him. Fleming had spent a heck of a lot of time fretting about severed heads. Could he really (so to speak) just put them on a shelf? And what had it all been about, anyway? Fleming's tendencies as a broad-brush theoretician made me wonder if a more interesting guiding philosophy was at work under the surface.

"Chet, I'd like to get together," I ventured. "I'm living in New York these days. Do you ever come to the East Coast?"

"Well, I'm coming to D.C. to do some patent work next month. Could you make it down then?"

"Tell you what. I'll pick you up at the airport."

∞

The human yearning to live forever is an ancient literary theme, usually delivered with a castor-oily dose of warning: immortality is for the gods, not men. Greek mythology tells of the Cumaean Sibyl, a young woman whom Apollo gave eternal life but (mean guy) without eternal youth. The Sibyl grayed and shrank until she fit inside a tiny bottle, a forlorn creature who peeped out a sad, endless refrain: "I only want to die!"

In *Gulliver's Travels,* Jonathan Swift presented the *struldbrugs,* rare beings who were born with the gift of immortality. Gulliver assumed they would be "happiest beyond all comparison." In fact, they just kept getting older, sicker, and crabbier, and they too longed for death's release. Swift also presented an ultra-rationalist attitude toward mortality by introducing the Houyhnhnms, the wise horse-beings Gulliver met during his final set of adventures. The horses regarded Gulliver as a beast, indistinguishable from the Yahoos, the noxious, carnal, cowardly humanoids who lived only for their grossest material pleasures. The horses saw death stoically, as the natural, unremarkable end to a life properly lived, and expressed "neither joy nor grief" when a fellow horse passed on.

Swift wasn't necessarily endorsing this as the right attitude for people, which is good, because I doubt many humans could be so Houyhnhnm-cool about death. We're passionate creatures, and most of us assume that when the time comes we'll splutter and yowl like a Yahoo who's stubbed his toe. Life-extension believers represent a third attitude: steely defiance. They believe in directed rage, fighting back, refusing to accept the final defeat.

Obviously, many informed people consider this outlook bizarre, ignorant, and silly. One prominent critic of the immortalist fantasy is Dr. Leonard Hayflick, a biogerontologist whose name is attached to a term that life-extension buffs love to hate: the Hayflick Limit. Hayflick earned fame in the sixties when he and a colleague debunked a long-standing belief that normal human cells in a tissue culture were immortal. His work showed that normal cells die after about fifty divisions, indicating that they have a built-in mortality "clock." Recent work has suggested that his "limit" may not, in fact, be insurmountable, but he still doubts that scientists will ever devise a way to string out the current maximum lifespan of around 125. Moreover, pointing at the social problems super-longevity would bring— start with overpopulation—he just thinks it's a bad idea.

"Let's say a little white immortality pill does become available tomorrow," Hayflick told me. "Do we really want people to have it? I can think of a lot of people—Hitler, Stalin, serial killers, rapists— who I wouldn't want to see live forever. We should leave these things to nature."

The immortality faithful certainly don't buy that. "Hayflick is tired," said Will Block, a co-founder of Life Enhancement Products, Inc., a California-based outfit that sells life-extension stuff. "He falls into a group that has an almost federal-department-of-aging view, which is one that ignores enormous amounts of exciting work and doesn't have a visionary quality."

The "federal" snipe is a reference to the National Institute on Aging, a government research body that tends to look at aging from a droopy "let's keep people healthy longer" perspective that both bores and annoys the buffs. Enough people share Block's conviction—tens of thousands, I'd estimate, based on the sales figures claimed by Block and others—that a thriving service sector exists to fill their needs, made up of private research groups, mail-order supplement providers, a publishing mini-genre, and renegade clinics that provide powerful substances like human growth hormone (another body-juice that declines naturally as you age) to anyone willing to pay for expensive injections.

Block's group is one of about a half-dozen whose entire business consists of selling anti-aging nostrums like DHEA and multisubstance wellness blends with names like Life Extension Mix and Super Radical Shield. Elsewhere, mass-market longevity books make dazzling promises that beckon readers to share the dream. *The Melatonin Miracle,* a best-seller in 1995, focuses on melatonin's alleged anti-aging benefits. *Reversing Human Aging* says the answer lies in telomeres— tiny chromosomal tips that are depleted every time a healthy cell divides—and predicts that within twenty years science will learn how to replenish them and deliver lifespans of "200, possibly 500 years." *Grow Young with H.G.H.,* a book by an energetic Chicago-based buff named Ronald Klatz, touts human growth hormone as the "amazing medically proven" way to "reverse" the effects of aging.

All of these claims are a stretch. Most mainstream gerontology researchers maintain that the anti-aging benefits of HGH, DHEA, and melatonin are unproved or nonexistent. Furthermore, since the aging process is still largely a mystery, victory dances are a bit premature. Whatever causes aging (it may be the ravages of metabolism on cells, the environment, a genetically encoded cellular lifespan, or something else), the battle is far from being won, and it may never be.

And yet, as the buffs are keenly aware, some serious scientists *do* suggest that research could add several healthy decades to the human lifespan.

"The idea that lifespan can be extended has moved from being a fringe idea to a subject for serious research," said Dr. Thomas Johnson, a geneticist at the University of Colorado who, in one promising area of inquiry, has manipulated roundworm genes in a way that doubles the creatures' lives. He's convinced that a drug could someday be developed that would neutralize protein products that lead to aging in cells, and he's involved in a new company—GenoPlex, based in Boulder—that hopes to do this. He believes that doubled human lifespans are possible, perhaps in our lifetimes.

Another optimist is Dr. Roy L. Walford, a pathologist and researcher at UCLA who served as the team physician during the Biosphere 2 project, in which a squad of humans lived for two years inside a sealed-off indoor ecosystem. Walford's baby is calorie restriction. This sounds strange, but it's based on a long-recognized fact: reducing calorie intake in lab mice extends their lives dramatically, and it's the only technique proven to do so in a mammal. Whether it works for people is still an open question—data released in 1997 indicate that it works in lower primates—but Walford is a believer. He told me that the de facto calorie restriction practiced inside Biosphere 2 (the Biospherians weren't able to grow enough food in there, so they fasted involuntarily) resulted in a range of quantifiable benefits, like dramatically decreased cholesterol levels.

Some of Walford's colleagues think he's gone off the deep end with his extrapolations, but at 73, he was still practicing the gospel, living on an 1,800-calorie-a-day diet, as opposed to the recommended 2,000 to 2,500 for adults. He insisted that a person who started calorie-restricting at 18 would have a chance of living to 160.

In good health? "It's possible. People make the mistake of getting into a *struldbrug* obsession," he said, referring to those miserable Swiftian immortals.

"That's not the case," he added with gruff certainty. "The health curve will increase with the survival curve."

And what would be the upper limit on that survival curve?

"Limit? I don't see a limit."

∞

Intrigued by such pronouncements, I decided to visit a few prominent life-extensionists. Not the research people, but the buffs in the
trenches, the strivers and self-picklers and supplementers who live in
painful awareness of the miracles that might (or might not) await
them in the years ahead. A few calls revealed a clear pattern of buff
concentration. Florida, Arizona, Nevada, and southern California—
Meccas of youthful narcissism and elderly roosting—were all hotspots. For efficiency's sake, I settled on a swing through the Southwest.

First stop: Nye County, Nevada, a high-desert outback several
hours north of Las Vegas. Nye County is home to a pair of founding
figures in the popular longevity subculture, Durk Pearson and Sandy
Shaw, a husband-and-wife team who in 1982 published *Life Extension, A Practical Scientific Approach,* an 858-page summary of the free-
radical theory of aging. Free radicals are byproducts of chemical
processes in the body; some researchers believe they damage cells in
a way that produces the effects of aging. Durk and Sandy, drawing
partly on the research of Dr. Denham Harman, a researcher at the
University of Nebraska, recommended taking massive doses of anti-
oxidants to reduce the free radicals' effects. Although critics slammed
the book as a factually sloppy farrago of other people's work, a fascinated public kept it on best-seller lists for months, making Durk
and Sandy the closest thing the movement has had to celebrities.

I heard about them from the first life-extension buff I ever encountered: Jack Wheeler, a flamboyant libertarian and adventure-travel
guide whom I met in 1993. Wheeler said Durk and Sandy introduced
him to life extension way back in the sixties, when they became
friends on the Southern California libertarian circuit. Durk and Sandy
had an additional interest in life extension, which dovetailed nicely
with their unhappy-with-government ideas. (The buffs are often

prickly about government, their gripe being that heavy-handed federal regulators are clumsily, stupidly standing between the people and the life-extending substances that could save them.) They'd read about Harman's work in science journals and were already whipping up their own experimental batches of antioxidant mix—using bulk tubs of pharmaceutical-grade vitamin powder.

"They had this formula—lots of Vitamin C, Vitamin E, and lots of B—that they made in their own lab," Wheeler recalled. "I'd go visit them and help mix it up. They didn't have any encapsulation equipment, so we would just carry this powder around in plastic bags and choke it down by the spoonful. It tasted awful. Oh, god! You have no idea!"

Wheeler helped make Durk and Sandy famous. He'd built a name for himself as a boy adventurer and globe-trotting action man—he guided tourist fly-ins to the North Pole, for example—and he was a frequent guest on *The Merv Griffin Show*. In a stirring moment of show-biz synergy, Wheeler told Merv about Durk, an act that led to many *Merv* appearances by Durk and Sandy and, eventually, the book contract. Durk and Sandy spent much of the eighties stoking their career, touring life-extension gatherings and health-food expos, creating and licensing products, and pushing their ideas while wearing glitter-rock costumes that made them look like refugees from *Starlight Express*.

Durk and Sandy remained high-profile during the late-eighties' "smart nutrient" craze, but when I talked to Wheeler in 1997, I realized I hadn't seen any sign of them for a while. Had they given up? Or died?

Nope, said Wheeler. They were fine, and as far as he knew, they were still figuring to live a long, long time. How long?

"Well, they say 30,000 years." Wheeler explained the reasoning: Durk and Sandy's mixes would keep them going for another fifty years, long enough, perhaps, for the "rapid doubling" of scientific knowledge to solve the last riddles about aging. Wheeler shared their hopes, though as a "safety net" he was looking into a technique they weren't interested in: cryonic freezing after death, with the hope that he could be thawed someday and revived.

"That's the bet, anyway," he said.

My road trip from Las Vegas involved a five-hour northward squiggle through a mountainous, increasingly Martian landscape. Nye County is old silver-mining territory that these days is better known for a streak of libertarian cussedness. (A few years ago, Nye County officials tried to declare federal environmental laws null and void in the county.) Durk and Sandy moved there from Southern California to stretch their freedom-loving legs; the breaking point came when local zoning nannies refused to let them build a personal "library" in their backyard.

On a cool summer afternoon, Durk met me on the tiny commercial strip in his hometown, smiling behind the wheel of a big white truck. I followed him up winding roads to his house, which was perched on a dry, scruffy hill above town. In his emphatic, analytical voice, he explained that the truck itself factored into his personal life-extension program.

"The vehicle weighs forty-six-hundred *pounds*. It has a chrome moly-steel roll bar in it. So if some drunk *idiot* in a twenty-five-hundred-pound car crashes into me, he's likely to get killed, and I'm likely to get a few bruises and aches and pains."

At fifty-four, Durk looked healthy—he was a big, strapping guy—but he also looked his age, maybe older. His signature feature was a frizzy mane of Peter Frampton hair that had turned gray. Sandy, also fifty-four, looked her age too. A slim, dark-haired woman who spoke in an excited bray, she greeted me inside a modest dwelling that was unbelievably cluttered with bric-a-brac, art, and scientific journals. The walls and rooms were crowded with images of Durk and Sandy in their glitzy eighties prime, but as they showed me around, they explained that these days they rarely left home. They made money by licensing their mixes and preferred to stick around the pad, beetling through scientific journals and books. They subscribed to roughly 50 of them—everything from *Cell* to *Free Radical Biology & Medicine*—at a cost of $15,000 a year. Out back on a dusty lot they were building a new library and lab to hold it all.

We cozied up outside. Durk stretched out on an old chaise longue, Sandy sat in a chair. Wheeler's 30,000-year figure turned out to be a stretch, but they did have great anticipations.

"I really don't expect to live forever because, if nothing else, *accidents* will get you sooner or later," Durk said. "That could be a very long time, though. If it were possible to maintain a person's health at what it was in the early twenties—and we don't know how to do that yet, we may never know how, but it's certainly a worthy goal— you would have an average time to death of about 800 years. So you eliminate things like common accidents, slips and falls in the shower, which is easy enough to do. You eliminate all that and it might be like 2,200 years mean time to death. That's a *very* long time."

"There's an awful lot an individual can do to reduce the risk of accidents," Sandy put in quickly.

Those were large "ifs." I asked them what, exactly, would do away with aging. Durk assumed that genetic research will eventually identify the precise genes that both cause and counteract aging and disease. "The next step, then, is to find out what those good genes are and *get* them. I really think that type of therapy will be as common fifty years from now as giving a kid a *shot* to immunize him against diphtheria and whooping cough."

"I think twenty-five years from now," Sandy said.

"How will you 'get them'?"

"You put the genes *in*," said Durk. "You inject an adenovirus that contains that good gene, and it affects all your cells. Like a cold."

"The doubling for knowledge in the area of aging mechanisms is now, say, five years," he continued. "We're fifty-four. The idea that science will *not* understand what causes aging and be able to deal with it in another half century is *ludicrous*. By the time we're eighty, aging will be as irrelevant as smallpox."

That's a major leap of faith, but Durk and Sandy have made it. And they were surprisingly blasé about it all, like a pair of lounging cats waiting for someone to give them an immortalizing scratch on the belly. Whether they believed this deep down or not, I can't say, but they seemed very happy, and there was something musky and disheveled about their "crib" that hinted at great delight in Yahoo carnality. Maybe they were living in a dream world, but I had to admire their quirky *joie de vivre*. I asked them to walk me through their daily routines.

"OK," said Durk, sitting up. "We get up in the morning and we take our first dose of nutrient supplements for the day. We also take brain foods, nutrient supplements designed to help the brain."

"These are substances the brain can use to make neurotransmitters," Sandy interjected.

"Um, all right. Are all these things pills?"

"No. These are *drinks*. It's a very nice-tasting iced tea."

They laid out the rest, explaining that, basically, they glug this stuff four times a day, try to avoid stress, and eat what they want. They didn't buy calorie restriction as a viable option for themselves—why live that way?—a conviction they vividly demonstrated later, when we went to lunch at a local Mexican food restaurant and downed beef tostadas topped with enough sour cream to clog the Chunnel.

Jack Wheeler, I recalled, was capable of gluttony, but he always performed penance with intense physical activity. "You both probably exercise a lot, right?"

"No," Durk said shamelessly, "we really don't do *any* formal exercise."

"We do believe we should be doing more exercise," Sandy said, sounding guilty.

"Ahhh, frankly, we prefer to read."

"Hey," I said. "I'm not judging you. I was just asking."

"Neither of us really cares for repetitive-type exercise," Sandy confessed with a gush of relief. "It just bores us silly."

Fine, no exercise. Plenty of red meat and fat. No interest in freezing. Clearly, Durk and Sandy might need a safety net. What about cloning? Would that be useful to them?

"Aaaah, a clone is just a twin, it's not you," Durk sighed, adding that the technology did have tangy potential. It would eventually be possible to take a cloned human liver cell, implant it in a pig, and grow a new human liver that could then be transplanted to a person.

"And there you go," he said brightly, "you'll get yourself a new liver *and* a bunch of bacon!"

I'd read somewhere that it would be possible to clone yourself and "harvest" organs from your twin. "But I don't understand that," I said, hoping to steer our talk into shadowy, Chet-esque territory. "Wouldn't that be rather . . . ghastly for the clone?"

Sandy: "I think they're talking about a clone that would have no brain. It would be decerebrate. So it wouldn't really be a person at all, it would just be a factory of organs."

"Aaaah," said Durk, waving that off. "They won't need that. It'll be a *lot* easier to use a pig."

Last question: Did they really expect to be alive far, far, far in the future?

"I'd be more surprised if it didn't happen than if it did," said Durk.

Sandy nodded. "We've got a tremendous opportunity."

∞

I expected many things of my afternoon with Chet Fleming: strange conversations, dark broodings. What I didn't expect was to be bored a lot of the time.

Don't me wrong: I liked Fleming, and the day was not without its rewards and astonishments. But I'd built him up in my mind as the ultimate weirdo, a man burning with an irrational interest in severed heads, ready to spill everything in a confessional freefall highlighted by phrases like "this damnable obsession."

Alas, as a character, Fleming at first seemed more like Bartleby the Frequent Flyer, a mundane and pleasant businessman who was reluctant to "play" any role I hoped to assign him. He came off his plane wheeling a luggage tote and extending a hail-fellow paw, an ordinary-looking guy with a tall, big-boned frame, sandy hair, and wire-rim glasses. If I hadn't already known he'd been burned as a child I wouldn't have noticed. He looked just fine, and his defining feature was something else entirely: his expression was often just the slightest bit . . . startled.

We exited the airport and staggered to my truck through a cold, cutting springtime wind. "I forget, where did you go to school?" I asked as we buckled up.

"My family was living in ―― when I started college," he said, "and I didn't feel old enough to go away, so I went my first two years at ―― State. I thought that was a good way to make the transition." Pause. From reading *Severed*, I knew already that Fleming was a speechmaker. Now I sensed that an anchor was being hoisted in advance of a long rhetorical voyage.

"And I'll tell you what," he said. "My preference with my kids would be for them to at least stay home the first year, to get out of the drinking stuff and all that. In fact, I wish *all* colleges would have some kind of system which is really designed to help young people make the adjustments. Instead of saying there's this flat-out prohibition where the law says you cannot drink until you're twenty-one, my feeling is that colleges should have a rule where you're a freshman, you don't drink. Simple as that. It's just flat-out prohibited. And then sophomore year―"

"I don't know, Chet. I think college kids are going to booze it up, regardless of what you tell them."

"Could be," he said agreeably. "There's a line from a Creedence song that talks about stealing a pie. 'You can have it by asking for it if you wanted to, but you'd rather have it on the run.'"

That was an awfully quick fold, but as I was starting to realize, that was typical Fleming. He was good-natured; he liked to discuss more than argue.

I drove him to his hotel, a Holiday Inn tucked away in the generic, dark-windowed cubes of Crystal City, Virginia, near the Patent Office. He registered, dumped his stuff, hopped back in, clapped his hands, and offered to buy me lunch.

"Thanks, but you don't have to do that."

"Hey, it's no problem. I don't even want to tell you what my royalty check is for this medicine."

"You're riding high, huh?"

"I'm ridin'—phhhhhewww. Man, it's extraordinary."

As I crept toward Alexandria I asked Fleming to walk me through his bio, from birth right up to the pivotal moment when he decided to invent "Device for Perfusing an Animal Head." He said he was born in 1952, and that his parents settled in the Midwest by the time he was ready for high school. He took a college degree in engineering, worked a while, and then decided to go to law school because "I felt the world needed more lawyers who actually understood how science and technology really work."

"I think in terms of bridges a lot," he continued. "Bridges are not designed to be as strong as a road on the ground, but as strong links. And—"

The mighty ship was again breasting wine-dark seas. I changed the subject.

"Wasn't it in law school that you first had this whole idea of discorporation? What happened?" I already knew: the moment is tinglingly described in *Severed*. During his first pressure-packed year in law school, Fleming used to go for long runs to let off steam. As he loped along, thoughts would intrude, "accompanied by visual images so vivid and disturbing I had to stop in my tracks, shaking my head in disbelief and feeling as though I had opened my front door to find a baby in a basket on the doorstep, with an anonymous note saying, 'Please give this child a good home, because I can't.'" One day a terrible, mewling newborn arrived in just this fashion.

"One set of questions in particular kept coming back, no matter how hard I tried to shake them. *What would happen if a team of scientists cut the head off of a lab animal and kept it alive?* . . .

"And if scientists can do that to animals, what about humans dying of terminal disease or mortal injuries?"

Fleming, a science-fiction buff, decided to explore this startling notion by writing a novel about it. As he realized, creating "tension" would be tough, hence the "great man" theme.

"I was thinking in terms of Albert Einstein, Martin Luther King, a genius who has contributed to humanity, and he's dying," Fleming said as I hunted for a parking spot. "What if we could keep him alive a little longer? Or keep his entire mind alive longer? And not in some disembodied-brain thing."

"Why not?"

"Between you and me, I find that extraordinarily gruesome—the whole idea of a completely isolated brain, pink tissue that's still generating waves. Because you know it can't communicate. It's trapped. You don't even know if it's in pain. To some people the severed head thing might be completely grotesque, but to me *that* is grotesque."

Agreed. Let's eat!

After lunch we drove back to Crystal City, and I started pondering the obvious contradictions in Fleming's writing. On the one hand, severed heads are treated as abhorrent. On the other, there's this persistent theme that the "good" they could provide is tempting. I started to wonder if he might be a pro-decapitator hiding in anti-decapitator clothing. So I asked him what he thought about cloning, hoping his answer might reveal hidden Dr. Frankenstein agendas.

Nope. Typically (and consistently), he saw cloning as inevitable and a little scary—if we can clone people we will; the rich and greedy will have access to it first—but also as a chance for a large-scale social-improvement experiment. If Fleming had his way, he would set up a committee of wise people to decide, right now, who gets cloned and why, as a way to promote the recycling of worthy genetic material.

"Let's say that at any given time on Earth there are a hundred or five hundred or a thousand people the caliber of a Benjamin Franklin or a Thomas Jefferson," he said. "Society could say, 'Hey, this guy was truly great. Let's give him another round.' That could be done with these cloning groups, but I would pass a rigid, solid law that says—"

"I dunno, Chet. Do you think there's *any* chance cloning will be handled in such an orderly way?"

"You're probably right. The odds are pretty remote, but that doesn't mean we shouldn't try."

A pattern was taking shape. Fleming built up these idealistic edifices in his mind, but their props were shaky. I wondered: Were the termites of pessimism gnawing away at the supports? I took a chance and lobbed a big question that might provide a hint.

"Chet, what do you think will really happen with mankind? What's most likely in terms of, you know, day to day reality a hundred years from now?"

He pondered it for a moment. "In terms of most likely," he sighed, "I think in terms of overpopulation leading to environmental collapse, leading to basically dictatorships. I see mankind as being in just an epic struggle against overpopulation and I think we're gonna lose. I am absolutely convinced we are raping the resources of this planet. I think we're going to have some form of population wars, and these epidemics. I am definitely afraid that we will get into truly serious environmental problems. I'm talking wipeouts of insect populations because their wings can't stand UV radiation with all the ozone depletion, I'm talking about agricultural collapse. If we get to that level, it's going to turn into flat-out racial wars and religious wars. It's gonna be just an utterly horrifying, desperate, grim battle to see which groups will survive—and not all of them will."

I had only one more eensy question: *What?* I was completely caught off guard by this apocalyptic spiel. It hadn't turned up in any of Fleming's writings.

"Have you explored these themes in print?"

"I've written an extended article on evolution and religion," he said. "I'll give it to you later."

∞

Durk and Sandy may be happy to "wait and see" about immortality, but some life-extension buffs feel compelled to take action. No one exemplifies this spirit better than Saul Kent, a gray and craggy fifty-eight-year-old based in Southern California. Kent is no scientist, but he has long been involved in amateur animal experiments designed to "perfect" that famously controversial backup technique: cryonic freezing. Among other things, Kent and his pals have lowered the body temperature of lab animals close to the freezing point, and warmed them again, to see what they can withstand and to study the effects of frigid temperatures on cells.

"For several years now, we've been able to take dogs to a few degrees above freezing and revive them," Kent told me soon after we met. "I have a pet dog named Franklin who went through that process."

Kent was fielding my questions on a sunny Saturday morning in the lobby of a generic, one-story office building, home to his fringe-scientist's lair, a lab called called 21st Century Medicine. Mild, clinical chemical smells wafted through the lobby, and as we sat there, I couldn't help but notice how much Kent actually *looked* like a mad scientist. He had a leathery-lipless Frankenstein mouth, wild, stringy Igor hair, and very, very intense eyes.

Surprisingly, I found myself warming to the man. Kent had been a serious grouch when I first called him up, but in person he had a (moderately) lively sense of humor that animated his funereal bearing, and he was able to joke about his strange fixation. "At the age of four," he said, smiling, "I realized that people die, and I decided that would *not* be a good idea."

On the downside, there were those pooch experiments, which sounded icky and senseless. Kent made me promise not to reveal his office's address, because he feared attack by animal-rights advocates. As well he might. Over the years dozens of dogs have died in the name of Kent's certitude that cryonic preservation or low-temperature "suspended animation" can work, despite obstacles that have convinced mainstream scientists that these ideas—particularly freezing—are absurd. First, icing down bodies is a destructive process: when you freeze someone, spiky ice crystals form that rupture cells and wreck organs. Second, when people are frozen, they're dead. Its many miracles notwithstanding, science has yet to figure out how to bring anyone back to life.

All the same, Kent decided long ago that he could not just sit on his hands waiting for science to deliver longer lifespans. The 21st Century Medicine operation is the research arm of the Life Extension Foundation, a supplement-selling, Florida-based outfit that Kent founded with a fellow buff named Bill Faloon. In 1997, flush with cash from the sale of anti-aging nostrums and other supplements,

Kent and Faloon embarked on the Life Span Project, a multiyear, multimillion-dollar private research effort designed to "blaze new pathways" in longevity research.

The project had various parts, including a tie-in with credentialed researchers at the University of Wisconsin and the University of California at Riverside to test the rejuvenation properties of substances like melatonin on lab mice. Dubious-sounding canine experiments would continue at this facility and a new, larger space nearby. Kent introduced me to Brian Wowk, a pale, portly young Canadian Ph.D. who was coming on board to investigate how to deal with the problem of ice crystals rupturing cell tissue. I also met Mike Darwin, forty-three, an uncredentialed researcher lacking so much as a college degree, who was studying the effects of ischemia—the cutoff of blood flow—on the brains of dogs. Darwin was a prematurely white-haired man with tense features and a crisp speaking style. Kent handed me off to him for a tour of the main lab, and Darwin showed me around a warren that looked like a veterinarian's surgical theater. He wasn't very smiley; he was visibly unhappy with my presence.

"I'm antimedia," he said grimly.

It's hard to blame him. Cryonics has been a public laughing stock for decades, and it seems that every few years some scandal or pathetic episode pops up to remind journalists to poke fun at it.

The idea of freezing bodies for future rejuvenation apparently was first conceived by a man named Robert Ettinger, in a 1962 book called *The Prospect of Immortality.* And while the freezing part has proved simple enough, thawing and revival still elude discovery. There are currently a handful of companies in the United States that will freeze you, but there aren't many takers. (Contrary to popular myth, Walt Disney did not choose to be frozen, though Dick Clair, a writer for *The Carol Burnett Show,* did.) Alcor—one of the best-known outfits, and one that Kent and Darwin were affiliated with for years before splitting off on their own—had thirty-three customers on ice as of early 1997: thirteen bodies and twenty "neuros," or heads without bodies. (Many cryonics buffs believe that science will one day be able to grow a new body to match a preserved head.) The full-body freezing process, simplified, works like so. After you die, technicians pump out your blood and replace it with antifreeze. The body or head is wrapped in protective materials and suspended in a tank of liquid nitrogen.

Therefore, what "cryonics" really entails is a limbo world of cold storage and black comedy. Kent has been an active player on this stage. He became a fringe superstar after the 1987 death of his mother, Dora Kent, who had signed up with Alcor as a "neuro." Dora was beheaded—and her head was prepared for freezing—before the proper official arrived to declare her legally dead. Disgruntled, the Riverside County Coroner's office labeled the case a possible homicide after an autopsy revealed a lethal amount of barbituates in Dora's body. The matter was eventually dropped, but the allegations touched off a lengthy, highly publicized investigation that featured gruesome sideshows, like a find-the-head raid on Alcor that occurred after the cryobuffs refused to reveal its whereabouts. (The authorities didn't find the head, but they did find Dora's hands in a plastic jar.) Caught in the middle of it all were Saul Kent and Mike Darwin, who defied officialdom every step of the way.

Darwin is media shy, in part, because he's been caught up in such fiascoes, but also because he fears for his life if the animal-rights people know where to find his lab. The rightsniks, no doubt, would not be pleased with his antics: the research protocol he described to me was the stuff of a Chet Fleming nightmare. It involved stopping a dog's heart for fifteen minutes or more, trying to learn which drugs (or combinations) would help lessen the effects of ischemia in the dog's brain.

The application to cryonics? Just this. When you die, the blood flow to your brain is cut off, causing neurological damage. The cryobuffs would like to come up with a drug soup that would be administered to a dead "patient," preserving the brain as fully as possible.

On behalf of this questionable goal, many dogs were being "sacrificed" by Darwin, at a rate of one every two weeks.

"It's a brutal thing," he said, looking anguished. "The work we do here is punishing, for us and for the animals. We're very good at pain management, but if somebody slit me up both sides of the groin and put all kinds of instruments in me, and killed me for fifteen minutes, and then reperfused me and put me on a ventilator for a day, I don't think I'd be feeling too hot, no matter what you gave me."

Uh huh. Call me an old sentimentalist, Mike, but I'd say it's more punishing for the animals.

Such episodes give "suspended animation" a ghoulish air that strikes many people as highly unamusing. Should dogs really die so that obsessive men can fantasize about living longer?

Darwin and Kent made no apologies, and for both men, there was an obvious desperation in the hurry-up nature of this research. Neither looked like he was cheating death with dietary supplements.

"It's not an optimal situation," acknowledged Kent, who wears a metal bracelet on his wrist that tells physicians and paramedics to whistle in the freezer boys if he's found dead. "I coined the phrase, 'Being frozen is the second-worst thing that can possibly happen to you.' But whether the odds are high or low that I can be revived, I don't care. I just want to make the odds better."

∞

At the end of my visit, Kent introduced me to Dr. Stephen R. Spindler, a professor in the Department of Biochemistry at the University of California at Riverside. Spindler was funded to help conduct the Life Span Project's rodent research on the effects of supplements. He's also an old hand at researching calorie restriction, which for decades has been known to extend the life of lab mice and rats.

(The mystery is how.) A dapper, compact man who practices a mild calorie-restriction regimen himself, Spindler offered to show me his lab at Riverside, so I followed him over.

En route, I sorted my thoughts on all this stuff. Larry and Herb and Durk and Sandy seemed harmless enough, but obviously, I had to be against the dog-slaying. Calorie restriction seemed OK, but I did have to wonder if that would be a desirable way to "live" just to tack on a few more years. A typical platoon of calorie-restricted mice eat about 40 percent less than their unrestricted counterparts. Put in terms I could understand, that comes out to about 100 percent fewer trips to New Orleans. The idea of living life as an extended pursed-lip tightrope act seemed too rational to be much fun.

Put another way, it seemed too "Houyhnhnm." Say what you will about the superior moral virtues of the horse people in *Gulliver's Travels*, but admit this: they were awfully boring. Little wonder that no one mourned when they died. They probably couldn't tell the difference. The Yahoos weren't proper role models, either—they were too animalistic, nasty, and ignorant—but at least they knew how to have a good time, even if their primary amusements were howling, fornicating, and defecating.

Inside his lab, Spindler introduced me to his wife and lab partner, Patti Mote, a kindly woman who loaned me a white coat. We took an elevator upstairs to a small room where the racks of mice are kept. Against one wall was a rack of individually caged, calorie-restricted mice; against the other, the so-called ad libs, furry fatties who could eat whenever they wanted. With dramatic consistency, I was told, the fatties were unhealthier and died sooner. I leaned in to study them closely. They looked sluggish, lazy, and swollen, like little fur-covered sausages with hangovers. By contrast the dieters were alert, pert, and active. Even though I'm a naturally too-skinny guy myself, I felt no kinship bond with the fit-and-slim mice, who struck me as too smug and Houyhnhnm-like to love. I liked the fatties. The Yahoos.

The Spindlers grabbed a Houyhnhnm mouse and a Yahoo mouse and showed me the "dowel test," a measure of mouse dexterity. They laid a long wooden dowel over a dry sink, creating a sort of Dowel Bridge over Sink Canyon. They put a dieter on the dowel and slowly turned it. It kept its balance, no problem. Then they put a Yahoo through the same paces. The hapless tub clutched and blobbed and quickly fell. But . . . was I imagining it? He seemed to be smiling as he tumbled.

"He fell off without me even rolling the dowel," Spindler observed dispassionately.

Good for him. As far as I was concerned, that made him a champion. His sloppy-but-heroic effort brought to mind Alexis Zorba, the "life force"-y character created by Nikos Kazantzakis in *Zorba the Greek*. At one point, describing his vision of the afterlife, Zorba imagines God as a big, strong, hard-partying guy who greets newly arrived souls with a huge wet sponge. At Heaven's gate, you cower before him and confess your sins until he's heard enough.

"Flap! Slap! a wipe of the sponge, and he washes out all the sins," says Zorba. "'Away with you, clear out, run off to Paradise!' he says to the soul."

The "scolding" points at the rustic-but-elegant truth of Zorba's theology: God is proud of you for arriving a little stained and sinful. Blessed are those who live a little.

∞

"Have you ever read *The Denial of Death,* by Ernest Becker?" Chet Fleming asked me. "It's one of the great, great books ever written. It gets into comments that Otto Rank made, who was one of Freud's students. He said Freud was on the right track, but he put too much emphasis on sex, that it isn't sex that explains the human psyche so much as it is death."

We were sitting in a carry-out food joint across the street from the

Patent Office, sipping Cokes. We'd spent the afternoon poking around in the towering shelves that contain the paper patents. Though Fleming had serious work to do, he generously took the time to hunt down his patent so I could thrill to seeing the original. I gazed at the illustration on the first page, familiar to me from the book—it was of a crudely sketched simian head, seen from behind, resting atop a schematic diagram of the cabinet's plumbing and functions. Then I saw the sad addition made after the patent got reexamined: "Claims 1–20" . . . that is, everything . . . "are canceled."

Fleming told me more about *The Denial of Death*. "It's all about how humanity is caught in this gigantic conflict between these two opposing things," he said. "One is that our bodies are finite. They're mortal, they get sick, they die, they rot and stink. But we think our intellects are so incredible that somehow, damn it, they ought to be able to live forever. Some people satisfy that need by having kids. Others do it by trying to accomplish things, you know, by creating monuments that will live on after them as a testament to their time here on Earth.

"And some people," he said, giving me the startled look, "do it with the most hideous and heinous behavior you can possibly imagine. A lot of people join groups, and this does a lot to explain why some people would become fascists or Nazis."

I later leafed through *The Denial of Death,* which was very useful for understanding the immortality seekers. Becker, obviously, didn't know about Durk and Sandy and Saul and Mike when he wrote, but I doubt he would have approved of their capers. Becker was more aligned with the "deal with it" approach to death. In a chapter on the "Heroic Individual," he discussed various responses to mortality, searching for a path that ran somewhere between the pat answers of organized religion and the great failing that Otto Rank saw in Freud, this being that Freud "saw things too 'realistically,' without their aura of miracle and infinite possibility."

Becker wrote admiringly of the "knight of faith," a philosophical ideal described by Søren Kierkegaard in *Fear and Trembling*. This is a man who (in Becker's summary) "has given over the meaning of life to his Creator. . . . He accepts whatever happens in this visible dimension without complaint, lives his life as a duty, faces his death without a qualm. . . . He is fully in the world on its terms and wholly beyond the world in his trust in the invisible dimension." That is, he tries to do the right thing, have fun, and not whine.

That's a tall order, but as it turns out, it's how Fleming, in his own nerdy, earnest way, tries to live. Earlier, while he toiled away at his patent labors, I read his paper on evolution and religion. Chetishly titled "Evolution and Religion: An Honest Search for Truth," it covered vast stretches of territory, but boiled down to an idea I found easy to work with.

The way I read it, the paper is about how religion is sometimes used perversely, as a way for genetically similar tribes of people to identify "others" to whom they are hostile. Fleming believes that, in the future, religion can and must be shaped into a life-affirming force that, along the way, rescues mankind from falling into the trap of soulless biological determinism that is one possible response to the cold views of many evolutionary biologists. That is, that we aren't creatures sparked by souls, but well-programmed carriers of "selfish genes." Fleming is devoted to science, but he also hopes to cling to a scrap of religious mystery. "[S]cience cannot prove," he wrote, "that some power—call it God—which is higher and more complex than what humans have been able to measure, did not somehow guide and steer the course of evolution . . . to bring us to the point where we are today."

Simplified considerably, Fleming's argument is for a new fusion belief called Religious Darwinism, which holds that, whether there is a God or there isn't, man should behave and "evolve" as if there is. By which he means, toward greater cooperation, selflessness, even holiness—especially in regard to the natural world, which Fleming thinks is under dire threat as human populations grow. The individual's role is to make specific contributions, small and large, to the overall betterment. Hence the severed head patent, which on one level was Fleming's attempt to contribute to the common good by alerting the world to a potential evil. Beyond that, he argues for living with an awareness of "the extraordinary bargain we get to make with God."

So Fleming actually believes in God?

"I use God to refer to the entire collection of everything that is beyond our understanding," he told me. "Something has created this extraordinary planet, which is the most extraordinary place anyone could imagine for supporting life, diversity, and the richness of everything we could want. And you have to realize that the only real comfort anyone is going to find on this Earth comes from a satisfied feeling of being in love, and loving your family, and feeling good that you tried to help someone that day."

All very sweet. Still, if you believe Chet believes this (and I do) you have to ask: Then why is he so pessimistic?

Because he figures there's only about "a 10-to-20 percent" chance that mankind will evolve toward a higher consciousness. More likely, we'll evolve in our normal tribal, greedy way—driven by the blind self-interest of genetics—and he shudders to think where this might lead on a planet with diminishing resources.

"I'm convinced that [environmental] warnings are valid," Fleming wrote, "and if the human race doesn't begin solving those problems, then they will either destroy the human race or they will condemn any survivors to live . . . in a nightmarish vision of hell on earth. If an active God has taken steps to preserve the diversity of life on earth, the human race had better yield to God's will. That is part of the message, and part of the warning, of Religious Darwinism."

Looking up from the page, I realized I rather liked it, and I later folded the elements into a handy little mantra that seemed like a good alternative to the "hopeful selfishness" of the immortalist drama. Its elements: Don't be a jerk. Do be nice to your family, pets, and fellow man. Hope there's a God and, even if there isn't, live like there is. And above all, *don't whine.* Fleming didn't. The guy was facially disfigured during childhood, and we all know how warm and loving gangs of children can be about such things. But here he was after all these years, still banging away at his optimistic manifestos.

Looking at Fleming as we sat there, I felt oddly grateful. He hadn't given me too many severed-head thrills, but he gave me something better: a philosophy I could work with.

∞

My last stop in California was with Max More and his wife, Natasha Vita More, buff bodybuilders and cryonics believers who live in a perky, white-walled apartment in Marina del Rey. "More" is an assumed name that they adopted in keeping with a futuristic philosophy that guides their lives. It's called Extropianism—as in, "away from entropy"—and its 5,000 or so adherents long for a day when technology, in various ways, will carry people past the limits of the human form.

On a brilliant southern California Sunday morning, the Mores told me about the final days of Timothy Leary, who, before his death in early 1996, had signed up for cryonic treatment with an outfit for which Mike Darwin performed technical work, CryoCare. Freezing Leary would have been a notable coup, but he backed out, apparently citing his family's wishes that he not turn his death into a sideshow. To his credit, Darwin delivered a moving speech supporting Leary's right to choose death.

The Mores weren't there, but they didn't find this a happy conclusion. In an issue of *Extropy,* a magazine Max edited, Max and Natasha both lamented Leary's decision as a cop-out, a capitulation to "deathist" thinking.

That's a novel way of looking at it—death as a bad lifestyle option—but it was no joke to the Mores. They seemed sincerely stricken.

"Tim was not a long-range planner," Natasha said sadly.

"He was surrounded by people who were hostile to cryonics, who were very much into reincarnation and Buddhism, things like that," Max added. "Plus, a close confidante of his, John Perry Barlow, had this idea that—"

"That death was to be honored."

"That you were to die with dignity and grace and that death is this wonderful and natural thing. I think Barlow got Leary to see himself as a new Socrates, taking his hemlock."

And what was Barlow trying to prove?

"That dying is still an acceptable choice," said Max.

∞

My life-extension travels left me with serious doubts about the prospects of Religious Darwinism. Granted, the buffs represented a tiny fringe, but the selfishness inherent in their cause could (and, in Kent's and Darwin's case, already did) lead to bad things. During my last half-hour with Chet Fleming, he talked about the creepy "prior art" that he encountered while researching his patent. This, too, made me feel shuddery and pessimistic.

"If it can be done, it will be done," Fleming opined, and he should know. He lost his patent because, during his research, he overlooked a 1964 paper, published in *Nature,* describing an actual experiment on dogs that closely matched what he only imagined. (Give Fleming a gold star for ethics: it was he who brought this fact to the Patent Office's attention.) In the experiment, called "Extracorporeal Perfusion of the Isolated Head of a Dog," a team of scientists cut the heads off fifteen "adult mongrel dogs" and kept them alive briefly with tubes, fluids, and a pump.

The real big daddy of severed-headery, however, was Dr. Robert White, a neurosurgeon and researcher at the Case Western Reserve School of Medicine who was interested in isolating the head and brain to allow for more precise study of its functions. In one set of experiments, White removed the head of a monkey and grafted it to the side of the neck of another monkey. In another, he severed four monkey heads and transplanted them onto the heads of decapitated monkey bodies. The reattachments were vascular only, so the heads and bodies were not neurologically connected. But the four heads (technically called "cephalons") did "live," one of them for thirty-six hours, and it experienced consciousness.

"In three to four hours, each cephalon gave evidence of its awareness of the external environment by accepting and attempting to chew or swallow food placed in its mouth," said the paper by White and his team, which was published in *Surgery* in 1971. "The eyes tracked the movement of individuals and objects brought into their visual fields and the cephalons remained basically pugnacious in their attitudes, as demonstrated by their biting if orally stimulated."

White, who has long been demonized by animal-rights activists, was not doing this research in a quest for "immortality" or life extension, but he has said that head transplants could, in theory, become a viable medical technique. "I believe in the twenty-first century, we are going to transplant a human head, just as you transplant a person's heart today," he told the *Washington Post* in 1988. "If someone wanted to come through here and give us $5 million to build the machine, we could do it."

As far as Fleming knows, that line of research isn't being pursued anywhere, but what he wrote in *Severed* is, strange to admit, still true. Who's to say it won't happen someday?

During our final minutes together, I beseeched Fleming to share chilling stories about "strange experiences" with his patent. *Severed* has been advertised for years in catalogues, like *Loompanics* and

Amok, that sell fringe books to edge-seekers and cranks. Had he ever heard from anybody . . . bizarre?

"I never got a piece of hate mail," he said happily. Then he got serious. "But there was this one guy who called me—and this, this is real—who called and said, 'I'm not gonna tell you who I am, but I'm in the military. I'm in military intelligence. And I want you to know that this experiment has been done on humans.'"

"Noooo," I said.

"He did. He said it was done a number of times by French surgeons on Indo-Chinese soldiers who were mortally wounded back in the fifties. He said these surgeons basically regarded the Asians as just a couple of notches below humans, as basically expendable commodities. He said he'd seen written reports of this stuff being done."

"Did the guy sound like a nut? Did he have any hard evidence?"

No and no. The man "sounded rational" and called three times, but he never produced anything tangible. "He said reports existed, but he doubted I could ever find them. He mentioned Bethesda Naval Hospital, or Walter Reed, but there would be no way to trace it."

I thought about this. "But at this point, do you feel like it's all over?" I said. "Are severed heads a thing of the past?"

No again. "I still think it's going to happen someday," he said. "It would not surprise me in the slightest to hear that some contract research company is doing the research under carefully structured contracts in other countries."

The startled look appeared again. This time on my face. But who would get it? What kind of person would want it?

"Who knows? But I still think it will happen. Some guy's gonna get lung cancer or something and he's going to say, 'Let's try this. Let's try this. Because that's the only way I'm going to live.'"

A phantasm leaves a sleeping man, as depicted in Sylvan Muldoon and Hereward Carrington's classic soul-travel primer, The Projection of the Astral Body.

8

Take Me Home, Mr. Wiggles

[E]xteriorization of the astral body is, in fact, the first step into that mysterious realm called "death." So, reader, if you are interested in this dark phenomenon, if you have stood o'er the casket and gazed upon the cold corpse, and in silent awe have wondered how that being who only shortly before was animate . . . could now be but a lifeless clod, the same as you shudder to think you too will become, then you are interested in astral projection, for astral projection and death are not unlike.

—FROM *THE PROJECTION OF THE ASTRAL BODY,*
BY SYLVAN MULDOON AND HEREWARD CARRINGTON (1929)

"Think of the most important act you can accomplish today. Think of it now . . ."

I was asleep but hearing strange things. A baritone southern voice; synthesized musical tones; bizarre thumps and squeeps that got steadily louder, like a heartbeat with android backup singers. I opened my eyes to blackness, dimly remembering that I was waking up away from home, but not much else. What was this?

I felt around. I was lying on a mattress, not a slab. My hair was messed up, not neatly combed, parted, and patted by undertaker fingers. *Good.* A few inches to my left was a hard flat surface. Behind my head, more of the same. Feet? I scriggled in that direction and hit another wall. Yikes. *Bad.*

"*This day I perform my intended purpose,*" said the voice. "*This day I am more than my physical body.*"

Time to test another direction, like over my face, possibly to hit a coffin lid. Here goes . . . aaaand . . . empty space. Yay! I wiggled my arms and fingers like a deranged marionette and flopped to the right. Instead of wall there was a coarse, floppy curtain. I grabbed an edge, yanked, heard a Velcro rip, saw light, and remembered what was going on. I was waking up on the first morning of my week at the Monroe Institute, a private paranormal research foundation in the Blue Ridge Mountains of Virginia. The Institute uses esoteric methods to teach you how to have an "out-of-body" experience, or OBE, with a fairly ambitious goal in mind: to prove to yourself that you do, in fact, exist after death. I was sleeping inside one of its most important tools, a recessed sensory-deprivation bunk called a CHEC unit, an acronym for Controlled Holistic Environmental Chamber, a sort of perceptual tomb.

I also had a wife somewhere. Where was she?

Poking my head out, I looked at the generic decor of the larger room. Across the way, Susan was sitting in her CHEC with the curtain open and a light on, reading and looking glum. Her hair was wet from showering; she'd obviously been up a while.

"Hey," I said.

"Hey," she said without glancing up. "You overslept. They rang the bell for 'exercise period' a while ago, so it'll be time for breakfast soon." Pause. "I don't want to do this."

That I remembered. We'd been here since the previous afternoon, and events of the night before—cringe-inducing events—had already convinced her that the Monroe experience was going to be a New Age squishathon rather than the rigorous paranormal experiment we'd bargained for.

"Sorry, but we're doing it. You begged to come and we paid already." $1,495! "Come on over and let's bitch about it together."

She scrambled into my CHEC.

"What's the weather like?" I said.

"Yucky."

I looked out a window. So it was. The sun was up and it was late May, but you'd never know it. A gray-ceiling low had rolled in that would squat for three days, spitting out cold, sticky rain.

"See, this is good," I said. "The weather sucks, so we might as well be in here doing this. It's like a sick day."

"Except it's a whole sick week."

"I am going to count down now . . . when I reach the count of one, all your five physical senses will be operating clearly, sharply, and beautifully."

"And I'm already tired of Monroe's voice."

She meant the tape-recording, the voice that woke me, which was rumbling through the speakers mounted in our CHECs. It featured the vocal stylings of the late Robert Monroe, who founded the Institute. Monroe is not a household name, but to many fans of the occult and the paranormal, he is one of the great under-recognized geniuses of the twentieth century. They believe he invented a rational method to teach virtually anyone to embark on soul flights and come back again, at will, something he supposedly did countless times before passing away in 1995 at seventy-nine. The tapes were being played by Institute tekkies who, eerie thought, were twiddling knobs somewhere in this building even now. One of them punched in a new selection that replaced Monroe's voice: "Cable Car," an annoying synthesizer song that he wrote as a final wake-up call for us Institute campers.

"I had a weird dream last night," I said, changing the subject.

"What?"

I sat up and described its surreal textures. I was standing in a large room full of jabbering Monroe students, but I couldn't talk because my mouth, strangely, was stuffed with canned-corn kernels. Then everything changed, and I was in line to enter a bouncy, futuristic costume party. Every person in line was dressed as Mr. Spacely— George Jetson's crabby, runty boss—except me. I was naked.

"What do you think it means?" I said.

"That you don't want to be here either?"

"I mean deeper than that. The next level."

"That you have hackneyed dreams about not wanting to be here either?"

A new voice cut in on "Cable Car," speaking in the hushed tone of a "quiet storm" FM-radio jock. It was one of our three Monroe "facilitators," speaking live into a microphone, welcoming the day, telling us that breakfast would be served shortly.

"So come on down," the voice crooned, *"and let's all have a wonnnnderful day."*

"I hate the food here," Susan said, efficiently squeezing in a final gripe.

"Let's try to look on the bright side of this," I said as we crawled out to get dressed. "This will be an entire week of doing nothing but eating, sleeping, lying around, and listening to tapes. And maybe, just maybe, having out-of-body experiences. Won't that be neat?"

"I do want to go 'out of body,'" Susan said. "But I'm also scared to."

"It'll be safe. And even if we don't get that far, the tapes will be pretty wild." As she knew, the tapes were supposed to actually affect our brains in some tangible way, almost like hallucinogens, that brought on mind-expanding states of consciousness.

"Those tapes won't do anything."

"Now, stop it. I don't want to hear that."

"Ha," she said flatly. "Funny."

No, I was serious. I'd been through a lot in my pursuit of millennial and utopian understanding, and this week, my grand finale, was supposed to provide "closure" *and* a vacation. Although the coming episode did look to be potentially icky, I felt confident I could handle whatever Monroe dished out . . .

But not if the tapes weren't really like drugs.

∞

This may be hard to believe, but we had shown up at Monroe with a sunny attitude. Harder to believe: we left with one, too. Between times, it's true, we occasionally sounded like two pinch-mouthed old ladies who didn't like their cruise-ship berth, and the glow we carried away had little to do with Monroe's "planned activities," which struck both of us as a crock. It had more to do with the people we met there: our strange, mixed bag of fellow students. The worst of them were self-indulgently emotive saps. The best were ordinary people on a mission—an earnest mission to somehow comprehend the timeless uncertainties on the other side of death, and they displayed a sad, endearing nobility that was genuinely moving. They also taught us by example that, even if the soul can't really be "validated," there's something to be said for making the attempt.

The Monroe Institute consists of three moderne-rustic buildings plopped on lush green Blue Ridge foothills south of Charlottesville, Virginia. We drove through the main gate at mid-afternoon on a sun-blazed Saturday, following a winding, rising road that soon topped out, curved right, and morphed into a natty, tree-lined lane that led straight to the Monroe compound. We parked and gazed at the main building, the Nancy Penn Center, so named for Monroe's third wife, Nancy Penn Monroe, a fellow astral flyer who "went to the other side" in 1992. The center was a large, well-landscaped split-level with a glass tower jutting up at one end. I'd seen an illustration of this place that showed eel-sleek spirits squirting out of it at night, and I felt a flip-flop in my brain's apprehension lobe. We'd been treating this adventure as a lark, a game, but the fact was, we really didn't know what we were getting into.

We looked at each other. What *were* we getting into?

Time to find out. Leaving our stuff behind, we surged into the entrance hallway of the main building, coughing and clunking to herald our presence. The interior smelled richly of cedar, and I could hear, but not see, laughing people. Large, moon-faced portraits of Bob and Nancy hung on facing walls made of rustic planks, both rendered with luminous, spiritualized daubs.

Our greeter was a smiling Monroe employee named Dianna, who wore a blue T-shirt embossed with the official Institute logo: a ghostly spirit, shooting skyward from an etheric vortex. She took us downstairs to a bright gathering room called the Fox Den, plied us with pretzels and lemonade, and left us with a few other newbies who sat around a table, chattering fitfully.

Introductions all around. . . . Among the students were Ray and Kay, friends and cheerful blue-collar tubbies from the Chicago area who shared an interest in out-of-body experiences and a plateload of first-cousin esoterica like dowsing, UFOs, and runestones. Their "Joe Sixpack" personas bode well for the group's diversity. Walter was another good sign. He was a stressed-out, chain-smoking airport-operations manager from Strongsville, Ohio, who was hungrily looking for a pathway to serenity. Paul, a ponytailed twentysomething from Palo Alto, California, seemed whimsically "spiritual"—with alarm, I heard him mention that he played the didgeridoo, the spooky-sounding wooden trumpet played by Australian aborigines. Eileen, a short, friendly faced woman from Florham Park, New Jersey, defied easy categorization, as did Greg, a silent young man from Poland.

The group was amiable enough, but understandably stiff, given that we were strangers on the cusp of a very strange week. After a few minutes of interpersonal dead air I developed a "need" to find a john.

"Anybody know where a bathroom is?" I said, trudging up the squeaky staircase.

Ray laughed. "Hey. Try *not* finding one."

Huh? Then I saw. At the top of the stairs there were two bathrooms to the left, each fitted with a red light that shone when it was occupied. Walking down a much longer hall on the right, I saw red lights decorating several more doors. I never counted, but I'm pretty sure there were a dozen toilets on this floor alone, many more elsewhere in the building. Why such bounteous plumbing?

Heading back to the Den, I ran into Dianna, Susan, and a different batch of new arrivals whom Dianna had collared for a tour. First, she led us down the Great Hall of Potties, explaining sweetly that "there is approximately one toilet for every two people," but not saying why. From there she took us downstairs to the dining room, and then down more stairs to the exercise room, a mirrored space complete with a treadmill, dumbbells, a Soloflex, a stationary bike, and other stuff.

Dianna said daily exercise was advisable, given our invalid-like, bedsore-generating routine. In this program—the beginner's OBE class, known as "Gateway"—we would spend several hours every day inside our CHECs, listening to consciousness-expanding tapes as we worked toward the blast-off state.

"All those days of lying on your back," she cautioned, "*can* take a toll."

After showing us a carpeted meeting room next to the Fox Den, and the gift shop and lending library (where I snagged a copy of *Catapult*, a biography of Monroe written by a Gateway grad), Dianna released us to find our rooms. She took Susan and me to a closed hallway door and gave us puzzling directions.

"This door opens onto a small office that you have to go through to get to your CHEC units, which are numbers 23 and 25. Normally the office is empty. They're having private interviews in there now, but it's OK, you can just knock and walk on through."

"Really? We can just walk through when they're having private interviews?"

"Yes."

"That's OK?"

She chuckled. "It's definitely OK."

I went and got our stuff, knocked, opened the door. It wasn't OK. One of our three counselors—Cheryl, a gym-coachy person with chopped blond hair and a natural scowl—poleaxed me with a glare.

"I'm sorry," I said. "She said we were supposed to come through here. Even though . . . you're in here." Argh. It sounded weak, even to me.

"Who said?"

I forgot her name. "The woman."

"You can get to your room just as easily through the room on the other side."

"She didn't tell us that, but sure, we can go that way."

"Noooo," she sighed, "it's fine, it's fine. Jusssst . . ." With a puffed sigh, she waved us through. We toted past her, slump-shouldered, shut our door, after which I used exuberant mime calisthenics to convey that Cheryl could kiss my butt. Granted, it was a meaningless encounter, but it left me feeling crabby, almost sullied. It was our first hint that the Monroe Institute might be a lot like summer camp—complete with jerk counselors.

Susan and I inspected the CHEC units, then she announced that she had to get out and find a bathroom. She tried the alternate route through the other room, but that was a no go: she opened it and saw a man and woman in there, giggling and dry-humping on a CHEC bed. She shut it instantly and wide-eyed the Cheryl door.

"Can't you wait?" I begged. She bulged her eyes: not a choice. I knocked, took my lumps, Susan left. She didn't come back, either, so I assumed she'd been ambushed by a counselor. I slumped on the floor, examining *Catapult* while Cheryl interviewed students. As it turned out, her grousing about privacy was silly—this building was put together with beach-house craftsmanship, and there was a big gap at the bottom of the door. Thus I couldn't help but overhear as

Cheryl prebriefed the Gateway hopefuls. Eileen was in there now, not exactly meshing with "coach."

"What do you hope to get out of Monroe?"

"I'm here to try to reach the theta level," Eileen said. "I mean the theta *pattern*. I don't know what you people call it, but that's what I call it."

Cheryl, crisply: "Let's just call it an altered state."

"Sure. Anyway, that's what I want!"

∞

Feeling guilty about eavesdropping, I climbed inside my CHEC, sniffing it like a kitten in its first litter box and fretting about facing Cheryl. (Which never happened. The counselors forgot me.) I hadn't thought once about what I really "wanted" from Monroe. I'd better start.

On the most literal level, I was here as a voyeur, but I'd also come because my experience with the life-extension obsessives and Severed Head Man had brought on an unwelcome funk about the body-as-meat problem. I decided to investigate belief in the human soul, which struck me as the most "utopian" dream of all for a species whose members are pangingly aware of their inevitable demise.

Did the human spirit exist? I knew, of course, what Christianity had to say on the subject: Yes, it does, and it winds up in Heaven. Have faith, be good, and you'll get there. But I also knew there were "others" out there, people of a metaphysical bent who desired a more take-charge answer to this eternal question.

Unfortunately, I didn't know where to start. Ghosts and astral projection and gurgling ectoplasms had never been among my interests. Fortunately, Susan knew this area quite well. Raised in an atheistic household, she had long pursued personal spiritual interests, outside the boundaries of formal religion, in a quiet but determined search for evidence that we are more than just bodies, and she'd long been fascinated with OBEs. Earlier, at home, when I asked if she had any books on the topic, she snuffled about happily in our shelves and pulled out a stack of yellowed paperbacks that I'd never seen before. There was *Out-of-the-Body Experiences,* by Robert Crookall. *The Projection of the Astral Body,* by Sylvan Muldoon and Hereward Carrington. And *On Life after Death,* by the only name familiar to me, Elisabeth Kübler-Ross.

I opened the Muldoon and Carrington. It was vintage stuff, originally published in 1929, and it contained scary old drawings of a spirit floating out of a body, attached head-to-head by a wispy cord. "Arrows show the route the phantom takes in projecting," the caption said. "Phantom often uprights here."

"You're into this!" I said, kidding her.

"I'm not into it," she said defensively. "I'm just . . . interested."

Her tone also said: no wisecracks, please.

No problem. As I told her right away, of all the subculture beliefs I'd taste-tested, *this* would be the one I found it easiest to root for. Despite my skeptical shell, I've always vaguely wanted to believe we will exist again as whooshing spirits. Ever since my dad died, in 1979, I'd slowly moved further in that direction, even though my "head" scoffed that it was all a fantasy. It complicated matters that my mom—a level-headed person—had delivered straight-faced reports of contact with dad's talkative wraith. Maybe she was dreaming, maybe it was wishful thinking. Whatever it was, I liked the idea of it, and I had to admit that Dad seemed a natural candidate for ghost-dom. A tall, looming, white-haired M.D. who had been forced to confront too many of life's gutty realities during his career as a pathologist, he was a quiet and sometimes morose, but also benevolent and religious man whose mind often seemed lost in a troublesome cloud. He even gave himself an unintentionally ghostly nickname late in life: the Great White Father, a label he jokingly took during a brief enthusiasm for C.B. radios in the mid-seventies.

According to the family contactee, the Great White had soothing things to say about Eternity, and the sense was that encountering his presence conferred a tremendous feeling of peace about what awaited in the beyond. I grew envious when I heard about it. Many times I'd wished he would drop in for a basso-profundo chat with me. Among other things, he'd never met Susan. I wanted to hear him say he liked her.

As for Monroe, we quickly gathered from Susan's books that he was The Man, a figure who had supposedly brought rigor and rationality to OBE research. A wealthy radio and cable-television executive, he believed he began having out-of-body experiences in 1958, involuntarily at first, but later at his own behest and under his control. Monroe kept mum about this until 1971, when he published *Journeys out of the Body,* a widely read account of his astral adventures on this world and beyond that made him famous, even in the mainstream. (The *Wall Street Journal* once featured Monroe on its front page because the Institute was popular with mind-expanding executives.)

Monroe had star power in part because he didn't fit the fringe-person stereotype—he impressed observers as a nuts-and-bolts guy—and in part because, if you believed him, he was something of an out-of-body Edison. Over the years he tinkered with methods to help the less-gifted reach altered states conducive to astral travel. He developed a patented technique called "Hemispheric Synchronization," or "Hemi-Sync," a pattern of sounds, used in the Monroe Institute's audiotapes, that supposedly made going out of body much easier for beginners, like learning to ski on super-sidecut parabolas.

How did it all work? We had no idea, but from quick glances at two other Monroe books—*Far Journeys* (1985) and *Ultimate Journey* (1994)—we gathered that things had gotten fairly freaky by the time Monroe "left the physical" for good in 1995. Working mainly in the seventies and eighties, he and a team of hard-traveling volunteer

"Explorers" had mapped out the beyond, assigning numbered "levels" to various zones in the spirit realm.

As I cozied up in my CHEC, I opened *Catapult,* which was written by Bayard Stockton, a former *Newsweek* correspondent and recovering alcoholic who took the Gateway class in 1987, during a quest for spiritual footing. Gateway produced incredible, revelatory experiences for him—at one point, blissing out in one of the "levels," he enjoyed "a bolstering, warming conversation with the energy I identify as Jesus Christ." As a result, he swooned. The book depicts Monroe as a visionary, a genius, a sort of out-of-body Hugh Hefner: "Monroe—the Ultimate Adventurer. The Ultimate Player. . . . A Scorpio who's a man's man, and a woman's man as well. He protests he's unaware of the flirtation issuing from his liquid, appealing eyes."

Chucking *Catapult* for the moment, I decided to try hard to suspend my sarcasm and make this work. But first: a nap. The CHECs seemed incredibly cozy to me, so I snoogled in, clicking off the wall light, exhaling loudly, smacking lips. The bed was wide and firm and offered a fluffy comforter. There were three knobs for adjusting blue, red, and amber "mood" lights overhead. A metal-plate console on the wall contained various dials, jacks, and a switch labeled, simply, READY.

I didn't know what the switch was for but I flipped it anyway. "I *am* ready," I declared. "Let's get metaphysical."

∞

In *Catapult,* Stockton fondly recalls "amazingly appetizing vegetarian" food during his Gateway week. Lucky him. Our first dinner was slop—glutinous Chinese mishmash, "southern" vegetables boiled in sugar water—and the fare went downhill after that. During the week I developed logy indigestion. I grew increasingly swollen and inert.

Susan and I did enjoy our table mates, however. Especially Ray, who didn't like the food either, but for his own special reasons.

"Too many vegetables," he carped, working his rubbery face into an indicative frown. "I won't lie to you. I gotta have junk-food burgers."

I interrogated Ray, curious about how he ended up here. It had a lot to do with his pal Kay, an older woman and the mother of three. Kay had turned Ray onto paranormal pursuits, and they filled the void that organized Christianity, which he'd grown up with but now disdained, had left in his soul. Ray said he'd experienced two OBEs in his life. He was here, flat out, to score another.

"If you've already had them, why do you need the training?" I asked.

He shrugged. "No control." He meant that in baseball-pitcher terms. Ray hadn't been able to "direct" his astral body to go where he wanted, so it bumped around like an unmoored dirigible.

After dinner we trooped over to the second building, David Francis Hall (named for a rich benefactor and friend), a two-story structure that was the site of our evening lectures. We gathered in a big space with chocolate-brown ceiling beams, two large flip charts, a jumbo projection screen up front, and four gigantic speakers that looked like "custom" jobs circa 1973. Swiveling chairs were grouped around large Formica-top tables pushed together in a zigzag pattern.

Taking a seat, I was whammied by a sense of olfactory déjà vu. The entire building reeked of stale cigarettes, an odor I knew all too well. The Great White Father (and Mother) were heavy puffers, especially in his car.

I snoofed deeply and frowned. There was no doubt about it: this building had a nicotine fiend lurking inside it, a tar-stained troll, which confused me. Signs on the walls commanded that smoking was prohibited throughout the building. So who was lighting up? Phantoms?

After everybody sat down and stopped buzzing, Joe Gallenberger—a square-jawed psychologist and Gateway trainer with a mustache, serene eyes, wire rims, and sandy hair—brought things to order.

"'Trainer' is a funny word for the Gateway process," he said gently, tapping his fingertips together, smiling enigmatically. "It's more like . . . flight attendant." That got a laugh.

Joe said we would do our introductions "a bit differently." We had to pick a buddy, interview him or her, and then describe our new pal to the group. I turned right to watch Susan and a stranger start gabbling away. I turned left and saw a huge, square-shouldered man in his fifties. He had dark brown hair, a regimental mustache, a set of white teeth that looked strong enough to bite through lumber, shoulders like Frankenstein, and a grip like a Norwegian whaler.

"Hellooo!" he boomed in an elegant foghorn voice. His name was Craig, and he said he was a commercial printer from Newport Beach, California.

Stiffly, I continued the interview. "So, Craig," I said, "how long have you been interested in . . . phenomena like this?"

He smiled, inhaled, and answered in a theatrical boom.

"I'll tell you, Alec, when I was nine years old my DAD started having out-of-body experiences that continued for years and years. His experiences were a HELL of a lot like Bob Monroe's, a HELL of a lot." He paused to deliver a *sotto voce* aside: "I know it sounds crazy, but my friend, believe me, I wouldn't shit you. Ha ha ha haaaaa." Then it was back to the regular bray: "And this was in the FIFTIES, mind you, before anybody had even HEARD of Bob Monroe!" Craig added that he'd been trying since childhood to go out of body himself, but without success. He was here looking for "some assistance."

The rest of the group was a mix that Monroe probably would have liked and loathed. Monroe could be grumpy about the people who were interested in his methods—he prided himself on attracting serious metaphysicians rather than "unreasoning misfits."

The class contained a little of everything: professionals (a lawyer, a dentist), several "misfits" (no hints: you make the call), and some people who had come for genuinely moving reasons. To name just a few from a freshman platoon that numbered twenty-five . . . Lisa was a free spirit from Levittown, New York, who walked with a bouncy gait that hinted annoyingly at prior training in "the dance." She said she had a "magical connect" with Bob, the dentist. Nancy from Colorado and Karla from Connecticut were forlorn women who had both lost loved ones in recent years (a husband and two fathers between them) and got into OBE research hoping to reconnect. Jim worked in computers, wrote poetry, had achieved OBEs before, and tended to kvetch about small details like the food (a soul mate!) and his lumpy bed. Oriyin published a New Age magazine in Sedona, Arizona, and seemed to inhabit her own daffy orbit.

Joe was buddied-up with Curt, an electrical engineer from Pennsylvania who had good reasons for putting faith in OBEs. He'd been diagnosed with amyotrophic lateral sclerosis, or Lou Gehrig's disease. There's no cure for it—there's no treatment for it—and it is invariably fatal, following a prolonged period of decline. So far, Curt's only noticeable symptom was a slight slurring of speech.

Last, we heard the astral résumés of our Gateway staff. Joe was from North Carolina and had experienced "minor" OBEs as a kid and "major" ones as a young man, after he suffered a motorcycle wreck that put him in a body cast for six months. He'd also written a book detailing his attempts to forge an OBE bond with his dead brother, who had committed suicide. Karen, a middle-aged brunette from Sausalito, California, was a hard-flying Monroe veteran from way back in the seventies, when Monroe briefly launched a West Coast branch. Cheryl, a nurse from Las Vegas, was spearheading a Monroe expansion into "German-speaking countries." She'd had a near-death experience at age twenty-one and had been affiliated with the Institute since 1984.

"Uncle Bob and I loved each other," she recalled, "even when we would be at loggerheads." Uh huh. I could certainly buy half of that.

Cheryl outlined the daily routine. We'd rise, exercise, eat breakfast, "do tapes and discussion and break," eat lunch, have a long break, "do" more tapes, eat dinner, sit through some kind of evening program, maybe do another tape, and go to sleep.

Karen and Joe then briefed us on techniques. The Monroe tapes, they said, deferring a full techno-lecture until later in the week, used special tones that somehow synchronized the brain's two lobes in a way that helped bring on out-of-body states. Gateway also employed standard relaxation methods (like saying *ommmmm* until our skulls vibrated, known as "resonant tuning") and spoken instructions from Monroe to guide us through a series of escalating "base camps" of consciousness. Monroe was big on lingo, so he assigned numbers to each level. First we would "go" to a state called Focus 10, which Monroe defined as "body asleep, mind awake." Our final stop in Gateway was Focus 21, which marked the transition area where Here became There.

Karen said marvelous things happened at this Focus, and that once we reached it, we should "explore freely." Reaching any of these states required total concentration, so it was strongly, strongly recommended that we "empty our bladders before each tape." Ah, that explained the bathroom bounty. It seemed like a silly detail, but it ended up mattering to Jim—from start to finish, what he called his "aqua problem" kept waking him up, and he suggested half-seriously that the CHECs should be fitted with catheter tubes.

"Bob's favorite saying and famous saying was, 'Go and find out for yourself,'" Karen said, pausing to let that sink in. I heard faint murmurs of resonant grokking. *Mmmm.*

"Let it be large," she continued. "Let it be unfamiliar. Let it be different. Let it be new. Let the experience teach you. Or tell you." *Mmmm.*

"Bring in a quality of love. I'm talking about the highest resonant energy that we can operate in." *Mmmm.*

"This week may be a lot about remembering. You're *not* new to this." *Yessss.*

While Monroe still lived, the first evening's highlight came when he descended from his home on nearby Roberts Mountain to slurp a cup of coffee and say howdy. We got him on video, shown on the big screen up front. The tape, regrettably, was shot with the same dead-on style used by Marshall Herff Applewhite for his suicide farewell, so Bob looked rather spooky and cult-leadery. But he sounded soothing, like a craggy old gentleman who sincerely hoped we enjoyed happy flying.

"We have only one particular piece of dogma that you have to consider," he said. "And that is that you, and the essence of you, are more than your physical body. . . . Gateway helps you explore the borders, the edges of consciousness as we know it."

Tape over, the trainers took our watches away (the better to free up our consciousnesses with) and asked for questions. I had one—If I encountered Cheryl's spirit in the astral, would it be all right to trick her into entering a jar and then screw the lid on?—but I said nothing. Flesh or spirit, I didn't want her coming after me with revenge in mind.

∞

Several major religious movements were created in the United States in the nineteenth century, including Mormonism, Christian Science, Seventh Day Adventism, Jehovah's Witnesses, Spiritualism, and Theosophy, an important feeder current of what we now call the New Age. The last two are direct influences on the Monroe Institute's m.o., though the Monroe-ites would hotly deny it. Monroe saw himself not as the heir to mossy old crackpot traditions but as a hard-science guy who, as a bonus, happened onto a fantastic yet "provable" spiritual realm. But that night, as I stayed up late studying his books, Susan's esoteric collection, and works from my personal weirdo stash, it seemed obvious that the Monroe training was a pastiche of the Spiritualist tradition and Theosophy.

Spiritualism came into prominence back in 1848, when the Fox sisters of Hydesville, New York, attracted national press coverage with their claim that they had made direct contact with the spirit world. The *Encyclopedia of Mystical and Paranormal Experience* describes the genesis:

> [Margaret] (Maggie) was fourteen and her sister Catherine (Katie) eleven when they and their parents began to hear strange thumping noises at night, which Mrs. Fox believed were caused by a ghost. Maggie and Katie discovered that if they clapped their hands, the raps answered back. By rapping in response to yes-no questions and the spelling out of letters . . . the spirit allegedly claimed to be a murdered peddler named Charles Rosa, whose throat had been slashed by John Bell, a former occupant of the house.

The Fox sisters became famous in the years ahead. Joined by their older sister, Leah, and initially promoted by P. T. Barnum, they mounted stage acts in New York, where they performed public séances, talking to departed luminaries like Ben Franklin. Attacked by religious authorities and skeptics, Spiritualism nonetheless spread to Great Britain in short order, where it thrived, even among the educated classes. (This was true in America, too: among Spiritualism's fans were Harriet Beecher Stowe and Horace Greeley.)

Over time, the Fox sisters slouched through a checkered career that helped discredit Spiritualism as a mass phenomenon. Both became alcoholics as the years wore on; Maggie later converted to Catholicism and denounced her old beliefs as fraudulent and evil. In 1888, Maggie and Katie made a joint debunking appearance in New York, explaining the tricks they used during séances. Spiritualism began a long, slow decline after that, but it never really died. In fact, its spirit exists all around us today, manifested in our society's thrumming obsession with near-death experiences, angels, and even old-fashioned spirit communication. Best-sellers like Betty Eadie's *Embraced by the Light* (about near-death experiences) and lesser-known books like Harold Sherman's *The Dead Are Alive: They Can and Do Communicate with You!* make claims that sound like updates of the Foxes' original rap:

"You'll listen to the actual voices of the dead—contrary, lyrical, entrancing," says *The Dead Are Alive*. "You'll also discover how *you* can communicate with the dead—and capture their voices on an ordinary tape recorder!"

Helena Petrovna Blavatsky, who died in 1891, left a similar legacy. A Russian émigré with a stout body and a bulldog's face, "H.P.B." traveled the world for years in the mid-1800s and claimed to have spent a mysterious period studying with wise masters in Tibet, beings who taught her all about the occult, telepathy, the wisdom of the ancients, and out-of-body projection. She emigrated to New York in 1873, where she founded the Theosophical Society in 1875. The years ahead were filled with perambulation (in 1878 Blavatsky and her sidekicks moved to India), feverish writing (she produced two mammoth volumes of dense Theosophical mumbo, *Isis Unveiled* and *The Secret Doctrine*), controversy (Blavatsky's claims that her spiritual masters, Koot Hoomi and Morya, produced tangible artifacts from beyond, including written messages, were investigated and debunked by the British Society for Physical Research, a group devoted to open-minded but tough investigation of occult claims), and deflation. Theosophy lived on as a formal organization—indeed, the Theosophical Society exists to this day—but it never became as important as Blavatsky hoped.

Spiritualist and New Age themes both pop up in the Monroe teachings, as does a Yankee obsession with doing it yourself. This goal, too, predated Monroe. The *Encyclopedia* credits a Frenchman, Marcel Louis Forhan (born 1884), for being the first to lay out practical OBE methodology. Here in the United States, a famous early practitioner was a lovable character named Sylvan Muldoon, who co-wrote (with a British-born enthusiast named Hereward Carrington) *The Projection of the Astral Body,* an OBE classic that offered step-by-step advice. The men met after Muldoon, then in his twenties, read Carrington's work, which discussed the ancients' interest in the subject and claimed to find biblical support for the then-popular notion that a "silver cord" connected the body and soul during astral travel. (In Ecclesiastes 12, it's written that when a "silver cord" is "loosed . . . Then shall the dust return to the earth as it was: and the spirit shall return unto God who gave it.") Carrington lamented that, with the exception of a few pioneers like a Frenchman named M. Charles Lancelin, there was a dismaying lack of practical information on "this vital theme."

That comment inspired a tangy letter from young Muldoon, who said, "I can write a book on the things that Lancelin does not know!" So he and Carrington did. Muldoon's own experiences had started as a boy, when his mother, an avid occultist, took him to the Mississippi Valley Spiritualist Association camp in Clinton, Iowa. His first night there, the twelve-year-old Muldoon began "vibrating at a great rate of speed, in an up-and-down direction, and I could feel a tremendous pressure being exerted in the back of my head. . . ." He soon realized he was floating over his body, to which he was attached by an "elastic-like cable."

For beginners, Muldoon offered several techniques, including the "'Dream Control' Method of Projection," which involved a Focus 10–like state ("Try to remember that you are awake, but still going to sleep"), followed by the willed application of a dream. Its "plot" should symbolically lift the spirit out of its physical housing.

"Imagine that you are steaming out of the body—coming out of all the pores," Muldoon advised, in words that suggest why skeptics usually dismiss OBEs as auto-suggestion. "Now this steam is collecting just above you and is forming a replica of yourself and is then carried upward on the air."

∞

Monroe's big innovation was using sound to flip the switch. The various beeps, buzzes, and tones used in Hemi-Sync are supposed to promote synchronicity between the left side of the brain (the dominant, "rational" side) and the right (the intuitive, "artistic" side). The hows and whys are complicated, but it's supposedly done by filling each ear with sounds played through headphones, which are synchronized by the brain into "binaural beats" that Monroe said "appear to contribute to the hemispheric synchronization evidenced in meditative and hypnagogic states of consciousness." Which is a fancy way of saying that when you put on headphones, different sounds come in from each side, your brain reconciles them, and you feel really, really good.

To me it sounded like the college freshman's timeless recreational favorite: getting drunk or high, slapping on the headphones, and listening to Pink Floyd. How did it promote an altered state? I've never fully grasped that one. The Monroe explanation (summarized in "The Hemi-Sync® Process," a paper by F. Holmes "Skip" Atwater, who works in the Institute's Research Division) consists of mostly incomprehensible jargon. Not surprisingly, Monroe has been sharply criticized over the years—plenty of skeptics *and* paranormal supporters have said his theories are simply garbage, and that he spent decades making too much of what were probably just vivid dreams—but I knew that was irrelevant. For all I know, he really was experiencing the soul flights that he described. The people who'd paid for Gateway definitely believed in him. Every one of them was poised for lift-off.

Monroe's claims were certainly intriguing. During the week I read all three of his books, fully absorbing the staggering nature of his claims. By the end he was saying he'd traveled to where the dead go—he called it "the Park"—and that Monroe-trained soul flyers were going on phantom-world rescue missions, serving as escorts for the sometimes addled spirits of the recently departed. One Monroe graduate sprang into action after the Oklahoma City bombing to aid and abet its victims during their hasty transition to the beyond.

Things weren't quite so flashy at first. *Journeys out of the Body,* which was based on Monroe's experiences in the button-down fifties and sixties, is written in a no-nonsense prose monotone that conveys Monroe's utter seriousness about his research:

> Let's look for a beginning to this candid report of a highly personal experience.
>
> In the spring of 1958 I was living a reasonably normal life with a reasonably normal family. Because we appreciated nature and quiet, ours was a country environment. The only unorthodox activity was my experimentation with techniques of data learning during sleep—with myself as the chief subject.

The first abnormal episode came during an auto-experiment on a Sunday afternoon. With the family away, Monroe listened to a tape he'd worked up. Nothing much happened. The family returned and they all sat down to brunch. Later, Monroe was seized with a severe torso cramp and nausea.

Not so remarkable, except that this episode—which Monroe figured had to do with the tape rather than the grub—evolved menacingly over the next few weeks and months. At one point he experienced a continuing series of vibrations, "like an electric shock running through the entire body without the pain involved." Months later, half asleep, Monroe draped an arm over the right side of his bed, touched the rug, pushed, and was surprised to feel his arm go through the floor. He tried to convince himself this was only a hallucination, but he understandably remained troubled.

Finally, four weeks later, the first big fly-out occurred. The vibrations, which had disappeared, returned. As Monroe lay in bed "trying to decide how to analyze the thing," he thought about going up in his glider the next day—his hobby at the time. That's when it happened:

> After a moment, I became aware of something pressing against my shoulder. Half-curious, I reached back and up to feel what it was. My hand encountered a smooth wall. . . .
>
> Then I looked again. Something was wrong. . . . It wasn't a wall, it was the ceiling. I was floating against the ceiling, bouncing gently with any movement I made. I rolled in the air, startled, and looked down. There, in the dim light below me, was the bed. There were two figures lying in the bed. To the right was my wife. Beside her was someone else. Both seemed asleep.

The "someone else" was Monroe himself. Shaken, and concerned that he had survived a near-death experience, Monroe went to see a psychologist, who told him not to worry, that this sort of thing happened all the time to "some of the fellows who practice yoga and those Eastern religions." Seeking answers, Monroe methodically investigated what was known about the "Second Body." His foraging led him to a surprising "underground" made up of people from all walks of life who shared his interests—a hidden, proto–New Age subculture. During this time, Monroe encountered the vintage writings of people like Sylvan Muldoon, but something about their work and the underground as a whole irritated him: namely, its lack of scientific rigor. From the start, Monroe insisted that if OBEs were real, they had to yield quantifiable results.

"The most consistent problem encountered in associating with the underground," he wrote, "has been to avoid submergence of the analytical approach in the vast morass of theological thought and belief. . . . Perhaps the Second Body operating in the Second State can provide the quantum jump to *prove* God empirically. Then there will be no more underground."

"Proving" God? Awfully big talk. But Monroe meant exactly what he said.

∞

Sunday morning, winded by our grumping, Susan and I slouched down to breakfast late, where I stoked my developing bolus with rubbery bacon. I skipped my shower and showed up, scritching my scalp, just in time for our first pretape briefing in the carpeted conference room. It was a sock-feetsy place, apropos to the half-sleepy state in which we existed all week. Everybody was dressed in sweats, shorts, jeans, or billowing New Age clown pants.

The trainers reviewed the protocols. Before each tape, we would meet here to "debrief" (discuss) the previous tape and prepare for the next one. We were told to meticulously "journal" our experiences.

"Keeping a journal is almost a command," said Joe, who explained that we might experience "puzzle pieces," seemingly disconnected images that could fit together later.

"I kept getting images of a red wagon," he recalled. "I finally got the whole experience of being *in* a wagon. The message was, 'Play more, Joe.' I was at a Mr. Serious point." *Mmmm.*

Karen outlined the first tape, "Intro to Focus 10." In this and most subsequent tapes, Monroe would guide us with his voice, saying things like "Do this now" and "I will meet you there." After relaxing to the sound of surf, we would imagine an "energy conversion box," a container that would temporarily hold all our real-world problems while we squinted and wished for transcendence.

"On the energy conversion," one woman asked, "is it overkill to just put your whole analytical brain in the box?"

Not at all, Karen said. "Just *love* that left brain. And just send it on vacation."

Using resonant tuning—the *ommmm* and *ahmmmm* business—we would become aware of the energy flows in our bodies. Then we'd form a "resonant energy balloon," an imaginary cocoon of "positive" mojo. In Monroe-ese, forming this balloon was called "popping a Reball."

Karen closed with a homily about step four: the all-important Gateway Affirmation, an astral creed that begins, "I am more than my physical body. . . . I can perceive that which is greater than the physical world."

"Focus 10 is the foundation upon which you will do your expansion work," Karen summed up. "So get into it like you've never gotten into it before."

With that we shot off like twenty-five six-year-olds heading for Christmas Eve bunks. An hour later we reassembled, sitting on pillows or portable floor chairs, everybody looking dozy. How had it gone?

"I found it exceptionally incredible," said Iona, a short-haired woman who spent the week drawing loopy-stroked cartoons of what she'd experienced. "To me as a visual artist, I just got so much material. Heart be still! It was the most wonderful way to see color."

"I went deep into the Focus 10 state, came out, and went back into Focus 10 again," the dentist sniffed cockily.

Lisa, his bouncy schmurgle buddy, said: "It was amaaazing. I kept thinking of when I was a kid taking the Nestea plunge!"

Was I missing something? I didn't get results like that, and I sure as heck tried. I taped myself "doing" the tapes, and there's an embarrassingly loud commitment to my Reball popping, which sounded like operatic hiccups.

And the tapes did seem to have an effect. They were surprisingly hypnotic, and throughout the day, when I managed not to pass out, there was the faintest stirring, just a trace, of the early sensations of inhaling nitrous oxide, a feeling I remembered vividly from college parties sponsored by thieving medical students. Once or twice as the Focus 10 tonal buzz kicked in, faint blue-white blobs of light floated into "view" behind my closed eyes, and I could feel the deep-brain drone that I recalled as the last "focus" before I entered the nitrous-oxide zonkosphere.

But incredible? The Nestea plunge? I wondered if my classmates weren't showing off.

Mercifully for my consciousness's ego, other reports were less remarkable. That first day, Craig became known (and resented by the trainers) for cheerfully, loudly admitting that he was getting nowhere. "I just have this DESPERATE feeling that I'm a TERRIBLE fake," he lamented.

Eileen and Ray said they caught nothing but a nap. "I couldn't do anything," Ray said, slouching and clad in a Bud Lite T-shirt. "I just got very relaxed and that was it."

"Were you lying down?" Cheryl asked.

"Oh, yeah."

"That just may be your process right now. Just go with it."

"Just use your imagination when you're not getting it," Karen said, adding advice that would draw a whistle and a technical foul from any half-vigilant skeptic. "And if you can't imagine it, *pretend* to imagine it."

This response—essentially, "whatever you say is valid, but in a meaningless way"—made for some interesting moments during the week, because the counselors voiced it no matter what the campers reported. Oriyin, the old New Age woman from Sedona, said one of the tapes caused her terrible pain, as if someone "took off the top of my skull and was slicing into my brain again and again with a knife! Is there something in those tapes that we don't know about?"

Comment: "Hm. Let us know if that happens again."

Paul the Emoter spoke of an elaborate dream. "I asked my guidance to tell me what I need to know right now. I didn't really get anything and I kept drifting off to sleep. But do you remember a toy called Mr. Wiggles? It was like this elongated squirmy water balloon that you couldn't hold on to. In the dream I had a Mr. Wiggles and it got away from me and it sort of slithered into a dark hole."

I'm no psychoanalyst, but young Paul obviously was either "coming to grips with" his sexuality or "losing his grip" on it. Either way, the dream seemed spicily discussible.

"What do you think the meta-message of that was?" Karen asked.

"That maybe I'm trying to grab on to something new?"

"Honor that," she said. "Feel *grateful* to Mr. Wiggles. It seems like he's trying to take you somewhere."

∞

During their glory days, Monroe and his Explorers didn't sit around mulling the hidden wisdom of playthings. They were blasting off, rocketing to the outer limits of consciousness, space, and time. In their soul travels they routinely encountered enigmatic spirits that offered deep thoughts about the nature and purpose of life on Earth, which they described as a meandering path toward higher awareness. As far as I can tell, Monroe never actually met God, but he sensed His existence, and he eventually codified all of what he and the Explorers found, developing new tape programs like "Lifeline" and "Going Home" that involved visits to the post-death planes. In Lifeline you try to visit "Focus 27," the spiritual resting place known as the Park. In "Going Home" the dying—and their friends, families, or caregivers—try to get out there together.

How did Monroe get this far? It took many years, and as skeptics like to point out, his discoveries tended to evolve as his life and influences changed. Monroe believers reject that. They say his research expanded simply because the Explorers made legitimate, fundamental discoveries.

Either way it was a very wild ride. In *Journeys,* Monroe had flown around the Earth and into strange zones like "Locale III," a parallel world where Monroe's Second Body inhabited the form of a sad and lonely man ("the 'I' who lives 'There'") who becomes involved in a failed relationship. (An event with a parallel in Monroe's life. In the late sixties, a few years after he and his wife moved from New York State to Charlottesville, they divorced.) At the beginning of *Far Journeys,* Monroe laments that he began to feel frustrating boredom with out-of-body travel. That changed starting in the seventies when Monroe was invited to Esalen—the famous mind-expansion-and-hot-tub retreat in Big Sur, California—to put on a workshop demonstrating his techniques. This was the genesis of Gateway, and it helped draw to Monroe young, groovy followers who energized his research.

"So that the picture is clear," Monroe wrote in *Far Journeys,* describing the research unit that he used during the pioneering days at a country estate he purchased, Whistlefield. "The subject lies on a water bed in a darkened, acoustically and electrically shielded 8-by-10 room. . . . Electrodes for monitoring physiological states are glued to head, fingers, and body."

The Explorers started flying hard and fast. At first they investigated the solar system, then "other suns . . . other planets." Depressingly, they found no signs of life, fleshy or spiritual. "It seemed to us a sterile universe," Monroe wrote.

The great shift occurred in 1974. Monroe said the "catalyst" was the addition of the Gateway Affirmation into each lab session.

"It was suddenly as if a curtain had been lifted," he wrote. "Almost every time one of our Explorers went into the out-of-body state . . . they encountered intelligent beings who were more or less willing to communicate—and could do so."

Much of *Far Journeys* is consumed by transcripts of "nonverbal communication" dialogues with the entities. These make for hard, boring reading. Monroe, always lingo happy, invented a "replica" vocabulary to convey the experience of "NVC." A "rote," for example, is a received "packet" of thought, memory, knowledge, or information. To "vibrate" is to show emotion. "Rolled" means "laughed." To "smooth" is to "get it together."

The result was page after page of dialogue that most readers probably "blanked" (failed to understand) or (my coinage) "chucked across the room." Here's Monroe talking to an entity named Z-55, who at first mistakes him for an ordinary person having a dream:

> Z-55/LOU opened. (*You're still in-human!*)
> I smoothed. (*Yep.*)
> He flickered. (*Oh, a sleeper. You got out this far? That's pretty good. Too bad you won't remember it.*)
> I opened more. (*It's not quite that way, Lou. I, uh, here.*)
> I tossed him a short rote covering the out-of-body beginning.

At the end of the book Monroe attempts to sort it all into a map of the afterlife. He uses the image of "rings" of existence that contain various species of beyond-physical beings. The first ring is home to the Dreamers (entities who still seem attached to a physical body, so they're probably the result of dreams or OBEs). There are also the Wild Ones, beings who are aware they are somehow no longer alive, but are still obsessed with using their physical bodies. On one of Monroe's travels, he sees a wriggling pile of Wild Ones having an orgy.

There are other taxonomic groupings, but none is quite as fascinating as the Monroe entity I call The Elisabeth Kübler-Ross. Yes, the world-famous bereavement theoretician and author of *On Death and Dying* hooked up with Monroe, with astounding results. Kübler-Ross visited Whistlefield in 1976, over the July Fourth weekend, where she enjoyed the ultimate Bicentennial explosion. Monroe put her into a CHEC but, according to her account of what happened, his techniques really didn't help her much. She was flying high on her own, and in the Whistlefield guest house one night, Kübler-Ross experienced an incredible vision. As she described it later to a journalist, it started horribly, with the sense that she was reliving the death of every one of her thousands of patients.

"The pain was beyond any description," she said, ". . . and I pleaded, I guess, with God for a shoulder to lean on, for one human shoulder. . . . And a thunderous voice came: 'You shall not be given.'"

Refusing to give in to the anguish, Kübler-Ross barked defiantly at whatever was causing it: "Okay. Give it to me. Whatever it is that I have to take. I am ready to take it." With that, the horrible vision turned to a perception of infinite, universal joy, "the most incredible rebirth experience."

> It was so beautiful there are no words to describe it.
>
> It started as my belly wall vibrating, and I looked—open-eyes, fully conscious—and I said, "This can't be!"
>
> . . . Everything vibrated at this incredible speed. And in front of me was a form.
>
> The closest way to describe it is like a vagina. I looked at it, and as I focused on it in utter amazement—there were incredibly beautiful colors and smells and sounds in the room—it opened up into the most beautiful lotus flower. . . . The vibrations stopped and a million molecules, including me . . . fell into one piece. . . . And I finally thought, "I'm okay, because I'm part of all this."

Later, Kübler-Ross decided she'd seen nothing less than a symbol of the heavenly bliss that awaits long-suffering humans, the "'home of peace,' which is where we all end up one day, when we have gone through all the hell and all the agonies that life brings. . . .

"That," she concluded, "is the reward."

∞

Heaven-Symbolized-by-Vagina was certainly an interesting notion, but Kübler-Ross's fab trip depressed me as well. What good were my pathetic visualized smoke rings next to that? The counselors had warned us against Focus Envy—worrying too much about how fast the other guy advanced—but it was hard not to feel it. For her part, Susan was already at a low point, which depressed me further. I didn't bring her here to challenge her beliefs, but that was the effect. By Tuesday morning she was lobbying for premature departure.

On my end, the early nitrous-y thrills had given way to discouragement. In session after session I enjoyed teensy "trips," but it dawned on me that these were probably a natural neurological phenomenon, like the behind-the-eyelids optical flashes you get when you fall asleep at the beach. On Tuesday afternoon I officially gave up on going out of body, calling out to my dad, "Sorry. Maybe another time, another place. And don't come here looking for me, either. You wouldn't like the food."

Or the counselors. The Great White had a low "cringe threshold"—we're alike that way—and the more the counselors said, the more convinced I was that the Monroe techniques consisted of worthless busy work that, if it had any power at all, derived from the students' heightened auto-suggestion.

Having chewed through the CHEC umbilical, I spent the last few days poking around and thinking. Following Karen's advice to Paul, I wondered: Where was my "Mr. Wiggles" urging me to go? I mapped out two paths. First, I wanted to hang around more with Craig and Curt. They were rooming together (with Walter), and they often turned up on a deck beneath our window to smoke and talk. All three were having trouble getting anywhere with the tapes, and for them it really mattered. An important aspect of their faith was being challenged. How would they handle it?

I also wanted to know why the Institute seemed so ragged around the edges, and so oriented toward the hard-sell. The main building had serious problems. The roof leaked whenever it rained, the air conditioning on one side konked out for twenty-four hours, and one night a pipe burst above the room next to us, sending a jagged chunk of wet ceiling foomping to the floor. (Susan and I somehow slept through it—thanks, Hemi-Sync!)

Moreover, considering how much money the Institute had skinned us for already, way, way too much hawking occurred, of products and future instruction. We were often reminded that additional courses were available, and much of Tuesday afternoon was devoted to indirect-but-vigorous selling at the hands of Skip Atwater, Monroe's research director. The payoff was a field trip to the third Monroe building, the research lab, which contained a super CHEC unit, a stand-alone structure constructed with several layers of drywall, wood, fiberglass, insulation, and sheet copper. It was carpeted inside and contained a saltwater flotation bed. Skip enticingly mentioned that "graduate" students got a chance to do tapework inside it.

That afternoon our work resumed. Joe announced a startling experiment: a no-tape exercise, without the "Hemi-Sync training wheels." We were sent to our CHECs and told to "guide" ourselves to a higher Focus using the "new neural pathways" that the tapework had allegedly created. I tried it, and I didn't like it—the tapes, warts and all, were still rather entertaining—but other students did, especially Unlucky Jim.

"This was the first time I haven't wanted to come back!" he enthused at the debriefing. "I requested that my guide just take me and let it be whatever it was going to be. Patterns of swirling stars formed!"

The counselors smiled.

Jim suggested that perhaps Hemi-Sync was only getting in his way. "Is there a chance it might be kind of, you know, limited?" he asked.

The counselors stopped smiling. That was an insight too far.

"Best I know," Joe said, folksy but firm, "it's the most effective system in the world for giving the brain freedom."

That night in the Ashtray House, piling on another demonstration of Hemi-Sync's wonders, the counselors played the Patrick Tape, a recording of a 1981 episode in which one of Monroe's most talented Explorers, Rosalind McKnight, went into the phantom zone on a special mission. McKnight channeled an entity named Ah-So, who announced through her that other entities were going to use McKnight's body as the "live" mouthpiece for a young Scottish sailor named Patrick O'Shaughnessy. The lad had drowned at sea in a nineteenth-century shipwreck and his soul had been "lost" all this time. Ah-So's intent was to guide Patrick to a place of rest in the spirit world. On the tape, you hear the voices of both Ah-So and Patrick as Ah-So aids the soggy unfortunate.

The Patrick Tape is one of the Institute's favorite pieces of "evidence," but it was sadly, comically lame. McKnight sounded like a six-year-old girl playacting, and Patrick sounded like a cross between a castrato and Mr. Bill. "Ohhhhh," he kept saying. "I'm in this water and it's so cold, oooooooh!"

Craig was sitting next to me that night and I didn't dare look at him, but I could sense his awesome cringing. I think I heard his skeleton creak.

According to *Catapult*, even Monroe had trouble buying the Patrick Tape, calling it "the worst bit of ham acting I've ever seen." But he must have believed it on some "level." The Institute mounted a search to trace records of the wreck or the sailor in Scotland, without success.

What did this say about Monroe? Only the obvious: that he probably let his imagination run away with him. In this instance, he even came up with a rationalization for the transparent hokiness of Patrick's squeals.

"I tend to consider that whole operation was a synthesis, just to show us something," he told Bayard Stockton, meaning that the entities staged it to teach mankind a useful lesson about the spirit realm. "I *know* 'they' have the technological capability."

∞

OK, point made. Heaven still must wait. The Monroe Institute hasn't proved it. In fact, it's arguably done just the opposite: made Heaven seem stupid.

And yet . . . I found myself resisting the easiest path, which was to snicker at everybody for three days and then leave. Craig and Curt were the main reasons why. Craig because he was simply too good-natured not to like—and to envy. I had to wonder where he got his seemingly inexhaustible supply of good spirits, especially in the teeth of his utter failure with the Monroe methods. During breaks and meals, Craig made it clear that getting out of body wasn't just a passing fancy with him. He'd worked at it for years, straining to prove to himself that the fantastic places his dad had described were real. He told me he'd relied on the "classic techniques" described by people like Sylvan Muldoon and had experienced a few moments— aching, elusive moments—when he believed he was almost there.

At lunch on Wednesday I asked how Gateway was treating him.

"I'm having a nice time. I like the people. I've been relaxed," he said. "You know."

And the Monroe techniques?

"They have almost PERFECTLY cured me of believing in the existence of whatever out-of-body precursor symptoms I may have had. Ha haaaaa ha."

Susan and I got to know Curt better, too, and he struck us as one of the nicest, gentlest people we'd ever met. He was funny, intelligent, and kind, and one of the few people I'd encountered during my fringe-world travels—Arthur Blessitt was another—who seemed to radiate a genuine inner glow.

This isn't to say Curt was "at peace," of course, otherwise he wouldn't be at Monroe. Unlike Craig, he believed he'd gone out of body before, but he had no control over it. With his disease bearing down, he seriously wanted, needed, to master out-of-body skills, but the tapes weren't doing it for him. Even so, he never whined about it.

"Ehhn," he said, smiling, shrugging off his dim results. "I guess I just have to stick with it."

On Wednesday the sun finally popped out. Along with this desperately needed illumination came action on the OBE front, which helped clarify my opinion on the wisdom of continuing to believe in such things. My opinion was: it probably isn't logical, but I still want to believe. I can't really explain why—partly I didn't like imagining Curt or Susan or my dad or me wiggling down a black hole where nothing awaits—but there was no denying it. We'd spent that morning in a "sacred silence" meditation, then we came back and did a tape.

Whether it was the sun or the silence, something broke. When we reconvened, Ray announced: "Well, I got out! There was a white boat. I felt a tug like from a rope. I was out for at least 2 or 3 seconds and it was *very* cool."

Everybody applauded for Ray. I did, too. But did I really believe it? Oh, what the hell. *Yes!* The Fat Man had flown.

On Wednesday afternoon I solved the Ashtray Mystery. I had an appointment with Laurie Monroe, Monroe's second-oldest daughter and the Institute's director. Her office was on the second floor of the Ashtray House, and the instant I walked in, I knew I had entered the universal epicenter of cigarette ignition. Laurie was a middle-aged blonde with a raspy cough who, as I knew from reading *Catapult,* had sometimes bumped heads with Monroe. She was brought in to run the place like a business, with an eye on the bottom line, and she looked right for the role. She was a hard-edged woman who had sold real estate in Florida before taking over here.

Laurie seemed nice enough—she greeted me with a big smile and a hacking-cough hello—but her place at the helm put things in perspective. The Monroe Institute acreage had, for a hopeful period in the eighties, been set up as a community called the New Land, which Monroe gridded out to sell to fellow higher-order colleagues. Stockton writes that New Land was intended as a classic utopian community, where enlightened metaphysicians would run a cooperative greenhouse, pasture for livestock, areas for poultry raising, a processing plant for alcohol, a fish-stocked lake, and more.

It didn't work. When guru becomes salesman, tensions usually result; Stockton writes that by the mid-eighties, the buyers' complaints about earthbound realities like traffic, dust, trespass by daydreaming Gateway students, and crummy job opportunities in the area had soured Monroe's dreams for New Land. He scrapped the idea and started selling off plots as nothing more than parcels in a quiet subdivision.

Laurie, I figured, represented the continuation of that "spirit." As I sat down, she seemed exceptionally nervous. After a few minutes I realized she was suffering intense nicotine withdrawal. Before long she broke.

"Do you mind if I smoke?" she wheezed.

"No! Hey, no problem." Any other answer would have been second-degree murder.

She lighted up fast, inhaled deeply, and an all-body look of relief washed over her, as if someone had injected scotch-and-water directly into her brain. After that we talked amiably a few minutes—about her dad and his spirit, about the benefits of taking graduate courses, about the Institute's research, which she described as "cutting edge."

"What's an example of some cutting-edge research?"

"Well," she said, taking a pleasurable drag, pondering. "There are some really, really exciting examples of messages from the spirit world—coming through to us on fax machines."

∞

Thursday *we* became the dead.

The morning exercise was an extended "silent walk" around the grounds, followed by a tape. Joe told us that local property owners referred to this as "Zombie Day," so named for the sight of Gatewayers plodding eerily about. We were to move verrrry slowwwly, carefully considering each perception and sight. This "active meditation" would end with a tape.

After we dispersed, I walked to my room and "silently" put on my boots and headed for the lake.

At first I moved slowly, but the zombie pace was a bore, so I started galoomphing downhill at normal speed. I never got to the water. The most direct path from the main road to the lake led through a posted cow pasture occupied by cattle and a local farmer in a battered pick-up. My recollection was that Gatewayers had dispensation to ignore the KEEP OUT sign, but what if that was wrong? I didn't want my silent meditation disrupted by a butt-chewing. I looked for another route. The only one I saw, on the unposted south bank of a meandering creek, was choked with high weeds. I squinted at it, contemplating the likely late-summer presence of ticks and snakes, and heard Mr. Wiggles tell me not to go there. So I went back up the road, gazing at the cow pasture as I walked. After a few paces I noticed a fat groundhog, colored red-orange from tunneling through the red clay soil of these hills. It stood on its haunches and rifled me with a crabby glare. A Cheryl glare.

I thought about how this might play with the class if I "shared" it.

"And what did that groundhog seem to be saying to you?" Karen would ask.

"It's hard to say."

"Accept the pieces," Joe would counsel.

"I think it was . . . yes, I understand! It was saying: 'Go away.'"

"Your guidance may be telling you something. What does that say to you?"

"That I should 'go away' from 'where I am now'?"

"Honor that."

"Oh, I intend to."

I ambled back toward the main building. As I topped a rise I saw, in the distance, a tall, pale figure gliding ghostly and slow across the lawn by the main building.

Could it possibly be the Great White Father?

No, but it was the next best thing: the Great White Craig. I hurried over and asked him if he would consider breaking the sacred silence and talking to me.

"HELL yes," he said. We sat on a picnic bench as he torched a cigarette. I asked him to describe the sensation of almost going out of body.

"OK," he whispered. "You know what a chill feels like, a little shiver? Multiply that shiver by five hundred. What you get is an emanation of discharge off the body. I've been working on this since childhood, and at times, with my eyes closed, very awake, I would see in my mind's eye, VERY vividly, nothing for the first six inches around my body. And then for twelve or eighteen inches, there was the apprehension of a discharge of sparks! I asked my dad about it and he laughed and said, 'Yes, that's one of the precursors.'"

He took a drag. "My dad said it helps ENORMOUSLY if you have a great deal of desire. Now, my desire is of a mediocre nature, so I figured, well, I'll come here to Monroe and hand it over to the experts. But these people are a little more . . ."

He stopped to choose his words carefully. "Well, I mean, my old man was a small businessman, a middle-class white Republican. A retired colonel of artillery. OK? He wouldn't fit the picture at a place like this, babe. *Capisce?* We've got enough love and bliss here to fill five thousand douchebags."

"I'll tell you something," I said. "Susan and I came here wanting to think that it's all really possible, but this place has made us doubt it."

Craig was touchingly mortified, as if he were a priest and I'd just weepingly renounced my belief in Christ.

"No, Alec! Tell Susan that there's something there! Are you going to tell me that a billion years ago there just was a pool of water and a billion years later, poof, you've got Spinoza? My dad said there was NO QUESTION about the afterlife. That was not a serious question. He said that emotionally, going out of body is like a revealed religious experience. You suddenly *know* what's in the next fucking realm, and most people don't!"

I already knew what he would say, but I wanted to hear it framed in full Craigian cadences. "So you're not giving up?"

"Noooo, hell no. I would even tell you that I still have a mild expectation that before I die that I'll have an out-of-body experience. But I know now that it will be by my own path." Meaning, his dad's path. "I'm gonna dance with the one that brung me."

And if it happens? How will it stack up in the old religious-ecstasy department?

"Oh, God," he roared. "I'd be like a bitch in heat. I mean, I'd stay on that baby and it would be like jacking off when you're twelve. It would just be an awful thing! Ha ha haaaa ha."

Thanks, oh Great One. I'll carry that expectation with me for the rest of my days.

The image, I'll try to forget.

Afterword:
My Thousand-Year Deep Thought

In 1998 I took one last millennial field trip, to a place I'd been years before, western North Carolina, where I met the Earth Changes prophetess Greta Woodrew and her husband, Dick Smolowe, in 1992.

In January of '98 the region was all over the news because Eric Robert Rudolph, the alleged bomber of the New Woman All Women Health Care Clinic in Birmingham, Alabama, disappeared into the hilly woods about fifty miles west of Franklin, near the town of Murphy. Rudolph was said to be a follower of the late Nord Davis, Jr., head of a group called the Northpoint Tactical Teams, an antigovernment, conspiratorial, reputedly apocalyptic outfit centered in an armed "compound" in Andrews. Rudolph was also supposedly a follower of Christian Identity, the strange right-wing religion that has it that the ten Lost Tribes of Israel migrated, fully intact as a group, to northern Europe and Britain, subsequently making their way to America. In other words: whites are the Chosen People, as opposed to the fraudulent "people who call themselves the Jews."

I went down for a couple of reasons: to check out the old Earth Changes crowd and, if possible, to meet at least one believer in Identity, which was the only "faith" I'd heard about during my various adventures that really scared me. Some Identity believers (not all) hold to what's called "seedline doctrine," which has it that Eve mated with both Adam and the Serpent. In this scenario, Identity followers are seen as the good people, the fruit of Eve's proper and sacred union with God's first man. The Jews are direct descendants of Satan, a notion that leads to deep-seated hatred. At its worst, Identity is virulently anti-Semitic and generally antiworld, and it may turn out that Rudolph was a seedline Identity believer. After he vanished, the Southern Poverty Law Center announced that it had evidence that Rudolph was an "active follower" of Nord Davis, who was "seedline," though it declined to offer proof.

The trip itself was sad and pathetic, in large part because it was another grim reminder that millennial strivers, like all of us, invariably lose out to change, decay, and death. Every Earth Changes believer I'd met in '92 had either croaked or moved away. I paid a visit to an elderly believer I'd never met before, a man named Ed Zane, who lives down the road from Greta Woodrew's mountaintop chalet. With various sad-looking Earth Changes tracts spread out on his kitchen table, Zane explained that Greta, regrettably, had felt a need to relocate to Winston-Salem, North Carolina.

Why? Had her outer-space intelligences—the Ogattan space brothers—told her that Winston-Salem was a safer place to survive the Changes?

"No," he said. "She had bad knees, and there were a whole lot of steps in that house. She just got to where she couldn't take it anymore."

Hmm. I guess the dictates of prophecy are powerful, but geriatric concerns are on another level entirely.

∞

I also had no luck getting into the Northpoint Tactical Teams. I called, and whoever picked up the phone told me to go to Hell. I drove out anyway, but the entrance to the compound—which was tucked away at the end of a long road, at the base of a wild-looking mountain outside of town—warned belligerently against unannounced drop-in visitation. Best to heed that, so I left a pleading note by the Teams' front gate, saying I'd be back the next day. If they were willing to talk, they should leave a note that it was all right to proceed up the road.

Then I drove up to Asheville, where I met with a right-wing contact who had promised to try and find an Identity believer who would talk to me.

Which he did—providing the name of a man I'll only call "Bob," who lived in a suburb of Asheville. I drove over, and though Bob was the real thing, he wasn't quite the nefarious dramatic spectacle I'd hoped for. He was a quiet, serious bachelor in his forties who lived alone in the musty but tidy basement apartment of a house owned by an old widow. His small, drab crib was full of Christian Identity books and a catalogued series of taped lectures by Identity bigwigs like the Reverend Pete Peters.

Bob wasn't seedline, though he made no bones about his longing for a balkanized nation split up into zones for the different races. His operative philosophy was a sort of white-separatist Golden Rule. "I don't hate black people and Jews, but I would choose to live separate from the other races," he said. "But if they're around, I'm going to treat them the way I would want them to treat me."

I leaned in, asking him how many Identity people were out there around Andrews and Murphy.

"Hundreds," he said spookily. "At least."

Hundreds? Were any of them apocalyptic in outlook?

"The doomsday mentality, unfortunately, is very prevalent among the Identity people."

Normally, just the sort of conversation I'd eat up, but instead I was suddenly overwhelmed with boredom and resentment about how silly it all was. I'd been through this drill so many times before—the careful questions, the slow peeling back of layers—but apparently I'd overdosed. Beliefs this baseless should not cause as much trouble as they do. I wanted to shake Bob and say, "You're *not* a Jew. Find a new hobby and get on with it!"

∞

But there was no need to be rude, so I thanked him and left, flooring it back to Andrews and occupying myself with a Big Question. Let's say we can choose right now how people will "be" in the year 3000. The choices are (1) they'll still be spiritual and irrational, in good ways and bad, as they are now. Or (2) they'll be stripped of such traits completely, becoming harmless but soulless beings who have no illusions about life and death and spirituality and the beyond.

Weighing the positive aspects of the human irrationalism I'd experienced (the people I was inspired by, like Craig Cordrey and Chet Fleming and Bob and Zoh and Brock d'Avignon and Arthur Blessitt) against the negative (Steven Greer, the Republic of Texas men, Saul Kent, and others), I decided . . .

Well, I didn't decide. It was just a thought game, but I couldn't come down one way or the other, except in favor of the obvious and empty conclusion that it would be "nice" if people stayed weird but somehow stopped being mean.

"What tripe," I said as I thought of it, which happened as I pulled up to the gates of the Northpoint Teams. After all this, was the only wisdom I'd accrued something that would work nicely as a "Ziggy" caption? I slapped my cheek twice to put some sting in my mind, and then thought, Ahhh, forget it. You can't "decide" this anyway. Humans are going to do what they're going to do. They cannot be steered.

Also obvious, perhaps, but definitely true. At the gate, my note was right where I'd left it, under a rock. As I stood there, forlorn, I heard a low, growly clanking coming from the hidden road inside the compound. This was it, I decided. The Teams were coming down the road in an armored personnel carrier.

Nope. It was a piece-of-junk little car jammed-to-bulging with a family of grinning mountain people. The car, which sounded like it might explode at any second, didn't seem able to go faster than 10 mph. I don't know if these people were friends of the Teams or "operatives" or what, but they didn't seem real scary. They stopped alongside my car, and a grinning young man in the back seat rolled down his window.

I tensed up, figuring I might get chewed out. Wrong again. "You need any hailp?" he said, jiggling with crazy mirth.

"No, but thanks. I'm fine."

"OK. Holler if you do!" They drove off again, still waving.

I mentally filed the moment. The terrifying specter of evil lunacy might always be loose in the world. But, fortunately, so will the amiable spirit of Goober Pyle.

Notes

INTRODUCTION

Epigraph and all other materials by Kenna E. Farris are taken from his correspondence to me.

WELCOME, SPACE BROTHERS

Epigraph: *Forty Years of Love and Light* (El Cajon, Calif.: Unarius Video Productions, 1994).

Unarius tax exemption: Form 1023, "Application for Recognition of Exemption," filed Dec. 27, 1974.

Thirty-three spacecraft to land in 2001: Ruth Norman–Uriel, *Facts about UFOs* (El Cajon, Calif.: Unarius Academy of Science, 1989), pp. 8–9. The predicted dates of the landing have changed over time. In 1976, for example, Norman predicted a "spaceship fleet" would land that year: "She's Expecting a Convention of Spaceships," *Sarasota Herald-Tribune*, April 14, 1977, p. 15A.

Unarius's Form 990 assets for 1992 totaled $524,942.

The relative poverty of Heaven's Gate in the mid-seventies is described by Joel Achenbach and Marc Fisher in "The Cult That Left as It Lived," *Washington Post*, March 30, 1997, p. A1.

Unarius's use of past-life therapy: R. George Kirkpatrick and Diana Tumminia, "Space Magic, Techno-animism, and the Cult of the Goddess in a Southern California UFO Contactee Group: A Case Study of Millenarianism," *SYZYGY: Journal of Alternative Religion and Culture* (Spring 1992): 159–69.

"They are both archangels . . .": The four-angel Unarius pantheon is described in *Unarius: A Biographical History*, vol. 1 (El Cajon, Calif.: Unarius Educational Foundation, 1985), pp. 73–74.

Atlantis snake cults: Unarius Students and Uriel, *A Beginner's Guide to Progressive Evolution* (El Cajon, Calif.: Unarius, 1987), p. 27.

"The Vehicles of Light" is reprinted in *Facts about UFOs*, by Ruth Norman.

"I am eternally grateful . . .": Louis Spiegel (Antares), *The Confessions of I, Bonaparte* (El Cajon, Calif.: Unarius, 1985), "Dedication."

"It all began millions of years ago . . .": Details about Antares's history are from *I, Bonaparte* and my interviews with Spiegel.

Spiegel as Pontius Pilate: *The Confessions of I, Bonaparte*, p. 413.

Details about Uriel's numerous lives are scattered throughout several Unarius books; I reviewed my summary in an interview with Spiegel.

Antares becomes good again: *The Confessions of I, Bonaparte*, "Dedication."

Uriel on Antares's conversion: Ibid., p. 9.

"Every year, Unarius celebrates the founding of the science . . .": In *Unarius: A Biographical History*, vol. 1, Ruth Norman wrote that she met Ernest Norman on Feb. 13, 1954, and married him in 1956.

"Disconfirmation" is a central theme of *When Prophecy Fails*, a 1956 study of a saucer-oriented millennial group that was conducted by Leon Festinger, Henry W. Riecken, and Stanley Schachter (Minneapolis: University of Minnesota Press).

"The Tesla Tower" appears in the *Unarius Light Journal* (Summer 1996): 13–15.

"The Cosmic Generator" and a schematic diagram of the 32-planet confederation are published in *Facts about UFOs*.

The aboriginal Zan: *The Arrival* (El Cajon, Calif.: Unarius Video Productions, undated).

"Red-and-yellow Jello . . .": *A Beginner's Guide to Progressive Evolution*, p. 49.

Crystal Mountain City: These details are from my tapes of Lianne's lecture; elsewhere, the "Crystal Mountains, Cities and Temple" are described as existing only in higher spiritual worlds (*Unarius: A Biographical History*, vol. 1, p. 5).

"Unarius is a 'contactee' group . . .": Jerome Clark, *UFOs in the 1980s: The UFO Encyclopedia*, vol. 1 (Detroit: Apogee Books, 1990), pp. 51–56.

Heaven's Gate's origins: Jerome Clark, *High Strangeness: UFOs from 1960 through 1979: The UFO Encyclopedia*, vol. 3 (Detroit: Omnigraphics, 1996), p. 477.

George Adamski: Jerome Clark, *The Emergence of a Phenomenon: UFOs from the Beginning through 1959: The UFO Encyclopedia*, vol. 2 (Detroit: Omnigraphics, 1992), p. 3.

Dorothy Martin: All details about Dorothy Martin ("Mrs. Keech") are taken from *When Prophecy Fails*.

Unarius discovered by academics: Kirkpatrick and Tumminia, "Space Magic, Techno-animism and the Cult of the Goddess . . . ," p. 165.

Uriel and Yancoskie: Adam Parfrey, "The Gods Must Be Crazy: The Latter Days of Unarius," *San Diego Reader*, June 6, 1991.

Uriel's use of guilt: Ruth Norman, *Effort to Destroy the Unarius Mission Thwarted* (El Cajon, Calif.: Unarius, 1984).

Antares updates the students: Unarius class transcript, "Sunday—Antares Speaks about Uriel's Condition & Working Out," February 2, 1992.

Uriel's death discussed: Unarius class transcript, "7/16/93 Friday Class."

". . . obsessional forces . . .": Ibid.

Antares scolded by Brothers: "Contact with Uriel and the

Unarius Brotherhood, August 18, 1996," as channeled by Lianne Downey.

THE SUNNY SIDE OF THE END

Epigraph: Reverend Clarence Larkin, *The Second Coming of Christ* (Glenside, Pa.: Larkin Estate, 1918).

History of the Temple Mount: Jerome Murphy O'Connor, *The Holy Land: An Oxford Archaeological Guide from Earliest Times to 1700* (London: Oxford University Press, 1998), pp. 80, 85–89; Karen Armstrong, *Jerusalem: One City, Three Faiths* (New York: Alfred A. Knopf, 1996), pp. 217–39.

Richman's hopes for the Temple: Chaim Richman, *A House of Prayer for All Nations: The Holy Temple of Jerusalem* (Jerusalem: Temple Institute and Carta, 1997).

Christian hopes for the Temple are described in several books; see, for example, Thomas Ice and Randall Price, *Ready to Rebuild: The Imminent Plan to Rebuild the Last Days Temple* (Eugene, Ore.: Harvest House Publishers, 1992).

". . . a red heifer without spot . . .": Numbers 19:2.

Richman's messianic ideas are described in his 1995 article, "Countdown to Redemption—Part 1," available on his Web site, "Light to the Nations."

". . . fate of the entire world . . .": Chaim Richman, *The Mystery of the Red Heifer: Divine Promise of Purity* (Jerusalem, 1997).

Facts about Melody: Kendall Hamilton (with Joseph Contreras and Mark Dennis), "The Strange Case of Israel's Red Heifer," *Newsweek*, May 19, 1997, p. 16.

Melody as four-legged bomb: Jeremy Shere, "A Very Holy Cow," *Jerusalem Post* (Internet edition), May 26, 1997. (This article refers to "a slightly hysterical story in one local paper" as having described Melody this way.)

Temple Mount violence: Tad Szulc, "Israel Denounces Arabs'

Campaign since Shrine Fire," *New York Times*, Aug. 25, 1969, p. A1; David K. Shipler, "Extremist Jews Blamed in Raid on Arab Shrine," *New York Times*, Jan. 30, 1984, p. A1; Lambert Dolphin, "Preparations for a Third Temple," published on a Web site called "The Temple Mount in Jerusalem"; David K. Shipler, "2 Arabs Are Killed as Israeli Attacks Dome of the Rock," *New York Times*, April 12, 1982, p. A1; Ehud Sprinzak, *The Ascendance of Israel's Radical Right* (London: Oxford University Press, 1991), pp. 251–88.

Etzion on Melody: "A Very Holy Cow," *Jerusalem Post*.

Garner's prophecy handbook: Guy Garner, Jr., *The Key to Understanding Endtime Prophecy* (Porterdale, Ga.: Voice of Liberty Ministries).

History of prophecy belief: Paul Boyer, *When Time Shall Be No More: Prophecy Belief in Modern American Culture* (Cambridge, Mass.: Belknap Press of Harvard University Press, 1992), chap. 1, "Origins of the Apocalyptic."

The "Apocalypse of Paul": Montague Rhodes James, trans., *The Apocryphal New Testament* (London: Oxford University Press, 1924), pp. 525–55.

"And he laid hold . . .": Revelation 20:2–3.

Revelation's authorship and dates: S. MacLean Gilmour, "The Revelation to St. John," *The Interpreter's One-Volume Commentary on the Bible* (Nashville, Tenn.: Abingdon Press, 1971), p. 947; C. Marvin Pate, gen. ed., *Counterpoints/Four Views on the Book of Revelation* (Grand Rapids, Mich.: Zondervan Publishing House, 1998), pp. 12–14.

Antichrist named in John: See, for example, 1 John 2:18, which says, "Little children, it is the last time . . . even now there are many antichrists . . ."

Amillennialism, preterism, and other forms of interpreting the Book of Revelation are discussed by Richard Kyle in *The Last Days Are Here Again: A History of the End Times* (Grand Rapids, Mich.: Baker Books), p. 33.

"... of that day and that hour ...": Mark 13:32.

Luther and Newton as millennialists: Kyle, *The Last Days Are Here Again*, p. 55; Michael White, *Isaac Newton: The Last Sorcerer* (Reading, Mass.: Addison-Wesley, 1997), p. 157.

Koresh as "another" Christ: Dick J. Reavis, *The Ashes of Waco: An Investigation* (New York: Simon & Schuster, 1995), p. 102.

The history of Montanism: Norman Cohn, *The Pursuit of the Millennium: Revolutionary Millenarians and Mystical Anarchists of the Middle Ages* (London: Temple Smith, 1957, 1970), p. 25.

Debate about the hubbub in 1000 A.D.: Charles B. Strozier and Michael Flynn, eds., *The Year 2000: Essays on the End* (New York University Press, 1997), pp. 13–29.

Joachim of Fiore's theology: Michael Grosso, *The Millennium Myth: Love and Death at the End of Time* (Wheaton, Ill.: Quest Books, 1995), pp. 42–47.

Cohn's thesis analyzed: Michael Barkun, *Disaster and the Millennium* (New Haven, Conn.: Yale University Press, 1974), p. 32.

House of Yahweh: David Wallis, "Does God Play Hardball?" *New York Times Magazine*, June 15, 1997, p. 13.

"The Blessed Hope ...": Larkin, *The Second Coming of Christ*.

The white man's genocidal plans: Charles B. Strozier, *Apocalypse: On the Psychology of Fundamentalism in America* (Boston: Beacon Press, 1994), p. 135.

"... a sound from Heaven ...": Acts 2:2–4.

Origins of Pentecostalism: J. Gordon Melton, *Encyclopedia of American Religions* (Detroit: Gale Research, 1996), p. 81.

John Darby's dispensational system and the Rapture doctrine: Larry V. Crutchfield, *The Origins of Dispensationalism: The Darby Factor* (Lanham, Md.: University Press of America, 1991), pp. 3–5, 166.

"The dead in Christ ...": 1 Thessalonians 4:16–17.

"Pre-Wrath": Marvin Rosenthal, *The Pre-Wrath Rapture of the Church* (Nashville, Tenn.: Thomas Nelson Publishers, 1990), p. 22.

Daniel's importance in eschatology: Ed Dobson, *The End: Why Jesus Could Return by A.D. 2000* (Grand Rapids, Mich.: Zondervan Publishing House, 1997), p. 57.

Nebuchadnezzar's dream is described in the second chapter of Daniel.

Daniel's "far" application: Robert Van Kampen, *The Sign* (Wheaton, Ill.: Crossway Books, 1992), p. 29.

Babylonian statue represents four empires: Dobson, *The End*, pp. 58–64.

The Seventy Weeks: Daniel 9:24–27.

Jewish torment during the Tribulation: Boyer, *When Time Shall Be No More,* pp. 209–10; John F. Walvoord, *Major Bible Prophecies: 37 Crucial Prophecies That Affect You Today* (Grand Rapids, Mich.: Zondervan Publishing House, 1991), p. 379.

John Darby, early American millennialism, and the Great Disappointment: Boyer, *When Time Shall Be No More*, pp. 209–10, 69.

"The Secretary General of the UN . . .": Hal Lindsey (with C. C. Carlson), *The Late Great Planet Earth* (Grand Rapids, Mich.: Zondervan Publishing House, 1970, 1977), preface.

Scriptural basis for the Third Temple: Ice and Price, *Ready to Rebuild*, pp. 197–200; Don Stewart and Chuck Missler, *The Coming Temple: Center Stage for the Final Countdown* (Orange, Calif.: Dart Press, 1991), p. 196.

Roy Manning's letter is published in Richman, *The Mystery of the Red Heifer*, p. 73.

Details about Arthur Blessitt's journeys are taken from an undated press release called "Arthur Blessitt, the Man Who Carried the Cross around the World."

EARTH IS A MOTHER

Epigraph: Dick and Leigh Richmond-Donahue, *Blindsided* (Lakemont, Ga.: Interdimensional Sciences, 1993), p. 18.

Earth as a shaggy dog: Sun Bear (with Wabun Wind), *Black Dawn, Bright Day: Indian Prophecies for the Millennium That Reveal the Fate of the Earth* (New York: Fireside), p. 51.

Gordon-Michael Scallion's Earth Changes map is described in his videotape documentary *Tribulation: The Coming Earth Changes* (Westmoreland, N.H.: Matrix Video, 1993).

Annie Kirkwood's visions are described in *Mary's Message to the World* (New York: G. P. Putnam's Sons, published by arrangement with Blue Dolphin Publishing, 1991).

Byron Kirkwood's advice is found in *Survival Guide for the New Millennium: How to Survive the Coming Earth Changes* (Nevada City, Calif.: Blue Dolphin Publishing, 1993).

Annie Kirkwood's description of the Aftertime and loss of life: *Mary's Message to the World*, pp. 255–56, 2.

My description of Matthew Stenger's message is from notes I took at the Whole Life Expo in New York, October 1989, and from Stenger's videotape *Earth Changes* (Maggie Valley, N.C.: Global Family, recorded at the 1990 Expo in New York).

Sun Bear's controversial career: J. Gordon Melton, Jerome Clark, and Aidan A. Kelly, *New Age Almanac* (Detroit: Visible Ink Press, 1991), pp. 438–40; Strozier, *Apocalypse*, p. 232.

"Hey, this isn't working, kids . . .": Sun Bear, *Black Dawn, Bright Day*, p. 54.

New severity of earthquakes: Ibid., p. 57.

Craig and Lex escape from New York: Richmond-Donahue, *Blindsided*, pp. 7–60.

The fraudulence of *The Protocols of the Elders of Zion* is discussed by Michael Barkun in *Religion and the Racist Right: The Origins of the Christian Identity Movement*, rev. ed. (Chapel Hill: University of North Carolina Press, 1997), p. 34.

Craig on "the afterbirth": Richmond-Donahue, *Blindsided*, p. 88.

"I'm not Catholic!": *Mary's Message to the World*, p. ix.

Nostradamus's prophecies are described in dozens of books. A typical contemporary example is John Hogue's *Nostradamus and the Millennium* (S.A., Switzerland: Labyrinth Publishing, 1987). For a skeptical view on Nostradamus, see James Randi's *The Mask of Nostradamus: The Prophecies of the World's Most Famous Seer* (Buffalo, N.Y.: Prometheus Books, 1993).

Cayce's dream of the future: Mary Ellen Carter (under the editorship of Hugh Lynn Cayce), *Edgar Cayce on Prophecy* (New York: Coronet Communications, 1968), pp. 12–13.

Atlantis rising: Ibid., p. 52.

Brother Philip, *Secret of the Andes* (Clarksburg, W.V.: Saucerian Books, 1961).

Jeffrey Goodman, *We Are the Earthquake Generation* (New York: Simon and Schuster, 1978).

Volcanic activity on Mt. Rainier: Gordon-Michael Scallion, *The Earth Changes Report: The Survival Guide for the Nineties* (Chesterfield, N.H.: Matrix Institute, February 1995), p. 15.

The "Hmmm" file: William K. Stevens, "Climatology Guru Is Part Curmudgeon, Part Imp," *New York Times* (Internet edition), March 17, 1998.

"Deep Ecology" coined: Arne Naess introduced this term in "The Shallow and the Deep, Long-Range Ecology Movements," *Inquiry* 16 (Oslo, 1973): 95–100.

"Within the framework of deep ecology . . .": John Seed, Joanna Macy, Pat Fleming, and Arne Naess, *Thinking Like a Mountain: Towards a Council of All Beings* (Philadelphia: New Society Publishers, 1988), p. 9.

Dire warning from the Club of Rome: Donella H. Meadows et al., *The Limits to Growth: A Report for the Club of Rome's Project on the Predicament of Mankind* (New York: Universe Books, 1972).

Paul and Anne Ehrlich, *Extinction: The Causes and Consequences of the Disappearance of Species* (New York: Ballantine Books, 1983), p. xiv.

". . . the human pox . . .": Dave Foreman, *Confessions of an Eco-Warrior* (New York: Harmony Books, 1991), pp. 55–58.

Craig and Lex call a meeting: Richmond-Donahue, *Blindsided*, pp. 95–101.

Greta Woodrew, *On a Slide of Light: A Glimpse of Tomorrow* (New York: Macmillan, 1981), pp. 1, 49, 61–63.

My description of Dolores Cannon's message is from tapes recorded at the Earth Festival in Richardson, Texas, March 1995, and from Cannon's book, *Conversations with Nostradamus: His Prophecies Explained,* vol. 1 (Huntsville, Ark.: Ozark Mountain Publishers, 1989, rev. 1992).

". . . like a spider . . .": Cannon, *Conversations with Nostradamus,* p. 192.

Earth Changes delayed: *Mary's Message/Newsletter,* June–July 1996, no. 28.

Craig and Lex's happy ending: Richmond-Donahue, *Blindsided*, pp. 162–71.

DRESSED IN FIRE, SHRILL OF SCREAMS

The epigraph is from e-mail. This and other e-mails about the Republic of Texas standoff were forwarded to me by a militia operative who requests anonymity.

Texas illegally annexed: *The Official Newsletter of the Republic of Texas,* Jan. 15, 1997, p. 7.

Cole's preference for 4-to-10-man cells: Correspondence from Ron Cole to me.

Death of Michael Schroeder: Dick J. Reavis, *The Ashes of Waco: An Investigation* (New York: Simon & Schuster, 1995), pp. 192–98.

"... someone within our ranks chucked a grenade ... ": Wayne Laugesen and Joel Dyer, "Americans against Americans," *Boulder Weekly*, April 27, 1995, p. 8.

Linda Thompson's allegations are contained in the videotapes *Waco, the Big Lie* and *Waco, the Big Lie Continues* (Indianapolis, Ind.: American Justice Federation, 1993, 1994).

McLaren denounced by Lowe faction: Web posting labeled "!!URGENT NOTICE!!," April 27, 1997.

SAFAN alert: E-mail traffic.

ROT group apprehended: Mark Babineck, "Police Arrest 7 Allegedly on Way to Join Secessionists," Associated Press, April 30, 1997.

Olson and Rayner: E-mail traffic.

McLaren's Mayday: Mark Babineck, "Authorities: McLaren's Wife Wants to Leave," Associated Press, May 3, 1997.

McNasby's description of the Aurora house: Federal affidavit, *United States of America* v. *Ronald D. Cole,* May 1, 1997.

McLaren sentenced: Eduardo Montes, "Republic of Texas Leader, Associate Are Sentenced," Associated Press, Nov. 5, 1997.

Woman wants McLaren lynched: Jesse Katz, "Neighbors of Texas 'Embassy' Seeing Red," *Los Angeles Times,* May 3, 1997.

"... I regret nothing ...": Ron Cole, "We're in solitary confinement; How did we get here?" North American Liberation Association press release, posted on the Internet, May 1997.

Motives of right-wing behavior: John George and Laird Wilcox, *Nazis, Communists, Klansmen, and Others on the Fringe: Political Extremism in America* (Buffalo, N.Y.: Prometheus Books, 1992), pp. 77, 82.

Dyer on right-wing motives: Joel Dyer, *Harvest of Rage: Why Oklahoma City Is Only the Beginning* (Boulder, Colo.: Westview Press, 1997).

Phineas Priesthood: Three members of this group—Charles H.

Barbee, Robert S. Berry, and Verne Jay Merrell—received life sentences in November 1997. John K. Wiley, "Bombing Defendants Sentenced to Life Prison Terms," Associated Press, Nov. 5, 1997.

Cole's high school years: Ron Cole, correspondence to me.

Cole's planned attack on Waco: Ron Cole, "What Wars Are Made Of: Waco, Texas, to Oklahoma City," manuscript.

Cole finds Branch Davidians too dependent: Correspondence to me.

Roden/Koresh feud: Reavis, *The Ashes of Waco*, pp. 64–65, 74–82.

Details about "The Gunnison Incident" are taken from Ron Cole's manuscript "What Wars Are Made Of" and "The Next Waco That Never Was," an article by Cole posted on the *Partisan* Web site.

Keyes search scaled back: "Texas Calls Off Search for Separatist Fugitive," Associated Press, May 6, 1997.

Joel Dyer's interview with Keyes was posted on *The Mojo Wire*, the Web site of *Mother Jones* magazine, June 24–30, 1997.

Keyes convicted: "Last of Texas Separatist Group Jailed for 90 Years," Reuters, June 19, 1998.

Cole's previous support for hit-and-run tactics: Correspondence to me.

"The Calling" is contained in Ron Cole's manuscript "What Wars Are Made Of."

SOMEBODY UP THERE LIKES ME

Epigraph: C. G. Jung, *Flying Saucers: A Modern Myth of Things Seen in the Skies* (New York: MJF Books, 1978; first published in German in 1958), p. 134.

Hynek's close-encounter labels: Jerome Clark, *The Emergence of a Phenomenon*, pp. xi–xii.

Andreasson case: Clark, *High Strangeness*, pp. 5–17.

Mack's theories about abductions: John E. Mack, *Abduction: Human*

Encounters with Aliens (New York: Charles Scribner's Sons, 1994), pp. 387–422.

Quazgaa: Clark, *High Strangeness*, p. 12.

Greer on "supersecret management" of UFO secrets: "The Art Bell Show," Feb. 21, 1997.

"The evidence is now clear . . .": Brian O'Leary, *Miracle in the Void: Free Energy, UFOs and other Scientific Revelations* (Kihei, Hawaii: Kamapua'a Press, 1996), p. 13.

Tewari generator: Ibid., p. 154.

Laws of thermodynamics: For a summary of why physicists rule out "free energy," see Robert Schadewald, "Perpetual Motion: The Perpetual Quest," in *The Fringes of Reason: A Whole Earth Catalog* (New York: Harmony Books, 1989), pp. 120–28.

Jung on alien superiority: Jung, *Flying Saucers*, p. 134.

Global cabal: Jim Marrs, *Alien Agenda* (New York: HarperCollins Publishers, 1997), p. 393.

Roswell saga: Clark, *UFOs in the 1980s*, pp. 60–72; William J. Broad, "Air Force Details a New Theory in UFO Case," *New York Times*, June 25, 1997, p. B7; William Claiborne, "GAO Turns to Alien Turf in Probe," *Washington Post*, Jan. 14, 1994.

Wilhelm Reich's battle with the federal government: David Elkind, "Wilhelm Reich—The Psychoanalyst as Revolutionary," *New York Times Magazine*, April 18, 1971; Irwin Ross, "The Strange Case of Dr. Wilhelm Reich," *New York Post*, Sept. 5, 1954; "Decree of Injunction: Civil Action No. 1056," United States District Court, Portland, Maine, March 19, 1954.

Reich's defiance: Wilhelm Reich, "Statement at Portland District Court, May 25, 1956, before Judge Sweeney."

O'Leary on "apocalypse": O'Leary, *Miracle in the Void*, p. 14.

"Polls show. . .": "Most in U.S. Believe in Extraterrestrial Life," Reuters, July 28, 1997.

CSETI Gulf Breeze event: Steven M. Greer, "Special Report: Close Encounter of the Fifth Kind Near Gulf Breeze, Florida, March 14, 1992," pp. 23–28.

Joe Newman's crusade: Eliot Marshall, "Newman's Impossible Motor," *Science*, Feb. 10, 1984, p. 571; "Report of Tests on Joseph Newman's Device," National Bureau of Standards, June 1986.

"A sad tribute . . .": Dan Davidson, *Breakthrough to New Free Energy Sources* (San Francisco: R & E Research Associates, 1977).

NakaMats's publicity: "Maryland Accelerates Efforts to Steer Enerex Engine Its Way," *Washington Times*, Nov. 15, 1990.

NakaMats's résumé: "Dr. NakaMats' Profile," 1990.

NakaMats's whimsical ideas: "Japan's Master Genius," *Asiaweek*, April 14, 1989, pp. 62–67; James Barron, "'Geniuses' Rub Elbows as Well as Their Heads," *New York Times*, Nov. 29, 1990, p. B1.

Stanley Meyer's free-energy formulas: Stanley A. Meyer, "The Birth of New Technology: Water Fuel Cell, Technical Brief" (Grove City, Ohio, 1990).

N.I.S.T. on Meyer's claims: George P. Lewett, correspondence to me, June 28, 1991.

My summaries of CSETI membership and Greer's travels are based on interviews and documents provided to me by Janice Williams.

Greer's Starlight goals: "Project Starlight Overview: Strictly Confidential," CSETI, undated.

Greer interviewed on Art Bell: Transcript of "The Art Bell Show," Feb. 21, 1997.

Greer accused of stealing UFO report: Greer's "D.C. Briefings" were held April 7 to 11, 1997. At this meeting he allegedly distributed a paper—under the aegis of CSETI Project Starlight—that was written by Don Berliner for the Fund for UFO Research. FUFOR subsequently denounced Greer's actions on its Web site, in an undated article called "Greer/CSETI Confronted."

Webster Hubbell on UFOs: Rober Sheaffer, "Psychic Vibrations," *Skeptical Inquirer* (March/April 1998): 22.

Greer on cancer: "Healing Fund for Shari Adamiak," CSETI Web site, July 3, 1997.

LET FREEDOMINIUM RING!

Epigraph: Michael Oliver, *A New Constitution for a New Country*, rev. ed., (Reno, Nev.: Fine Arts Press, 1968), back cover.

Strauss on new countries and nukes: Erwin S. Strauss, *How to Start Your Own Country: How You Can Profit from the Coming Decline of the Nation State* (Port Townsend, Wash.: Loompanics Unlimited, 1979, 1984); *Basement Nukes: The Consequences of Cheap Weapons of Mass Destruction* (Mason, Mich.: Loompanics, 1980).

Fruitlands described: Melton, *Encyclopedia of American Religions*, p. 594.

Joseph F. Coates and Jennifer Jarratt, *What Futurists Believe* (Bethesda, Md.: Lomonde Publishers, 1989).

1939 World's Fair: David Gelernter, *1939: The Lost World of the Fair* (New York: Avon Books, 1995), p. 53.

1964 World's Fair: My details are from the Discovery Channel Web site, "I Have Seen the Future."

Artificial islands on the drawing board: Frank P. Davidson, "Life on Artificial Islands," *Popular Mechanics* (August 1984): 76; Frank P. Davidson (with John Stuart Cox), *Macro: A Clear Vision of How Science and Technology Will Shape Our Future* (New York: William Morrow and Company, 1983); Ernst G. Frankel, "The Call of the Islands," *Technology Review* (November/December 1991).

Ecopolis is described in "Ecopolis: City of the Future," by Wolf Hilbertz, Newton Fallis, and Bill Wilson, undated.

Tract that influenced Brock: L. K. Samuels, *FREELAND: The Search for Free/New Countries* (Carmel, Calif.: Freeland Press, 1983), p. 5.

Compact for Orbis space colony: Spencer H. MacCallum, *Drafting a Constitution for ORBIS* (Rampart Institute).

A better version of Brock?: Marshall T. Savage, *The Millennial Project: Colonizing the Galaxy—In Eight Easy Steps* (Denver, Colo.: Empyrean Publishing, 1992), pp. 341, 15.

Oceania: Details are from the Web site "Oceania: The Atlantis Project."

Space projects on the drawing board: B. Alexander Howerton, *Free Space: Real Alternatives for Reaching Outer Space* (Port Townsend, Wash.: Loompanics Unlimited, 1995).

DEATH, BE NOT IN MY FACE

Epigraph: Herb Bowie, *Why Die?: A Beginner's Guide to Living Forever* (Scottsdale, Ariz.: PowerSurge Publishing, 1998), p. 14.

Immortality as birthright: Ibid., p. 269.

"In simple and blunt terms . . .": Chet Fleming, *If We Can Keep a Severed Head Alive . . . Discorporation and U.S. Patent 4,666,425* (St. Louis, Mo.: Polinym Press, 1987), p. ix.

"Discorp" mobility: Ibid., p. 178.

Technology coming at us: Ibid., p. xii.

Fleming's severed-head novel, *Pretend You're Strong,* is a manuscript written under the pseudonym "Darwin Edison."

Christianity and "Simplish": Fleming, *If We Can Keep a Severed Head Alive . . .* , pp. 214, 347.

Attempt to block ape-human "chimera": Rick Weiss, "Patent Sought on Making of Part-Human Creatures," *Washington Post,* April 2, 1998.

Leonard Hayflick, *How and Why We Age* (New York: Ballantine Books, 1994).

". . . amazing, medically proven" aging reversal: Ronald Klatz and Carol Kahn, *Grow Young with HGH* (New York: HarperCollins Publishers, 1997).

"Please give this child a good home . . .": Fleming, *If We Can Keep a Severed Head Alive . . .* , pp. xi–xii.

Cryonics as black comedy: Roy Rivenburg, "The Iceman Goeth," *Los Angeles Times*, March 2, 1994, p. E1.

Zorba in Heaven: Nikos Kazantzakis, *Zorba the Greek* (New York: Simon and Schuster, 1952), p. 105.

Fleming's patent denied: "Reexamination Certificate," U.S. Patent Office, Feb. 25, 1992.

Kierkegaard's "White Knight": Ernest Becker, *The Denial of Death* (New York: Free Press, 1973), pp. 257–58.

Fleming's views on "Evolution and Religion" are summarized from an unpublished paper written by him.

My details of the final days of Timothy Leary are from an interview with his companion, Vicki Marshall. Max More's lament ("The Heat Death of Timothy Leary") appeared in *Extropy: Transhuman Technology, Ideas & Culture*.

Dog-head experiment: David D. Gilboe et al., "Extracorporeal Perfusion of the Isolated Head of a Dog," *Nature* (April 25, 1964): 399.

Monkey-head experiment: Robert J. White et al., "Cephalic Exchange Transplant in the Monkey," *Surgery* (July 1971): 135–139.

White says head transplants are viable: Larry Thompson, "The Eerie World of Living Heads," *Washington Post*, Feb. 14, 1988, p. C3.

TAKE ME HOME, MR. WIGGLES

Epigraph: Sylvan. J. Muldoon and Hereward Carrington, *The Projection of the Astral Body* (New York: Samuel Weiser, 1973; first published by Rider & Co., 1929), p. 45.

Biographical details about Robert Monroe: Robert A. Monroe, *Journeys Out of the Body* (New York: Doubleday & Company, 1971; Anchor Press edition, 1977); Bayard Stockton, *Catapult: The Biography of Robert A. Monroe* (Norfolk, Va.: Donning Company/Publishers, 1989).

Monroe's popularity with executives: Bob Ortega, "Research Institute Shows People a Way out of Their Bodies," *Wall Street Journal*, Sept. 20, 1994, p. 1.

Stockton on Christ and Monroe: Stockton, *Catapult*, pp. 22, 33.

Appetizing Institute food: Ibid., p. 13.

"Several major religious movements were created . . .": The origins of all these faiths is described by J. Gordon Melton in his *Encyclopedia of American Religions*.

The origins of Spiritualism: Rosemary Ellen Guiley, *Encyclopedia of Mystical & Paranormal Experience* (London: Grange Books, 1991), pp. 568–70. This and other accounts of the Fox Sisters' career offer conflicting details about basic facts—like the girls' ages at the time the ghostly rappings began. I also relied on Ernest Isaacs, "The Fox Sisters in American Spiritualism," in *The Occult in America: New Historical Perspectives*, ed. Howard Kerr and Charles L. Crow (Urbana and Chicago: University of Illinois Press, 1983); Peter Washington, *Madame Blavatsky's Baboon: A History of the Mystics, Mediums, and Misfits Who Brought Spiritualism to America* (New York: Shocken Books, 1995); and Reuben Briggs Davenport, *The Death-Blow to Spiritualism: Being the True Story of the Fox Sisters, as Revealed by Authority of Margaret Fox Kane and Catherine Fox Jencken* (New York: G. W. Dillingham, 1888).

". . . actual voices of the dead . . .": Harold Sherman, *The Dead Are Alive: They Can and Do Communicate with You!* (New York: Fawcett Gold Medal Books, 1981, 1987). My quote is from the back cover.

"Blavatsky . . . left a similar legacy": My summary of Blavatsky's career is from Washington, *Madame Blavatsky's Baboon*; Jay Kinney, "Deja Vu: The Hidden History of the New Age," in *The Fringes of Reason: A Whole Earth Catalog* (New York: Harmony Books), 1989, pp. 23–25; Melton, *Encyclopedia of American Religions*, pp. 153–55.

Marcel Louis Forhan and OBEs: Guiley, *Encyclopedia of Mystical & Paranormal Experience*, p. 420.

Muldoon meets Carrington: Muldoon and Carrington, *The Projection of the Astral Body*, pp. 15–19.

Silver cord: Ecclesiastes 12:6.

Muldoon's first OBE: Muldoon and Carrington, *The Projection of the Astral Body,* pp. 49–53.

Muldoon's tips for beginners: Ibid., pp. 158, 161.

Mechanics of Hemi-Sync: Robert A. Monroe, *Far Journeys* (New York: Main Street Books, Doubleday, 1985), pp. 19–25; F. Holmes (Skip) Atwater, "The Hemi-Sync® Process" (Faber, Va.: Monroe Institute, 1997).

Skeptical views on Monroe's theories: Barry L. Beyerstein, "Brainscams: Neuromythologies of the New Age," *International Journal of Mental Health* (Fall 1990): 27–36.

The Park: Monroe describes the Park, also called "the Reception Center" and "Focus 27," in *Ultimate Journey* (New York: Main Street Books, Doubleday, 1994), pp. 245–64; and in "The Out-of-Body Experience: An Interview with Robert A. Monroe," Calvin Winston, *New Frontier* (November/December 1994): 7–11, 50.

The Oklahoma City "rescue": Bruce Moen, "Dining at Bennigan's—Wednesday April 19," in "TMI Focus: A Newsletter of the Monroe Institute," Winter 1996, p.1.

Monroe's early experiences: Monroe, *Journeys out of the Body*, pp. 20–44.

Locale III: Ibid., pp. 94–96.

Monroe's divorce: Stockton, *Catapult*, p. 98.

Origins of Gateway: Ibid., p. 114.

Early CHEC unit at Whistlefield: Monroe, *Far Journeys*, p. 37.

Explorer voyages: Ibid., pp. 39–49.

NVC communications with Z-55: Ibid., pp. 83–84.

OBE map: Ibid., pp. 238–47.

Elisabeth Kübler-Ross's OBE: Kübler-Ross described this event numerous times; I relied on her February 1980 interview with

Human Behavior magazine, reprinted in part in Stockton, *Catapult*, pp. 114–18.

Monroe's thoughts on the Patrick Tape: Stockton, *Catapult*, p. 144.

The New Land experiment: Ibid., pp. 215–22.

AFTERWORD

The Christian Identity is described by Michael Barkun in *Religion and the Racist Right.*

"Two Seeds" theory: Dan Gayman, *The Two Seeds of Genesis 3:15* (n.p., 1977).